Digital Collage and Painting

Digital Collage and Painting

Using Photoshop and Painter to Create Fine Art

Second Edition

Susan Ruddick Bloom

AMSTERDAM • BOSTON • HEIDELBERG • LONDON
NEW YORK • OXFORD • PARIS • SAN DIEGO
SAN FRANCISCO • SINGAPORE • SYDNEY • TOKYO

Focal Press is an imprint of Elsevier

Focal Press is an imprint of Elsevier
30 Corporate Drive, Suite 400, Burlington, MA 01803, USA
The Boulevard, Langford Lane, Kidlington, Oxford, OX5 1GB, UK

Notices
Knowledge and best practice in this field are constantly changing. As new research and experience broaden our understanding, changes in research methods, professional practices, or medical treatment may become necessary.

Practitioners and researchers must always rely on their own experience and knowledge in evaluating and using any information, methods, compounds, or experiments described herein. In using such information or methods they should be mindful of their own safety and the safety of others, including parties for whom they have a professional responsibility.

To the fullest extent of the law, neither the Publisher nor the authors, contributors, or editors, assume any liability for any injury and/or damage to persons or property as a matter of product liability, negligence or otherwise, or from any use or operation of any methods, products, instructions, or ideas contained in the material herein.

Library of Congress Cataloging-in-Publication Data
Application submitted.

British Library Cataloguing-in-Publication Data
A catalogue record for this book is available from the British Library.

ISBN: 978-0-240-81175-8

For information on all Focal Press publications
visit our website at www.elsevierdirect.com

10 11 12 13 14   5 4 3 2 1

Printed in Canada

Working together to grow
libraries in developing countries

www.elsevier.com | www.bookaid.org | www.sabre.org

ELSEVIER   BOOK AID International   Sabre Foundation

Contents

Part II *Step-by-Step Painting*

Part III *Artistic Considerations*

Dedication

Special thanks to my loving parents, Dorothy and Earvin Ruddick, who have supported my artistic efforts throughout my life. They launched my love of art with art classes at age five. They put up with the mess of paints, clay, and plaster throughout my college years. Dad was always ready to create frames in his woodshop to showcase my artistic productions. Mom, who is a fine artist on her own, was always ready with supportive comments and advice. They alone have seen the thread of art run through my entire life. Their presence in my life has been such a joy and blessing.

Susan Ruddick Bloom
October 2010

I

Planning and Inspiration

1

Concept

Where does that kernel of inspiration come from? Does it hit you when you are in the shower or when you are driving on the turnpike? Wherever it takes hold of you, it marks the beginning of the process of making a piece of art. Some artists agonize over each step of the creation process, whereas for some the work flows seamlessly from an inner fountain of inspiration.

There is an endless array of possible starting points. The *ah-ha* moment can be when you look at the texture of an old wall with peeling paint, the detail on a moth's wing, or the sweep of landscape contours on a hillside. As artists, we can be surprised by almost anything as we explore our world. Anything and everything is at our disposal to serve as possible elements for inspiration.

Often we are taken by surprise when a particular element "suggests" itself to us. The making of art is very intuitive, and the artist learns to follow his nose. The actual making of the art is seldom a

OPPOSITE PAGE: *"Autumn Vista"*

smooth ride. Instead, I would compare it to a roller-coaster ride. The process involves many unexpected twists, turns, and bumps. It is full of thrills and can be harrowing at times, but we wouldn't miss it for the world!

Once the seed of thought is planted, where do you go with it? It is important to think this thing through before you begin. What is the total concept? How can you integrate images into the completed work that might enhance that beginning concept? What additional imagery do you need? How do you see it coming together?

Visually, there are many things to consider. If you are using several images, as in a collage, how will you make them read as a whole? There needs to be a uniformity that unites the piece. You want to create a cohesive feel or mood. What will accomplish that for you? There are many unifying factors. Color can be the tie-in for you, or it might be scale, contrast, directionality, or more. We will cover some of these unifying factors in Chapter 2.

We will assume that the creative bug has gotten hold of you and you are now compelled to make a piece of art. So, hold onto your socks—here we go.

. . . .

What Is a Collage, Montage, or Assemblage?

What form will the imagery take? Artists throughout time have used marble and stone for sculpture, canvas and panels for paintings, paper for drawing and printmaking, and photographic paper for photography, to mention only a few formats. But, there is a dawning of a new age in art materials. We are fortunate to be living in the beginning of the digital age. For the artist, this introduces a whole new array of artistic tools and possibilities. The computer can be used to make imagery and is yet another tool in the imaginary tool belt that artists have at their disposal.

I attended a superb art college, where I was grounded in all the basics: strong drawing and painting skills, intense study of art history, and a good exposure to a variety of different artistic pursuits, from ceramics to fiber art, from lithography to photography. Mastery of the tools and techniques was a must in every field of endeavor. The artist needs to become so well acquainted with the materials and equipment available that creative applications become second nature. Once some mastery of the materials is in place, the work flows more easily. When a more complete understanding of the tools and techniques is in place, the inquisitive mind of the artist can explore variations on the techniques. So it is with the field of computer imagery. The artist needs to prepare by obtaining a basic body of knowledge about computers, software, and printing devices. Once these elements are in place, the artist can begin to fluidly make art using the digital tools at hand.

In this book, I have chosen to concentrate on two digital applications in the field of art: *digital collage* and *digital painting*. I will attempt to explore the endless possibilities in this arena with you. How does

Art is an affirmation of life.
—Alfred Stieglitz,
    in *Alfred Stieglitz:*
    Photographs & Writings,
    by Sarah Greenhough
    and Juan Hamilton
    (1983)

The role of the artist is
to hold up a vision of
spiritual reality.
—Joseph Campbell,
    The Hero with a Thousand
    Faces (1949)

the dictionary define *assembled imagery*? The *Merriam-Webster Dictionary* definitions include the following concepts:

- *Collage*
  An artistic composition of fragments (as of printed matter) pasted on a surface
- *Montage*
  A composite photograph made by combining several separate pictures
  An artistic composition made up of several different types of elements
  A varied mixture: jumble
- *Assemblage*
  A collection of persons or things: gathering
  The act of assembling
  An artistic composition made from scraps, junk, and odds and ends
  The art of making assemblages

For the sake of consistency in this book, I will refer to assembled images as collages, keeping in mind that in the field of art assembled images could mean many different things, in both two and three dimensions. Traditional collage materials might vary in form, from magazine photos to flattened chewing gum wrappers, from dried plant materials to beach pebbles. Everything is fair game if it can be used for a purpose that enhances the imagery. Our imagery will be digital in nature, but, as you will see later, that won't stop us from making artwork that has a more three-dimensional quality. No digital police will stop you from pushing the artistic envelope. I would encourage you to experiment and explore where these digital tools might take you with your artistic expressions.

All art is at once surface and symbol.
—Oscar Wilde,
The Picture of Dorian Gray (1891)

What Is a Digital Painting?

Digital painting, for me, usually involves just one image. I start with a photograph that I would like to transform into a painting. I use both a photo manipulation program (Adobe® Photoshop®) and a painting program (Corel® Painter™). I will show you in Chapters 4 and 5 how I approach creating a painting digitally. We will use tools that truly mimic real art materials, such as charcoal, colored pencils, airbrushes, pencils, and paint, but first a word on photography and its impact on the creation of artwork.

Let's put photography's contribution to making art in perspective. Since the daguerreotype appeared on the scene in 1839, artists have seized on the artistic possibilities that photography offers. Artists were the leaders in exploring this new medium. Itinerant portrait painters often converted to the craft of photography and emerged as the first traveling photographers. Samuel Morse, the father of American photography, was in Paris for the presentation of Daguerre's process to the French Academy of Sciences. Most of us know Morse for his invention of the telegraph and other scientific endeavors, but he was also an accomplished painter. Morse brought the techniques of photography to America and later trained one of the most acclaimed photographers of the nineteenth century, Matthew Brady.

The list of artists that have used photography as an aid in the creation of their paintings is long indeed, incorporating such esteemed names as Degas, Duchamp, and Eakins. For some artists, the camera was used to stop-action the position of a body in motion. This was a task easily captured by the camera but not possible for the human eye.

One of the certainties in the art world that seems to transcend time is the dialogue that emerges as soon as a new type of medium is explored. We see that discussion currently, with the advent of digital fine art. Is it really art, if it came from the computer? It is as if the computer has somehow mechanically stained or lessened the artistic output. This cry is an old and recurrent one. Ansel Adams, Alfred Stieglitz, and Edward Steichen are a few of the prominent names in photography that fought that artistic battle in the 1940s and 1950s, when they urged the creation of departments of photography in major museums.

Shortly after the announcement of Daguerre's photographic process was made in Paris, the painters in the French Academy declared, "Painting is dead." If the camera could capture in a few seconds what a painter would take months to paint, what was to happen to the painter? What did the artist have to offer that the camera did not? I think it is no coincidence that painting starts to take a new path in the years that followed. Artists began to paint the essence of a moment in time, creating the impression of the moment rather than a strictly realistic rendition. The Impressionism movement dominated in the years that followed the mass acceptance of the new technology of photography.

New technology has the force to propel art in new and unexpected directions. Change and growth always seem to come with controversy. I'm reminded of the quote that, "Only babies with a wet diaper want a change." The rest of us usually find reasons why we don't want to change. Change often requires retooling ourselves and a large chunk of time to learn new methods. It is easier to impugn these new methods than to learn from them, so beware! If you start to create art with the methods contained in this book, you may indeed be criticized and classified as a lesser artist. Wear the banner of pioneer proudly, though—you come from a fine tradition of artists who have dared to explore new materials and methods to see what those new technologies have to offer in the making of their art.

A word of caution should be extended early in this book. Using the computer to create art will not make you an artist, just as using pastels can't make you an artist. Ultimately, over time, the artwork will be judged on its own merits artistically. Your challenge will be to learn the techniques that this new form of expression offers to you. Once the vocabulary of the digital art world is well known to you and you can understand and practice the techniques, your artistic vision will be what separates you from others in the field.

In the works of Michelangelo the creative force seems to rumble.
—AUGUSTE RODIN,
Art by Auguste Rodin, by Paul Gsell (1912) (translated by Romilly Fedden)

What I do is the result of reflection and study of the great masters: of inspiration, spontaneity, temperament … I know nothing.
—EDGAR DEGAS,
In the Notebooks of Edgar Degas, by Theodore Reff (1976)

Ultimately, the tools really don't matter. They are quite simply the tools that allow the art to emerge. Picasso could use a discarded bicycle seat to make art, and Jackson Pollock could fling paint onto a canvas. It was a matter of some controversy whether the work of these artists deserved the title of "art," but over time their vision has come through and the work can be seen in context.

Expect to invite some flack as a digital artist. Some art shows do not allow the inclusion of digitally produced art. Lack of knowledge about this field is the primary culprit, but some of the fault lies with ill-conceived and poorly executed artwork, produced without much consideration of basic art and design concepts. Educate yourself as an artist. Continue to explore opportunities to learn more. Sign up for workshops and courses. Go to museums regularly to study at the feet of the masters. Get together with other artists to work, talk, and critique. The myth of the artist tucked away in an attic garret making masterpieces is just that—a myth. Art is both a visual and an intellectual endeavor. You can never be too knowledgeable. Art is not made in a vacuum but is created in context with our society and current events. It should be no surprise that the art world is being transformed in the digital age, when society and commerce are undergoing enormous upheavals in this new digital world we live in.

> Study the past if you would divine the future.
> —CONFUCIUS,
>   *The Analects (c. 50 B.C.)*

. . . .

Think It Out First, Assembling the Needed Images

It is very important to think through the intended project. What tools will you need? What imagery will be required? Try to extend the project out in your mind. Brainstorm a bit around your idea. Keep notes and draw thumbnail sketches. Maybe try a few little painting and sketching exercises around the concept. One of the things I have discovered in teaching, and in life as a whole, is that most people often pursue their first thought. Given a choice, most people will select the easiest and fastest track, and it is easier to go with that first idea than to take the time to think it through more thoroughly. It is often the case that the fifth or twelfth idea would really work better, but most people never allow that possibility to occur. Take the time to explore your initial concept in depth.

What do you want to communicate? Are you trying to go for a mood or evoke an emotion? Are you trying to create a political satire? What is your intended message? What would be the best method to convey that concept? These are the moments when the course of the project is determined. Take the necessary time to let the idea germinate well.

Will you need to initiate an artistic scavenger hunt to find the necessary imagery for this project? In these litigious times we live in, I think it is always wise to rely solely on your own imagery. Use your scanner as a camera. It is a cheap and very effective tool. Use your digital camera as a collection device. Freed from the consumption of costly film and processing, digital photography has created a willingness to gather a vast array of imagery.

On a recent trip to Italy, I took over 4000 photos digitally. On my return home, those images were burned onto two digital video discs (DVDs)

> Paintings have a life of their own that derives entirely from the painter's soul.
> —VINCENT VAN GOGH,
>   in *The Complete van Gogh*,
>   by Jan Hulsker (1977)

for a fraction of the cost that film and processing would have incurred. Digital photography frees you to explore the nuances of things. Did that scrap of paper in the gutter hold some appeal for you? Did that light beam outlining your toothbrush look interesting? Don't hesitate. Take the photo! Become a pack rat of imagery. Begin to create large files of photos to use later. This will result in a digital mountain of subject matter that will have to be cataloged and archived in some systematic manner, so be sure to spend some time with these issues.

Are You Drowning in Digital Files?

I recommend that you immediately burn a compact disc (CD) or DVD of your downloaded images before you alter them at all. Another way to archive your images is to store them on an external drive, which is becoming a more economically feasible alternative. These are your digital negatives. Treat them as such. You will never have more pixels than you have at that moment, especially if you are shooting RAW. Burn duplicates of your CDs or DVDs and store them in another location, in case of fire or a hurricane. Store an extra external hard drive in a safe deposit box or mail it to a friend or relative in a different location for safekeeping. That may sound crazy, but if your home area were hit by flooding in a bad storm, for example, it is possible that the bank with your safe deposit box could also be affected. I know photographers who mail their backups to relatives in a different state for safekeeping. In a way, the digital revolution has allowed us to duplicate that original base negative for safekeeping in ways we never could with film. Famed photographer Arnold Newman only had one negative of each image. If that had been destroyed, all would have been lost. Digital archiving gives us that advantage over film.

Get in the practice of writing on the container or envelope but not directly on the disc (this can harm your files over time). Develop a system of cataloging and archiving your imagery, for easy retrieval. I know many digital artists that are drowning in their multitude of files and can never lay their hands on the photo they are currently seeking. Give meaningful names to your files and folders. You can batch process a folder of images, giving them new sequential numbers and names, instead of the crazy numbers and letters that come with the metadata from your camera. You can make contact sheets in Photoshop and keep notebooks of thumbnail images contained on each disc. You can purchase a piece of software that will archive your work for easy retrieval. In short, find a system that works for you and how you work and think. This one small piece of advice can really facilitate the ease with which you will work.

What Is the Intended Output Size?

This one concept is huge in determining everything else. How big will you ever print this piece? You must match your file size to the requirements of the largest possible usage of your artwork. You can always make an image smaller, without sacrificing quality. The reverse of this is not true. You want to avoid asking the software to create more pixels than were originally captured. Think about medium- and large-format photography. Why did Ansel Adams go to the trouble of carrying big-view cameras and heavy tripods up dangerous mountainsides? The answer, of course, is detail. The larger the negative, the more detail it contains. On film, the detail was made by particles of silver. In the digital world, we use pixels. You want as many pixels as you will need to output your image at the largest size you will ever intend to print out. Err on the side of caution if you are uncertain and go for a larger file. The flip side of this, of course, is that a large file takes longer to manipulate and is a storage hog. Seldom, however, have I regretted making a file size large at the outset. I can always create a smaller file of the same image for a project requiring less detail and resolution. With those housekeeping notes aside, we will proceed to some basic design considerations.

When I see a tree … I can feel that tree talking to me.
—JOAN MIRÓ,
    ARTnews (January, 1980)

Figure 1-1
Scottish Cottage painting

2

Important Considerations Before You Begin

Unifying Factors

Unifying factors cannot be underestimated. They are not big and flashy additions, but they are frequently the glue that holds a composition together. Ideally, you would like to have a cohesive feel throughout a piece. Every item in the piece should appear to be woven from the same cloth. Collage is particularly susceptible to problems with disparate elements. Generally, collages are assembled from items taken from a variety of source materials. These items can come from photographs, magazine clippings, scannings, and elsewhere; frequently, the resolution of the images will vary. In order for your completed artwork to present a cohesive feel, you must consider the unifying factors of texture, color, contrast, and noise or grain.

The first truth is form. Put on paper what you know is true rather than what you see.
—Kimon Nicolaïdes,
  The Natural Way to Draw
  (1941)

OPPOSITE PAGE: *"Sacred Place #1"*

Texture

Texture in collage can be handled particularly well with the choice of your background layer. Where can you find a good background? Actually, background layers are all around us. I am constantly photographing textures and compiling DVDs full of these images. They become a visual vocabulary of backgrounds that I can pull from. Where can you begin to find these textures? Some of my favorites are skies, gardens, water, and rocks.

Figure 2-1

Catalog of sky images in Bridge

Skies

My first suggestion would be to look up! The sky is a fabulous source of backgrounds. The sky is constantly changing and the colors are great, with subtle variances. The scale can be easily manipulated for your needs later. Photographing the sky doesn't require you to travel to exotic locales; you can just step outside. You can live in a city or in the country and will still be able to gather good sky images. I find that people don't pay much attention to the sky unless they see a great, colorful sunset or threatening storm clouds. The ordinary sky of our everyday lives is frequently overlooked, but seldom boring. If you train yourself to pay attention to its marvelous changes throughout the day, you will quite simply be amazed at how beautiful it is. Take your digital camera out each day and build a catalog of sky images. You can sort the images, if you like, into folders by the type of cloud, color, etc. Begin today!

No bird soars too high, if he soars with his own wings.

—WILLIAM BLAKE, *"Proverbs of Hell," from The Marriage of Heaven and Hell* (1790)

Gardens

Another excellent source for backgrounds is the garden. Develop files of images that explore the textures of plant life, from ordinary grasses to leaves to exotic flowers. Try some extreme close-ups of the anatomy of a flower or leaf. The colors can range across the entire spectrum.

Figure 2-2
Catalog of flower images

You can find shiny surfaces or dull ones; delicate, transparent petals or thick, waxy cactus leaves. Try low light situations such as the early morning hours, allowing light to illuminate petals and leaves. If your camera will cooperate with multiple exposure images, try that technique. My camera will allow up to 10 images to be compiled into one, in the camera. That can create beautiful images, especially good for backgrounds.

Water

Take your camera everywhere. Photograph the beach with its rolling and crashing waves. Try some close-ups of the sea as it meets the shore. Photograph lakes and streams. If you can find an underwater housing for your camera, take some shots from under the sea. Another possibility for great water images is a ride on a glass-bottom boat or a visit to a local aquarium. Water, like the sky, can be an element that doesn't have an apparent scale. That can be a useful thing when you are constructing collages.

Rocks

Rocks are wonderful source materials. Rocks are everywhere: there are the smooth stones along Maine's coast, unique ochre-colored desert rocks, and ordinary rocks that you find in your driveway or along pathways. The boulder and pebble are interchangeable in digital images, as it often is not possible to distinguish between a boulder and a pebble by shape, contour, or color.

Figures 2-3, 2-4, and 2-5 illustrate the various types of views available in the Adobe® Bridge. Bridge is a wonderful file browser and much more.

Imagination is more important than knowledge.
—ALBERT EINSTEIN, *The World as I See It* (1934)

My artistic center is in my head and not elsewhere, and I am strong because I am never thrown off course by others, but what I do comes from inside me.
—PAUL GAUGIN, *Avant et Apres* (1923)

Figure 2-3
Thumbnail view in Bridge

Figure 2-4
View content as details view in Bridge

Color

What is the predominant color effect you want to achieve in your piece of artwork? Do you want it to have soft, pastel tones or vibrant, bright colors? Do you want a monotone or neutral effect? If you are combining many photos of people, you will be sure to notice the variance in skin tones and the variety of lighting conditions under which the photos were made. Undoubtedly, you will need to modify the color to achieve a uniformity of tone. If you are using color photographs from 20 or 30 years ago, you will notice extreme color shifts due to time. The dyes in the prints migrate and degrade over time, producing color shifts that can tend toward yellow, pink, or green. Photoshop® and some current color management programs are capable of more or less restoring the

Figure 2-5
View content as list view in Bridge

original colors of vintage prints. Figure 2-6 illustrates color corrections that can be made in Photoshop to restore the original look and feel of an old photograph or slide. Color correction is also often necessary on photos made today. Even photos taken on the same day under similar lighting conditions will vary and may require some color corrections.

There is no blue without yellow and orange.
—Vincent van Gogh,
In the Complete van Gogh,
by Jan Hulsker (1977)

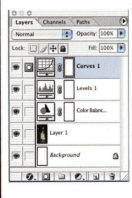

Figure 2-6
Color-corrected old slide (that had developed green tones)

Contrast

Contrast deals with the range of tonal values from dark to light. High-contrast images have strong dark and light tones with fewer mid-tones. Low-contrast images are full of lots of midtone values, but the tones are not as strong in the extreme ends of the tonal scale. In order to provide continuity in a piece of art, you may find it necessary to increase or decrease the contrast in an image to make it more adaptable to your composition.

Noise and Grain

Figure 2-7
Close-up of infrared grain and noise

Black is not a color.
—ÉDOUARD MANET,
   in *The World of Manet,
   1832–1883,* by Pierre
   Schneider (1968)

Why black is the queen of colors.
—AUGUSTE RODIN,
   Art, by Paul Gsell (1912)
   (translated by Romilly
   Fedden)

   Author's note: It
   appears that even
   the great artists will
   disagree from time to
   time.

The image on the left was scanned infrared film. The image on the right was created with a digital camera that was converted to solely shoot infrared images.

In film we are aware of the "grain." These particles are more apparent in higher speed film. I often use infrared film, which has a very noticeable grain. If you scan your negatives or slides, you will pick up the grain structure of the particular film type. In the digital world, we use the term "noise" for unwanted color aberrations, especially in darker areas. Noise is usually an unwanted by-product of low light conditions with digital capture or of images that have been manipulated too much. You will find it necessary to sometimes match the effect of noise or grain in the interest of uniformity.

Scale

Scale is an amazing element to use in your work. Reality is not a limitation in this design component. You are free to enlarge a small bird's feather to the size of a skyscraper or to shrink a giant tree to the size of a toothpick. You are in total control. As the temporary captain of the universe, your only true directive is to make the composition work. It should hold together visually and your choices should be valid ones. There are many different reasons for using an image that is not to scale. You may need a particular texture that the image affords. You may want the literal context of the artwork to be enhanced by the off-scale component. You may want to make your exaggeration a very deliberate showcase of the difference in scale, perhaps for a humorous pun. Whatever your motivation, pause to think about the effect that scale can have on your finished piece of art. Gigantic to minuscule—what's your choice? Let's take a look at an example.

Tree House Exercise

An enjoyable exercise in scale is to find a big, fat tree, to be your base image and then photograph various items such as windows, doors, or

Figure 2-8
Completed tree house with layers

steps that you can use to turn the tree into a tree house. This exercise will teach you scaling (through the Transform tool) and how to match up the colors, contrast, lighting, and noise. Roam your neighborhood with a digital camera to collect component parts.

Figure 2-9
Base photograph of a tree

The base photograph should be of a tree that is sufficiently large in girth to accommodate the imaginary elfin family within. There are no rules. Let your imagination run free. We are not making "fine art" on this one. It is just a wacky exercise to learn about scale. (A tutorial on scaling is included in Chapter 12.) The first element to set the scale of those that follow is the door. The red door that I photographed had plants sitting in front of it. I knew that I could later clone the plants out with the Clone Stamp Tool.

Figure 2-10
Imported door

Rotating, Distorting, and Transforming

Figure 2-11
Door transformed to proper scale

I simply love the Transform tool in Photoshop. This is one of my major tools for altering an image. If you don't use it currently, try it out. Take it for a test drive and learn the shortcut of Command + T for Mac (Alt + T for PC). Our tree example provides a simple exercise for working with layers and the Transform tool. Using the Transform command, I scaled the door down to size. The Rubber Stamp Tool was used to eliminate the plants in front of the door. One by one, I added other elements into the collage. Adjustment layers were used to correct color and contrast, and shadows were added to nestle the elements into place, avoiding a cut-out feel. If you are unaccustomed to using the Transform tool, be sure to try the exercise in Chapter 12.

Talent isn't genius, and no amount of energy can make it so.
—LOUISA MAY ALCOTT, *Little Women* (1868)

Figure 2-12
Close-up of tree house

Lighting

The very nature of collage usually requires pulling a multitude of images together from a wide variety of sources. You might sit down and peruse your contact sheets, pages of slides, scanned images, and clippings for inspiration. Once the idea starts to take form, begin to select images that you think will work well together. The items you gather might be ideal except for one thing … lighting. Maybe the light was coming from the wrong direction in one of the photos. Perhaps the light was flat when one photo was made and the rest of the images are more contrasty. The flat image stands out as a puzzle piece that

Of the original phenomena, light is the most enthralling.
—LEONARDO DA VINCI, *A Treatise on Painting* (1651)

doesn't fit in with the rest. Getting the lighting and the color of the light right is very important for believability.

Directionality of Light

Look at the photo and play detective. Where was the sun or light source when the photo was made? Follow the shadows and trace them back to the light source. Was the light overhead or from the side? In collaging, it is important that the light source directionality be consistent.

Quality of Light

What about the quality and color of the light? Was the photo made in early-morning gray light? Was it taken in the direct light of noon? Was it taken in those glorious minutes of golden-colored light before sunset? Was the sun already down and the light had blue tones? A good exercise is to photograph the same object at different times of the day to prove to yourself how the color of an object changes relative to the time of day and the type of light falling on it. Weather and cloud cover can also have a tremendous influence. Chances are that your collage components will be gathered from sources that vary in their lighting conditions.

Dramatic vs. Subtle

Light is the principal personage of a painting.
—Édouard Manet,
    in *The World of Manet, 1832–1883,* by Pierre Schneider (1968)

Full bright sunlight will render an object with sharp edges and deep shadows. Sometimes the highlights will blow out, depending on the range restriction of your film or digital camera. A foggy day may render edges in a soft manner. Shadows may not exist in highly overcast situations. As you assemble the component parts for your collage, you will need to determine the viability of each piece. Can you make the pieces work together? Not all pieces can be successful candidates for your collage. Let's look at a practical situation.

Projects: Places That Never Were

As part of a series, I made several collages depicting spaces that never existed in reality. Sometimes the images were sacred landscapes, like Ayers Rock or the Olgas in the Australian outback, that hold religious meaning to the aboriginal inhabitants. Sometimes they were awe-inspiring waterfalls or canyons. Collages in this series frequently incorporated a manmade piece of art or architecture with vast landscapes from different parts of the world. Could I make the created scene look like it really existed?

Figure 2-13
Turkish carving

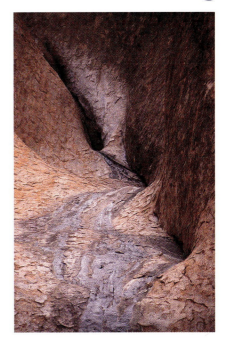

Figure 2-14
Ayers Rock, Australia

Australian Boulder

Our first example used a relief sculpture from central Turkey (Figure 2-13) and a portion of an Australian boulder that, although it exists in a desert, had at one time been subject to the effects of a flow of water (Figure 2-14). I imported the relief sculpture into the Australian landscape.

Place Turkish relief carving on top of the rock layer and blend with a layer mask.
Extend canvas (Image > Canvas Size).
The sky was a flat pleasant blue but not much of it showed. So, I extended the length of the canvas and imported a punchier sky that I thought would work with the other two images.

Add sky on a separate layer and blend using a layer mask.
I decided not to use the section of the sky that had birds in it. It was too much. The birds didn't help the composition, so only the lower portion of sky was used. Adjustment layers of Color Balance, Curves, and Hue/Saturation were used, with a clipping mask, to correct the color and contrast on the relief portion.

All artists, including sculptors, are children of light.
—ALEXANDER ELIOT,
   Sight and Insight (1959)

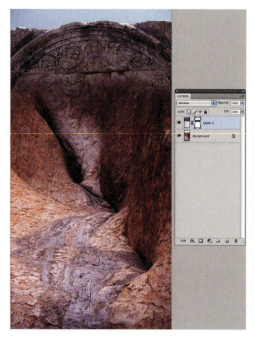

Figure 2-15
Turkish relief carving and rock face combined

Figure 2-16
New sky component

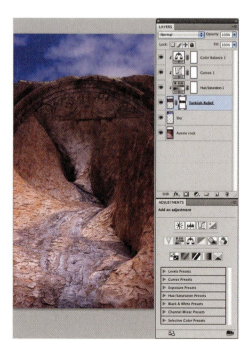

Figure 2-17
Sky area added to the composition

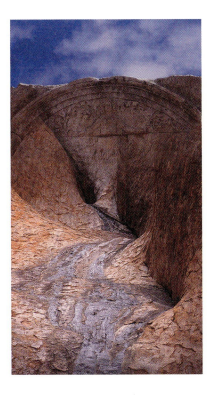

Figure 2-18
"Sacred Place #1" completed collage

Hawaiian Waterfall

Figure 2-19
Hawaiian waterfall

Figure 2-20
Columns under the city of Istanbul

There is no such thing
as shadow, merely the
absence of light.
—KIMON NICOLAÏDES,
The Natural Way to Draw
(1941)

Another collage that was made for the series involved a waterfall photographed in Hawaii. The tones tended toward a magenta cast. What could I integrate into this space? After several tries with various potential components, I settled on a photograph that I made in underground Istanbul. There is a fabulous world under the streets of Istanbul; the subterranean area is flooded with water and contains columns from ancient times. The photograph was a dark image that I thought might work.

Transform column image to proper scale.
Synchronize the color of the columns to the waterfall photo using Adjustment Layer > Color Balance.
Integrate columns into the waterfall setting using a layer mask.

Figure 2-21
*"Sacred Place #2" columns
added to waterfall image*

I sized down the image and tried to match the color tones that existed on the wall of the cliff. For this, I used a color balance layer adjustment. The columns were integrated into the cliff with a layer mask. The lighting on each component was similar enough that the only real adjustment was balancing the color and masking the image into the cliff. That was pretty simple.

Figure 2-22
Close-up of finished collage

Menace in Venice

Figure 2-23
Florida Everglades alligator

Figure 2-24
Venice canal

The preceding examples were pretty simple. How about a tougher project? This next little collage was just too much fun. We artists tend to be so serious about our art that we can lose our sense of humor.

Try doing something outlandish, just for the fun of it. In that vein, I offer up a little piece I call "Menace in Venice." The thought was to make the tranquil, magical city of Venice a little edgier. Tourists in Venice often wonder what is really in that canal water. The collage I created certainly won't be used by the tourist council of Venice, but it was worth a laugh to put together in a realistic manner.

Apply Adjustment Layer > Color Balance to the alligator layer.
Use a layer mask to integrate the alligator into the Venetian canal water.

The canal has a green color cast. The alligator has a magenta color cast. A Color Balance adjustment layer is definitely in order. The mask applied to the alligator took out the leaves and sticks floating near the alligator. The ripples were carefully conserved to show the motion of the alligator.

Use the Eyedropper to sample the color of the shadowed water.

A new layer was added, and the sample color was painted with a light opacity over the back of the alligator.

It was time to step back and analyze what else would help our deception. The bridge over the canal was casting a shadow onto the water, where our alligator was gliding. Using the Eyedropper Tool, a sampling was made in the shadowed water area. A new layer was made. With a very light opacity, the shadow was painted onto the new layer. The Blend mode was set to darken, instead of normal. This addition helps our menacing alligator to appear to be swimming under the

People always talk about the different light in different places. They say the light is different in Greece, or in the Galapagos. But light is light. It's all the same. I think it's subjective. I think it's the emotional state the person is in.
—ELIOT PORTER,
  ARTlines, vol. 5, no. 11 (December 1985/ January 1986)

Figure 2-25
Color Balance applied to adjust the alligator layer

Figure 2-26
Shadow from the bridge painted onto the alligator's back

shadow of the bridge, emerging into the sunlight. The shadow on a separate layer is more forgiving, if it needs to be corrected. It hasn't affected the actual alligator image.

In this type of project, try to allow yourself some forgiveness, and a way to back out, if you make mistakes. It goes without saying that you should save your work frequently. Mistakes happen, machines crash, power goes out in a storm, and you can lose hours of work very easily. Make it a habit to save your art frequently as you are working on it, not just when your session is finished.

Figure 2-27
Completed "Menace in Venice"

Although the completed collage is not likely to be used by the Venetian tourist board, it could lead to a new extreme sporting event for the gondoliers.

In short, it is wise to carefully select the component parts for your collages. Assess the feasibility of using the components together. Will the colors work? What are the directionality and quality of the light? How about contrast? Can the scales be adjusted? Does the grain or noise need to be altered? Consideration of all of these elements will ensure the success of your collages.

3

Inspiration

Digital Artists and Their Work

As we are thinking about the components that make a collage or painting successful, it would be wise to look at the work of several digital artists working today. I have selected them as stellar examples of how fine art work is being produced around the globe. Their techniques vary widely, and their subject matter and styles are equally diverse.

When looking at a piece of digital art we often want to know, "How did they do that?" In this chapter you will find out. Each artist was invited to submit one piece and to detail the steps that were taken in the creative process of constructing that piece of art. I also encouraged them to divulge what equipment they use, favorite papers, etc. This gives you a tiny peek into how each artist works. I hope you enjoy

OPPOSITE PAGE: Compilation of Digital Artists Contributions

their work as much as I do. May their work serve as an inspiration to you as you proceed in your own personal growth as an artist.

Dorothy Simpson Krause

Dorothy Simpson Krause

Marshfields Hills, Massachusetts
DotKrause.com
www.DotKrause.com
www.viewpointeditions.com

Equipment
Computers: Mac® Pro Quad-core, MacBook® Pro (2), HP® Pavilion Elite
Scanner: Microtek ScanMaker™ 9800XL
Printers: HP® Designjet Z3200, Universal Laser Systems® PLS4.60 laser engraver, Epson Stylus® Pro 9600
Favorite Papers: Hahnemühle Fine Art and Arches® Rives BFK
Color Management System: None
Cataloging and Archiving: Adobe® Photoshop® Lightroom®

About the Artist
Education: PhD in Art Education, Pennsylvania State University, 1965–1968; MA in Art Education, University of Alabama, 1961–1962; BA in Painting with honors, Montevallo University, Alabama, 1957–1960
Current Job: Artist (Professor Emeritus, Massachusetts College of Art)
Artistic Inspirations: Robert Rauschenberg, Antonio Tapies
Career Highlight: Being an Artist in Residence at the Smithsonian American Art Museum
Gallery Representation: Judi Rotenberg Gallery LLC, Walker Fine Art, 119 Gallery, Williams Gallery, Landing Gallery, World Printmakers, Digital Atelier

Dorothy Simpson Krause is a painter, collage artist, and printmaker who incorporates digital mixed media into her art. Her work is exhibited regularly in galleries and museums and has been featured in numerous current periodicals and books. Since being introduced to computers in the late 1960s when working on her doctorate at Penn State, she has combined traditional and digital media. Her work includes large-scale, mixed-media pieces, artist books, and book-like objects that bridge these two forms. Her work embeds archetypal symbols and fragments of images and text in multiple layers of texture and meaning. It combines the humblest of materials (plaster, tar, wax, and pigment) with the latest in technology to evoke the past and herald the future. Her art and bookmaking are integrated modes of inquiry that link concept and media in an ongoing dialogue—a visible means of exploring meaning. Krause is the author of *Book 1 Art: Handcrafting Artists' Books* (North Light Books, 2009) and co-author, with Bonny Pierce Lhotka and Karin Schminke, of *Digital Art Studio: Techniques for Combining Inkjet Printing with Traditional Art Materials* (Watson-Guptill, 2004).

Creative Process

As a part of the Boston Cyberarts Festival in the spring of 2009, I had a solo show at the South Shore Art Center titled "Losing Ground." The work is a plea for awareness. As our global population increases exponentially, the effects of our actions are changing the environment. With global warming and the melting polar icecaps contributing to rising ocean levels, we are literally and figuratively losing ground.

The exhibition included both large-format pieces and artist books that combined traditional art materials and digital processes. The wall-hung pieces were printed primarily on ultraviolet-cured flatbed printers on substrates such as aluminum and polycarbonate. The books included covers printed on copper or engraved with a laser into wood.

The showpiece book, also called *Losing Ground*, used images selected from series spanning more than a decade and incorporated text from the publications of the Intergovernmental Panel on Climate Change. This example shows the construction in Photoshop of one of the 44 pages in that book.

I began with photographs of three pieces of art:

- "Dark Passages" (12" × 12", encaustic, 2008)
- "Last One Standing" (24" × 24", pigment transfer to linen canvas, 2004)
- "Apologia" (8" × 5.75" × .5") (altered book with collage, colored pencil, pastel, and leather cover)

Figure 3-1
"Dark Passages," "Last One Standing," "Apologia" book cover and pages

Because the book was to be 12″ × 12″, I changed all images to 12″ × 12″ at 300 dpi. The screenshot shows the various layers that resulted in the final image. This image may have begun with the image layer at the bottom and worked its way up, layer by layer, as I will describe it, but most likely there were a dozen steps along the way that were discarded.

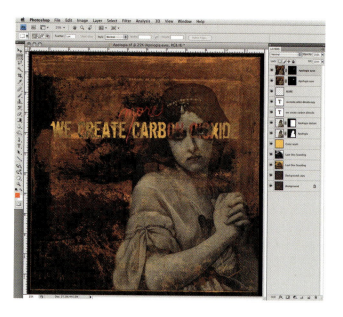

Figure 3-2
Layers

For continuity, I used "Dark Passages" as the background layer on many of the pages in the book. In this image, I duplicated the background layer and set the blend mode on the copy to Screen 28% to brighten it.

Figure 3-3
Background 28%

"Last One Standing" was the next image added to the layers using the blend mode (Multiply 57%). Because I was losing the tree form, I opened the file in Photoshop, duplicated the layer, and chose Image > Adjustments > Desaturate. I then chose Image > Adjustments > Curves and moved the dark slider toward the middle at the bottom to intensify the blacks and the white slider toward the middle at the top to intensify the whites. The resulting image was a high-contrast black-and-white image that I copied and pasted as the next layer using Darken 60%.

Figure 3-4
"Last One Standing" (Multiply 57%), "Last One Standing" black-and-white image, "Last One Standing" (Darken 60%)

Everything was getting too dark and muddy, so I made a new layer, filled it with a gold color, and set the blend mode to Overlay 59%.

Figure 3-5
Color wash (Overlay 59%)

Originally cut from a turn-of-the-century copy of *Godey's Lady's Book*, the woman in "Apologia" was added as a layer and placed in the lower right-hand corner of the image. From the bottom of the layers window, I selected the third icon, "Add Layer Mask," which gave me a mask icon beside my image. After clicking on the mask icon, I used large brushes with white to reveal or black to hide portions of the image. I set the blend mode to Screen 93% so that some of the underlying image of the background and tree came through the woman.

Figure 3-6
*"Apologia" (Screen 93%)
and "Apologia" (Mask
Screen 93%)*

To make the darks stronger, I duplicated the layer, changed the blend mode to Multiply 48%, and changed the mask layer to soften hard edges.

Figure 3-7
*Apologia (Multiply 48%)
and "Apologia" (Mask
Multiply 48%)*

I chose the appropriately named font, "Dirty Ego" (by Eduardo Recife), and typed "we create carbon dioxide" across the face of the woman in 72-point type using a gold color similar to the color wash. It was applied using the Difference 100% blend mode so it would interact with the underlying layer. To make it a little stronger and more colorful, I duplicated the type layer and applied it again using the Overlay 34% blend mode.

Because the entire phrase that would appear on the double-page spread was "burning fossil fuels we create more carbon dioxide," I added the word "more" by writing with a Wacom tablet in a bright red with the Normal 100% blend mode.

I wanted to shift the text color around the eyes, so I turned off the three text layers and saved a copy of the image as it appeared without text, then copied and pasted it as the next layer. I added a layer mask, filled it with black, and painted over the area of the eyes with white.

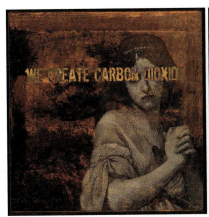

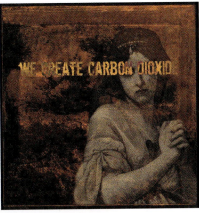

Figure 3-8
*Difference 100% blend mode
and Overlay 34% blend mode*

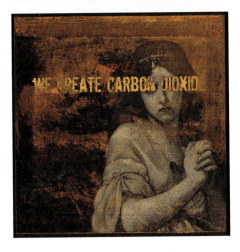

Figure 3-9
Normal 100% blend mode

I used the Overlay 100% blend mode so the underlying text color shifted from gold to red.

To bring the eyes to the surface, I duplicated that layer, worked more in the mask, and chose the Normal 100% blend mode.

When I think I have the final image, I usually save it with all its layers as a .psd file, then flatten it and save it as a .tif file. The .psd file allows me to make additional changes if needed.

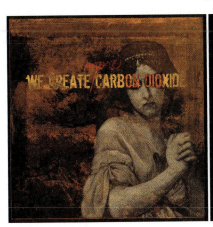

Figure 3-10
*"Apologia" eyes (Overlay
100%) and "Apologia" eyes
mask (Overlay 100%)*

Figure 3-11

*Apologia eyes (Normal
100%) and Apologia eyes
mask (Normal 100%)*

Each of the double-page spreads was worked on side by side but
kept separate because the pages were to be printed separately and
double-fan or perfect bound. The left-hand page was essentially
the same as the bottom five layers of the right-hand page, without the
figure and with different text.

This 12″ × 12″ 44-page book was produced in two editions: a deluxe
edition bound in aubergine Nigerian goat and a limited edition bound
in black Brillianta® book cloth. It is also available in a 7″ × 7″ soft-
cover open edition. The steps involved in making the book and each
of the 44 pages can be seen at www.viewpointeditions.com. The books
can also be purchased there.

Figure 3-12

Three books

Figure 3-13
Double page spread

Susi Lawson

Susi Lawson

Wytheville, Virginia
susi7lawson@yahoo.com
http://susilawsonphotography.biz

Equipment
Computers: Desktop PC, iMac®, MacBook® Pro
Scanner: Epson Perfection® V500
Printers: Canon® PIXMA® Pro, Epson Stylus® Color 1520
Favorite Papers: Red River Paper™
Color Management System: None
Cataloging and Archiving: I shoot my own "stock" photos and save
   them to named folders. I use portable hard drives as back up and
   archive to DVDs.

About the Artist
Educational Background: I believe I was born an artist and most of
   my "education" was doing what I love, which is draw, paint, write,
   and take pictures! I did attend a commercial art school briefly in my
   senior year of high school where I took Fashion Illustration.
Current Job: I really have no job, as I am a self-employed freelance
   artist, magazine writer, photographer, and instructor.
Artistic Inspiration: Norman Rockwell has been my all-time favorite
   since I was a child, and Harry Anderson was also amazing, even
   though he was not as famous. I also admire Georgia O'Keeffe as a
   person, Joni Mitchell for her various talents, Annie Leibovitz for
   her edginess, and my daughter, who lives life out loud. My favorite
   digital artist is Don Seegmiller, who was kind enough to answer my
   e-mails when I was first getting into this medium.
Career Highlights: Winning Best in Show at the 2007 NAPP Contest
   which included a trip to Rome with my daughter (I placed first in
   Portraits at the 2008 NAPP). In 2008, I won the WPPI Maob Print
   contest, which was a trip to Las Vegas for WPPI 2009; while there,
   I won first place in the Kodak Award of Distinction Book contest.

Creative Process

This is an intermediate-level project that can be made on Photoshop 7 and higher.

Have you ever sat and stared at a snapshot on your computer and knew you had something worthy of creating a great portrait but there was something missing? Sometimes it is something as simple as the background that can make or break the portrait that you are wondering what to do with.

Not every photographer has a vast array of expensive backdrops and backgrounds in their studio and perhaps you don't even have a studio. Well, this is where Photoshop comes to the rescue once again!

If you look around your house you will be surprised at the many patterns and designs you will find just begging to be used in your next digital art creation. Walk around and check out your curtains, shower curtains, gift bags, gift wrap. The design I used for the background in "Retro Wrap" is from a sheet of gift wrap found at my local dollar store. (Please keep in mind when using purchased designs that nondescript, generic patterns are all right to use, but stay away from unique artist renditions that may carry a copyright.)

Figure 3-14

Figure 3-15

I opened the portrait shot and the gift wrap design and made a duplicate layer of the retro girl. I next selected the entire image by clicking on Select All. I used the Move Tool to click on the girl and drag her on top of the gift wrap background, as shown.

Now with the retro girl on top of the gift wrap layer, I grabbed the #100 soft round airbrush at 100% opacity and erased the beige background on the top layer, revealing the gift wrap design beneath. I adjusted the brush tip to a smaller size as I got closer to the subject.

Both the girl and the background needed to be adjusted, so I clicked on each layer, one at a time, and used the Curves adjustment tool to pull the curve a little to the left to brighten and lighten each layer.

I then chose the Layers flatten option to combine the girl with her background. I made a duplicate layer, creating two of the same layer. Next I moved onto Image > Adjustments > Shadow > Highlights and moved the sliders until the details were showing in the hair. Be careful here, as this tool is commonly overused and can give a caramel cast to the skin. I then adjusted and tweaked each slider as shown.

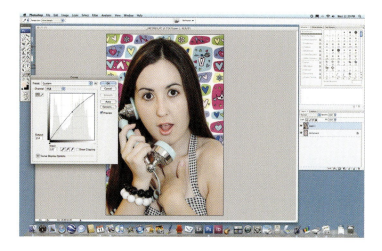

Figure 3-16

Figure 3-17

Figure 3-18

I made a new layer by clicking on the Layers icon, beside the trash can at the bottom of your Layers palette, and then clicking on the layer title and naming it "skin." I choose the #100 soft round airbrush at a 20% opacity. I sampled the skin on the face with the color picker and changed the color to a lighter shade, as shown.

Figure 3-19

Figure 3-20

Making sure the "skin" layer was selected, I brushed over the entire skin area using this light pink color at 20% opacity. I went over areas a second time that needed more coverage such as the dark circles under her eyes. Don't worry about this looking too flat as I will add more color in the next step.

To add cheek color, I used the same brush at the same opacity and sampled the pink lips as a natural reference for our blush. For security, one might want to add another layer and call that one "blush." I added color to the nose, forehead, and arms for a little extra life. Next I adjusted the opacity of the layer to make sure the effect wasn't overdone.

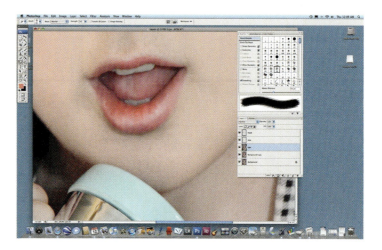

Figure 3-21

Now I did some smoothing using the Smudge Tool. I made a new layer by dragging the background copy layer to the Layer icon and naming it "Lips n Hair." I choose the Smudge Tool and the #59 spatter brush at around 50% opacity and brushed the lips, taking care to follow the natural shape and curvature of the lip. I also smoothed the tongue and teeth.

Figure 3-22

Next I repeated the previous step using the same spatter brush to smudge the entire head of hair as you might if you were actually brushing her hair with a hair brush. I adjusted the opacity as needed, finding that around 30 to 40% was good for hair.

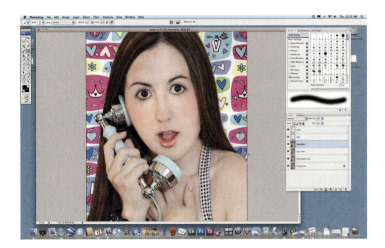

Figure 3-23

Now I added some great airbrush details to the hair. I made a new layer by dragging the "Lips n Hair" layer to the Layer icon, naming this new layer "highlights." I made sure it was selected and grabbed the #100 soft round brush at 30% opacity. I brought up the color box and picked a golden-brown color for the first highlights. I then made the brush tip smaller and smaller to make strands of hair that stand out from the brown base.

Figure 3-24

Using the same layer, I painted in some lighter beige highlights with the same brush. It is important to keep the brush tip small and have fun with this effect. I made sure to make those strands a bit looser and more playful, to give a natural look.

Figure 3-25

I made another layer and named this one "eyes." Using the same soft round brush, I painted some golden highlights into the eye irises. I went all the way around each iris, radiating outward like the sun, making a definite highlight on the left side of each iris using a circular motion.

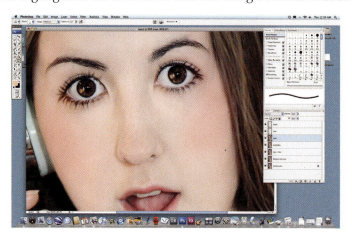

Figure 3-26

Now to define the eyes more, I used the Burn Tool and darkened the pupils, adding more detail to the iris and darkening and defining the lashes. I adjusted the opacity to achieve a natural effect.

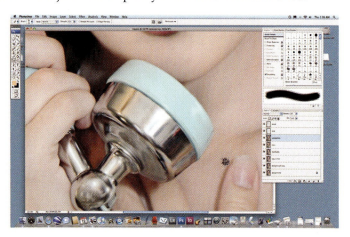

Figure 3-27

I made another layer and named this one "accessories." I then grabbed the Smudge Tool again and, using the same brush that I had used on the hair, I carefully smoothed the pixels on the phone and bracelet to give a more illustrative look. I was careful to follow the contour lines to avoid distortion.

Figure 3-28

Next was bringing out the shine in the accessories. On the same layer, and using the #100 soft round brush at a high opacity, I painted shine lights on the phone and bracelet using the existing shine lights as a reference. This exaggerates the shine for a more illustrative look.

Figure 3-29

Now onto the finishing touches! In traditional airbrush art, this step is very important, and it is no less so in digital art. I painted in bright white highlights to really give it the polished, smooth look of airbrushing. Choosing pure white and the #100 soft airbrush, I lightly but definitely painted shine highlights on the skin. I choose the skin layer already available for this; another option might be to create a "clear" layer. I painted white highlights on the edges of the hands, knuckles, collarbone, fingernails, tip of the nose, cheekbones, top brows, whites of the eyes, bottom lip, and forehead. This really made the image pop!

Figure 3-30
Finished Retro Girl

Mary L. Taylor

Mary L. Taylor

Marshfield Hills, Massachusetts
Mary@MaryTaylorArt.com
http://marytaylorart.com

Equipment

Computer: Mac® Pro (Quad-core Intel® Xeon with 10 GB RAM), Dell™ UltraSharp™ monitor (it feels ancient but I still use it a lot), 17″ Mac® PowerBook® G4 (1 GHz)

Scanner: Epson Perfection® 4490 scanner with VueScan standard edition software

Printers: Epson Stylus® Pro 7800, HP® Designjet Z3100, and an ancient office laser printer (Tektronix® Phaser® 740)

Favorite Papers: Soft, wonderful printmaking papers, such as Arches® Rives BFK and Canson® Edition; digital print papers, such as Hahnemühle Fine Art, Inkpress Duo Matte 80 two-sided; handmade ethnic papers; and, of course, my custom substrates!

Color Management System: Adobe® CS4 Suite color settings, no independent color management system.

Cataloging and Archiving: Not as well as I should; using Lightroom® and Bridge, my workflow for image organization is cumbersome and erratic at best. The best thing I've done for myself is to create a hierarchical folder system that I do maintain on large internal drives and back up to a redundant external system, using a 2-TB Western Digital® My Book Studio Edition II drive. I rely on the kindness of my brain and the strength of search engines, if I've misplaced something. For documenting and tracking my art pieces, I keep a database using FileMaker Pro. This is where I maintain the details about process, sales, and exhibitions.

About the Artist

Educational Background: My artistic training has come from years of daily immersion working with my mentor, professional artist Dorothy Simpson Krause.

Current Job: For over a decade I've managed Krause's studio and we have assisted each other in the development of processes and gorgeous art works. In turn, I formed my company, Mary Taylor Art, through which I assist other artists with their digital equipment and use of traditional art materials. More and more I teach artists' workshops in my Boston-area studio and by invitation at other venues. Away from my studio, I've given many workshops in such places as the International Center of Photography in New York City, Digital Arts Studio in Atlanta, and the Center for Contemporary Printmaking in Norwalk, CT. Each workshop is focused on integrative processes between traditional and digital printmaking. I also accept commissions and enjoy precious time to create artwork in my own studio which I exhibit in several shows each year. I love to experiment with innovative artistic processes and expand my artistic training by taking workshops with other artists: Beverly Carreiro, Ana Cordiero, Maureen Cummins, Peter Madden, Scott McCarney, Sharon McCartney, Keith Smith, Donald Glaister, Stephanie Stigliano, Wendy Hale Davis, Marcia Ciro, Shanna Leino, Kitty Maryatt, and Laura Wait.

Artistic Inspiration: Dorothy Krause, Irma Cerese, Anslem Kiefer, Wolf Kahn, and so many more

Career Highlights: Receiving the gift to work with artists and in turn sharing what I know—that exchange has been lifegiving for me. Teaching workshops while still working a part-time day job is both exhausting and energizing. Doing it well takes time to learn and requires a lot to deliver information in a way that others can use it, but the payback is that I learn so much in the process.

Creative Process

"White Trio" is part of an evolving local color series of art pieces primarily inspired by the New England landscape. I began with three very different photo-based images: "Rusty Train," "Duxbury Bay Sky," and a cyclamen scan. Ultimately, "White Trio" is more similar to botanical painting than landscape painting.

Figure 3-31
RustyTrain.jpg,
DuxburyBaySky.tif,
cylamen scan

Starting with the RustyTrain.jpg image that began as a tiny file taken in Vermont with an Olympus® E10, I cropped it slightly and expanded it to 24″ (h) × 36″ (w) at 300 dpi (7200 × 10,800 pixels) and saved as TrainWreck.tif. The original small image is very soft at this big size, but because it is only a layer of color the distortion becomes a feature. Generally I photograph images as RAW files, but that day the camera disk was full so I deleted some RAW files and took JPEGs for the rest of the day.

I unlocked the background layer by double-clicking on the lock (right-hand side of the background layer in the Layers palette) and named the layer so I could remove the train window curtains and create transparent windows in the train image. The white window curtains were roughly removed by using the Magic Wand Tool with tolerance set to 25. I held down the Shift key while selecting the white areas of the windows and then cut (Delete key) the pixels without refining the edges (no refined edges).

Figure 3-32
MagicWandTool.tif

By selecting the "Create new document from current state" button (bottom of the History palette), I now had a new image the size I wanted to work with; it had transparent windows and no locked layers. I did a "Save as" and named the file TrainWreck.psd. It is not necessary to save images in process, but I do it because I never know when I might want to return to an image in a previous state.

Figure 3-33
HistoryNewDocument Detail.tif

Next I opened the "Duxbury Bay Sky" image (captured with my Canon® EOS Digital Rebel XTi) and sized it to match the TrainWreck. psd image (7200 × 10,800 pixels). I copied and pasted it into the train image before closing it without saving.

I then duplicated the Duxbury Bay Sky layer and moved one copy to the bottom layer and named it "1 Dux Bay Sky Normal 100%."

I duplicated the train layer and kept both train layers in the middle. I made layer 2 "Train Hard Light 50%" and layer 3 "Train Difference 100%."

To the top layer ("4 Dux Bay Color 99% w/ Gradient") I added a layer mask, then used the Gradient Tool to add a 50% normal light to dark gradient to the mask. I dropped the opacity of the layer back to 99% and changed the blending option to Color.

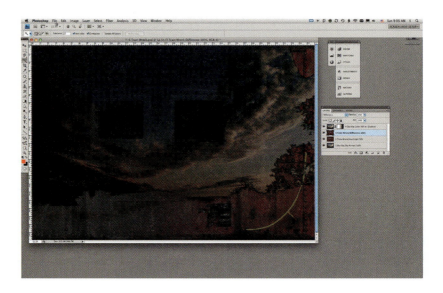

Figure 3-34
TrainWreckLayers.tif

I saved the TrainWreck.psd but it still wasn't quite what I was looking for at that moment. The entire image may become something else at another time, but I was looking for an area with abstract soft colors. Using the Crop Tool set to 24″ × 24″ at 300 dpi, I cropped around the right-hand window and saved the cropped image as "Train Window 24 × 24."

Now I had an extremely soft image with all four layers and I knew I needed to add something with a lot of sharpness for contrast. (The Train Wreck image has remained intact, offering other possibilities for images coming from different cropping choices or as a whole.) Next I opened "Cyclamen Scan," an image created from a scan of spent cyclamen flowers. The flowers were scanned at high resolution using my Epson Perfection® 4490 Photo Scanner with the output set to 20 (h) × 15 (w) at 300 dpi (6000 × 4500). The scanned image is sharp so it can handle being enlarged with out losing details such as the pollen. The cyclamen image was copied and pasted to the Train Window file. Now, as the top layer, the cyclamen image was dragged and slightly stretched to fill the dark area of the window and the blend mode was changed from Normal to Lighten 100%.

The completed image was saved in layers, then flattened and saved as WhiteTrioFinal.tif for output to my Epson Stylus® Pro 7800 printer.

Next, I began thinking about how to turn the digital file into a final art piece.

Figure 3-35
SSTrainWindow24 × 24.tif

Figure 3-36
White Trio final

I like to build cradled wooden boards (boxes) and mount my prints onto the surface. I print images onto materials that I can get through my printer and then glue them to the wood. The box I chose for "White Trio" was 24″ × 24″, so I designed a custom substrate by painting layers of paint onto a larger sheet of Tyvek® (a woven polyester house-wrap product).

To assist me with creating an underpainting on custom substrates, I create a mock-up using a quadrant grid. I use my grid file anytime I want to create a custom substrate with judiciously placed brush strokes, textures, or other materials. To build this grid file, I created a new file with a transparent background that was 8″ × 8″ (one-third the size of my final print but at a scale that I can print from my letter-size laser printer). Then, I used the Line Tool with the weight set to 0.014 and the color red, and I have set my workspace up to show rulers in inches. Holding down the Shift key, I dragged the Line Tool across the image horizontally and vertically at 2-inch increments to create a red grid. When I finished scoring the grid with red lines, I merged the visible layers, leaving me with a transparent red-lined grid. I keep this grid file in layers for continued use as a mock-up file. When I want to use it, I copy and paste my final image into the grid file and scale it to size. I print the mock-up on my laser printer and use it as a guide when I'm painting the custom substrate and for making notes as I paint.

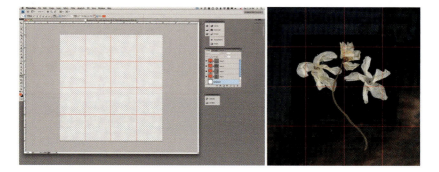

Figure 3-37
QuadrantGrid.tif and mock-up for Underpainting.tif

Next I painted the plain side of the Tyvek with deep creamy yellow (acrylic) paint and washed over it with black paint. I like the Tyvek because it can stand up to the painted surfaces without wrinkling. (The other side of the house wrap is quite busy with the branding information.) To prepare the painted substrate for inkjet printing, I coated it with iridescent inkAID™ (silver and pearl), a precoat that allows the ink to adhere to the painted surface. In the substrate detail you can see the layers of paint, creamy yellow and black, with iridescent silver and pearlescent inkAID on the top.

Figure 3-38
TyvekInfo.tif

I wanted the white of the flowers to pop and not be silver or pearl like the precoated substrate, so in the areas where the flowers would print I painted that area with white matte inkAID. This is where the

Figure 3-39
SubstrateDetail.tif

Figure 3-40
PrintedWhiteTrioDetail.tif

mock-up grid is helpful. The contrast of the white matte inkAID brush strokes adds further interest to the surface. The result is that the cyclamen flowers are white on an otherwise colored substrate.

Painting on the thin, very flat Tyvek allows the custom-painted and coated substrate to glide through the Epson printer. When the print was dry, I coated it with a matte acrylic varnish, trimmed the print to 23″ × 23″, and glued it down to the surface of the cradled wooden board. I prepared the box by painting it black and adding silver leaf around the edges. After the print was mounted I added a final finish by using a soft cloth and rubbing on a burnt-umber oil paint with cold wax medium.

TIP: To keep the scanner clean from pollen and other debris, I placed a clear piece of glass onto the bed of my scanner and then placed the spent blossoms on the glass and draped a black satin cloth over them. The result of that scan is that I captured the specks of pollen that add interest to the decaying flowers.

Figure 3-41
WhiteTrio.tif

Eric Scala

Eric Scala

Rennes, France
ericscala@yahoo.com
www.ericscala.com

Equipment
Computers: Mac® Pro (Quad-core Intel® Xeon®)
Scanner: EPSON®
Printer: EPSON®
Software: ArtRage, Bryce Vue modo®, Corel® Painter™, Adobe®
   Photoshop®
Favorite Papers: Heavy matte
Color Management System: None
Cataloging and Archiving: CD, DVD, hard drive

About the Artist
Education: Graduate of Lycee Henry IV, Arts Decoratifs of Paris
   (E.N.S.A.D.)
Current Job: Painter and illustrator
Artistic Inspiration: As a painter, Leonardo da Vinci, Alma Tadema,
   John Singer Sargent, and a lot of Preraphaelite artists; as an illustra-
   tor, Craig Mullins, Ashley Wood, Meats Meier, Sebastian Krüger,
   and more recently artists from Avalanche. For me, inspiration
   means looking at their work. I need to draw or paint, but inspira-
   tion could come from music such as that by Led Zeppelin or Peter
   Gabriel, or even a Bach cello suite performed by Tortellier.

Creative Process

Figure 3-42

At home or traveling, I always carry a sketchbook. The sketchbook could contain sketches or doodles. For "Ze Butcher," I started without knowing where I was going. I then scanned in the sketch.

Once it had been scanned, I opened Painter and added another layer. I then added my colors with chalk and used a water rake blender to blend the colors.

Figure 3-43

Figure 3-44

As my sketch had only the head of the character, I found I needed to add other details. I like to use two different pencils: a grainy cover pencil and a colored pencil.

By adding more color with the Chalk Tool in Painter, I can give a blurry effect. The next step was to begin to add a bit of the details needed.

More and more details were added. I changed the size of my drawing in Photoshop, allowing it to grow bigger and bigger. I also used Photoshop and the airbrush to work on the details.

Figure 3-45

Figure 3-46

I then added some characters either from a scan or directly drawn with ArtRage.

Figure 3-47

Figure 3-48

Next, I used a gradient filter in Photoshop to change the atmosphere. I also continued adding details in Photoshop, such as Remy Rat's reflection in the glass bottle.

I decided at the last moment to add the stamp. There's not that much difference between working on a computer or in a traditional method. I use one to three brushes. The only big difference is that I can change the size to work on the details … and that's Ze difference.

Figure 3-49

John Derry

John Derry

Omaha, Nebraska
derry@pixlart.com

Equipment

Computers: Power Mac® G5 (dual-core 2.3 GHz with 2 GB RAM); Power Mac® (2.4 GHz, Intel® Core™ 2 Duo, with 4 GB RAM); Apple® 20″ Cinema displays; multiple 500-GB external hard drives, Wacom® Intuos4 tablet, Wacom® Cintiq®

Scanner: CanoScan® FB 630U

Printers: Epson Stylus® Photo 2200, Epson Stylus® Pro 7600

Software: Adobe® Creative Suite® 5, Corel® Painter™ 11

Favorite Papers: EPSON® Velvet Fine Art (VFA), Arches® Velin Museum Rag 315, Arches® Rives BFK 310

Color Management System: Monaco OPTIX XR DTP 94 colorimeter and ColorEyes Display Pro profiling software

Cataloging and Archiving: I use a personal numbering system with backups to multiple hard drives.

About the Artist

Education: BFA in Painting and Drawing, University of Nebraska at Omaha; MFA in Painting, Cranbrook Academy of Art, Bloomfield Hills, MI

Current Job: Independent fine art professional. I do interpretive portrait commission work for professional portrait photographers, and I teach Expressive Photographic Interpretation workshops utilizing Painter and Photoshop. I write a regular column, "Express Yourself!," for Rangefinder Publishing's *AfterCapture* magazine, focusing on photographic postproduction work. I'm currently serving as Corel's Painter Ambassador-at-large.

Career Highlight: Co-authoring Painter with Mark Zimmer and Tom Hedges

Inspirations: Robert Rauschenberg has been a major influence, particularly in the manner that he mixed photographic and painterly content.

Creative Process

I'm passionate about merging the mediums of photography and painting. With the explosion of digital photography, it has become effortless to combine photographic source material with the expressive qualities of hand-applied brushstrokes via Corel Painter. These once disparate mediums now effortlessly coexist on what I refer to as the *new level playing field*.

For the past few years, I've been exploring the interpretation of photographic source content into the language of painting. Each medium is made up of a unique vocabulary. The vocabulary of photography includes sharp focus, depth-of-field, and lens distortion (which is not necessarily a bad quality). Painting's vocabulary, on the other hand, includes brushstrokes, canvas texture, and simplification of detail. To successfully translate a photograph into a convincing painted result requires transposing the photographic vocabulary with painting's unique vocabulary. Simultaneously, the artist's personal expression is intertwined with the result. In this project, I demonstrate this interpretive process using a still life of vases and woven baskets.

The immediacy of digital photography has made it easy to experiment with *light painting*. This technique involves interactively lighting a subject in a darkened space while the camera is set to a long exposure. With the shutter open, the subject is selectively painted with a directed light source. The resulting photograph exhibits a uniquely modeled lighting that imbues the subject with a painterly quality. This technique can act as a first step toward instilling an image with the vocabulary of painting.

Figure 3-50
SureFire® Z2 CombatLight®

Figure 3-51
Cone

For my light painting source, I use the SureFire® Z2 CombatLight®. This flashlight provides an extremely bright light source. Another advantage of the Z2 is that it has an on/off button on the rear of the flashlight. This enables the light to be instantly turned on and off at will, making it an excellent interactive light painting tool. I use black construction paper and tape to fashion a tight directional cone to further direct the light.

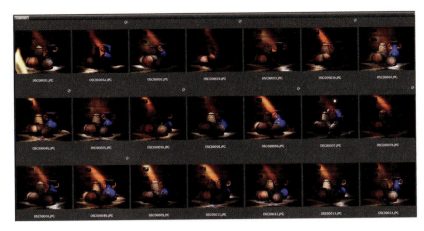

Figure 3-52
Proof Sheet

With my still life set up and the room darkened, I open the shutter for 30 seconds and proceed to selectively paint the objects with multiple stabs of light at different angles. It takes a while to perfect the desired lighting. This is where the advantages of shooting digitally come into play—I can instantly review my lighting and make corrections for the next exposure. The final result of the session is a photographic series of my subject painted with a variety of interesting lightings.

Combining Multiple Exposures

Light painting tends to be highly experimental. It is often difficult to get the exact look that you are after in a single exposure. Multiple exposures are built by stacking several exposures in Photoshop and

Multiple Exposure Layer Stack: *Lighten* **Blend Mode**

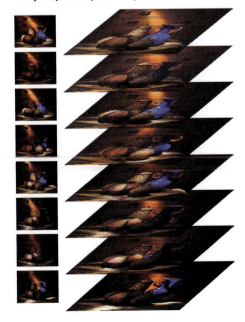

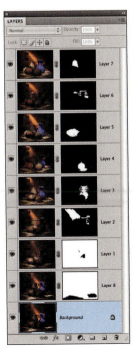

Figure 3-53
Layer stack

Figure 3-54
Layers palette

setting the blend mode for each to Lighten. Only the light-painted portions of each exposure are added to the overall composite image.

All the exposures are photographed on a tripod. As a result, the images are in registration with one another. Turning the various layers on and off in the Layers palette is like turning various lights on and off in the image. The additional use of layer masks further enables editing the lighting as desired.

Figure 3-55
Photo ready for painting

Once the desired lighting effect is created, I flatten the layers and perform a bit of retouching, color correction, and tonal adjustment. The initial step of light painting serves to provide the resulting image with an artistic idealization consistent with the vocabulary of painting. This image becomes the starting point for expressive interpretation in Painter.

Painter's layers possess the ability to treat any underlying imagery—no matter how many layers—as wet paint. In general, brushes that smear and blend on a layer can equally smear and blend any underlying color found below the current layer. This capability enables a highly useful technique that I refer to as *nondestructive layer painting*.

Interpreting a photograph into a painting utilizes the concept of *overpainting*. Overpainting is a process by which an existing image—a photograph in our example—is interpreted into a painting by utilizing non-paint-bearing brushes to smear the underlying color within the image. It is as if the photograph has been transformed into wet oil paint. A variety of brushes can be applied to the wet imagery to imbue it with a hand-painted appearance.

If you were to directly overpaint a photograph, you would be destroying the original detail, making it difficult to go back and adjust various elements that need additional enhancement. The technique of creating source and destination images via cloning is an option. You can overpaint the clone (destination image) and selectively soft-clone back any original detail (source image) as needed.

Nondestructive layer painting eliminates the need for a clone because the base image *is* the source image. The layers become the destination imagery. Instead of ending up with a flat overpainted photograph, you end up with the original photo intact on the Canvas and the dispersed cloning residing on as many layers as you wish. Each layer remains editable, enabling a great deal of flexibility. I refer to this technique as a *painting layer stack*.

This is a crucial step for successfully interpreting a photograph into a painting. Simplification is a key element in the vocabulary of painting. A painter typically *indicates* detail via expertly placed nuances of detail without literally stating it.

Paint Layer Stack *Schematic*

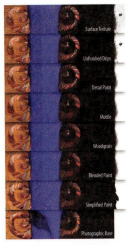

Figure 3-56
Painting layer stack

Figure 3-57
Simplifying process—Smart Blur filter

The human brain is wired is such a way that it delights in "connecting the dots." By providing well-placed indications of complex detail, the mind's eye of the viewer will fill in the details by connecting the dots. It is this engagement of the viewer's imagination that creates interest and depth within the image.

I begin by applying the Smart Blur filter (Underpainting palette) to the Canvas image in order to suppress the high-frequency photographic detail. Note that this can be optionally applied to a layer copy of the photograph. I prefer to apply it directly to the Canvas to avoid an unnecessary layer.

Figure 3-58
Simplifying layer clone source

Figure 3-59
Simplified paint

Next, I create a layer that is used to apply simplifying brush strokes. The goal of this step is to reduce the color complexity of the image to hand-applied, single-color strokes. For this step, I utilize a clone—or *source image*—of the Smart Blur layer as the color source for my simplifying brush. This simplification brush is a custom variant I created that samples the source image's colors but reduces it to a single-colored stroke. Visually, the painted result is reminiscent of opaque gouache.

Figure 3-60
Blended paint layer

Next is the blended paint layer. Apply a blending brush to this layer, which blends and smoothes the underlying color made up of the simplifying strokes. The blending brush does not apply color; rather, it imparts the expressive character of its brush bristles to the wet paint below. I do not attempt to completely eradicate the underlying simplifying layer—the result is more a visual mixture of both.

With the photographic detail now replaced by a simplified underpainting, I now begin to restore detail through various techniques. The still life's background is dominated by a dramatically lit oak chest of drawers. The simplifying steps eradicated the oak woodgrain. My initial step of restoring detail is to recreate this woodgrain in an artistic manner.

A key concept here is not to allow the original photograph to literally dictate the resulting expressive interpretation. If the original is slavishly copied, the interpretation will retain too much of the original photographic vocabulary. The artist must strive to subjectively interpret various aspects of the subject. This interpretive attitude is a key principle that firmly resides in the vocabulary of painting—as in many forms of artistic expression.

Figure 3-61
Addition of woodgrain

I first create a new layer to apply the woodgrain. To simulate the look of woodgrain, I use the Scratchboard Rake (Pens Category). This variant applies multiple parallel pen strokes. After painting the woodgrain to my liking, I apply Glass Distortion (Effects > Focus) utilizing a Paper Grain to rough up the woodgrain strokes. To further integrate the woodgrain layer with the painterly qualities of the image, I apply a layer mask and paint in the resulting mask with Square Chalk (Chalk Category) to impart a canvas texture the woodgrain. This is yet another technique that invests the image with the vocabulary of painting.

Figure 3-62
Mottle layer

The mottle layer is another technique that conveys additional arbitrary randomness. This layer imparts a random variation of density throughout the underlying imagery via the application of the Soft Light layer blend mode.

I create the mottle texture with the Pattern palette's Make Fractal Pattern dialogue. This useful tool generates a user-adjustable, seamless, random, fractal pattern tile. Because the tile pattern wraps around itself, it can be utilized to create a larger fractal texture (multiple copies of the tile can be placed adjacent to one another with no discontinuity of the fractal pattern). This fractal pattern is built and dropped on the mottle layer.

Because the resulting random mottle layer is made up of black-through-white values, the layer's blend mode can be set to Soft Light to impart the random densities to the underlying imagery. I adjust the layer's opacity to a low value (10% in this instance) to reduce the mottle to a just noticeable appearance. Note that this layer is optional, as is its order placement in the layer stack.

Detail Painting with a Saturated Color Source

Saturated Color Source

Clone Color painted on Detail Paint Layer

Detail Paint Brush set to *Use Clone Color*

Figure 3-63
Saturated lone source

Figure 3-64
Detail paint layer

The human visual system seeks out detail and contrast, ignoring areas of low detail and contrast. When applying detail, it is important to focus on the subject. In this case, it is the vases and baskets. This is where most of the detail painting should be applied as this will lead the viewer's eye to it, thereby investing the subject with greater importance. Less important areas—like the drawers and rug—receive less detail. It is a common beginner's error to apply equal detail to all areas of a painting. As a result, the mind's eye finds no points of focus and the image quickly becomes uninteresting.

The purpose of the detail layer is to restore the image's fine detail without literally stating it. Less is more in this instance—the goal is to allow the viewer's eye to fill in the detail by connecting the dots. Like the earlier-described simplifying layer, the detail layer employs the Smart Blurred clone source to stream color through the texture-aware detail brush. In this case, however, I oversaturate the source image. This serves to provide the resulting strokes with a painting vocabulary vibrancy not associated with photographs.

Figure 3-65
Unfinished drip layer

Photographs customarily have crisp edges delineating them. As such, this is an element in the vocabulary of photography. I often employ an unfinished edge to negate this photographic vocabulary element and interpret it with one from the painting vocabulary.

The unfinished edge has become something of a signature element in many of my expressive interpretations, and it is another visual element from the vocabulary of paint. To accomplish this, I provide the initial image with an *outset*. An outset is an additional margin beyond the edge of the imagery. This margin allows me to add random elements to the edges of the painting as I build up the layer stack.

I employ the drip layer to add random drips and splatters to the image with a custom-built Image Hose and Nozzles. My goal is to enhance the spontaneous character of the painted image.

Figure 3-66
Surface texture layer

Part of what we sense when viewing a painting is its physical presence. The appearance of canvas weave, the sparkling highlights of varnish—subtle though they are—invest a painting with a sense of physicality. These qualities may not even make a conscious impression on the viewer, yet they too are a subtle element of the vocabulary of painting.

Several blend mode algorithms (Overlay, Soft Light, Hard Light, Vivid Light, Linear Light, Pin Light, Hard Mix) treat 50% gray as transparent. Lighter gray values lighten the underlying imagery toward white; darker gray values darken the underlying imagery toward black.

This final layer adds the surface patina of canvas weave and lightly impastoed brush strokes to the painting. I use a custom grayscale-textured surface that relies on the 50% transparent gray value. The surface highlights are greater than 50% gray, and the surface shading is less than 50% gray. When this layer's blend mode is set to Linear Light, in this instance, the underlying imagery takes on the appearance of a canvas painted surface. The layer's opacity is substantially reduced (30%) to maintain the subtlety of the surface appearance.

In a twist of *trompe-l'œil,* my ultimate goal in this case is to present the final image as a photographic reproduction of a physical painting. The image has been drained of its photographic vocabulary and replaced with that of painting. The resulting reproduction in this book mimics the look of a photographed physical painting. It's kind of chasing its own tail!

There are basically two directions in which I can take this image. One is to print it on fine art paper. The other is to print it on canvas. Depending on the output, I can selectively delete layers to suit the substrate.

If I print on canvas, I can delete the surface texture layer and allow the actual receiving canvas's weave and subsequent protectant or varnish provide the physical cues. I could take it further and embellish the canvas with selectively applied paint strokes. If I print to paper, I can leave the texture layer intact and embellish with pastel pencils, extending the hand-wrought expressive character of the artwork.

In either case, I view the resulting image as a valid form of artmaking. When painting digitally, many of the same coordination and conceptual skills are required as painting traditionally. By embracing the *new level playing field,* I'm free to intertwine multiple mediums to any degree I desire. Being in a digital format—as all primary forms of communication now are—the artwork flows easily into these other forms.

The genie is out of the bottle.

Figure 3-67
Trompe-l'œil with a twist

Theresa Airey

Theresa Airey

Monkton, Maryland, and Bermuda
Aireyt@aol.com

Equipment
Computers: 15″ Mac® PowerBook® G4 for traveling and an iMac® Intel® Core™ 2 Duo, 2.4 GHz Processor with 4 GB memory in the studio

Scanners: Nikon™ Super Coolscan 4000 and Epson Perfection® 2480 flatbed scanner

Printers: Epson Stylus® Pro 4000, Epson Stylus® Photo R2400, Epson Stylus® Photo 2200

Software: Adobe® Photoshop® (CS4); Nik® Software: Dfine®, Color Efex Pro™, Silver Efex Pro™, Sharpener Pro™ 3, Viveza®; Akvis software: Sketch and ArtWork 2.0; Auto FX software: Photo/Graphic Edges 7, Mystical™ Lighting and Ambience; Boinx FotoMagico®; Microsoft® Office; Corel® Painter™ X

Favorite Papers: Crane® Epson Textured Fine Art, EPSON® Premium Canvas, Moab Entrada®, Crane® Museo® Max.

Color Management System: ColorBurst® in my printer

Cataloging and Archiving: Separate external hard drives for different folders, such as infrared work, books, text information, color shots; Canto® Cumulus® software for data on CDs and DVDs.

About the Artist
Education: BFA from University of Maryland, Baltimore Campus; double MFA in Fine Art and Photography from Towson State University, Towson, MD

Current Job: Instructor of creative studies (photography, collage, painting) at the university level, freelance photographer, and author.

Artistic Inspiration: Artists: Leonardo da Vinci, Vincent van Gogh, René Magritte, Georgia O'Keeffe; photographers (silver heroes): Ansel Adams, John Sexton, Jerry Uelsmann, Ruth Bernhard, Imogene Cunningham, Huntington Witherill, Henri Cartier-Bresson, Michael Kenna

Career Highlight: I hope I haven't had that yet; however, one thing comes close. One of my photographs was selected to be on the cover of *Photography in the 21st Century,* written by Katie Miller for Delmar Learning. My name was also listed in the index directly under Ansel

Adams, the one who showed me that photography could be a fine art in 1980.

Gallery Representation: Bermuda Society of Art Gallery, MasterWorks Gallery

Creative Process

I have been fascinated with Corel's Painter software for several years. I love creating paintings from my photographs, and while doing so I came upon the Kaleidoscope option under "Dynamic Plug-ins" at the bottom of the Layers palette.

At first I considered it too gimmicky but then started to explore the possibilities. I soon became excited about the numerous variations that I could create with just one image ... and use in my work.

You can use color, infrared, or black-and-white images to create kaleidoscopes in Painter. You can also combine black-and-white kaleidoscopes with color inserts or color kaleidoscopes with black-and-white inserts for more interest. It is great fun and gets your creative juices going. Try it and you too will become totally addicted.

Once you understand the concept of how the kaleidoscopes are created, the fun will be endless and you will end up with great useable images. Here is some important information and pointers to review before you begin.

Kaleidoscopes are square only. The more pixels in the image, the greater the selection of higher kaleidoscope dimensions from which you can select. If you have an image around 6.789 × 10 at 300 ppi, you have a pixel dimension of 3000 × 2037. So, in your Kaleidoscope dialogue box your highest Kaleidoscope option will be 2000 × 2000. This will give you a final kaleidoscope of 6.667 × 6.667 at 300 ppi with a pixel dimension of 2000 (width) × 2000 (height) pixels. You can later enlarge the size of your kaleidoscope in Photoshop by using the Bicubic Smoother in the Image Size dialogue box.

A good kaleidoscope of 12″ × 12″ at 300 ppi is ideal for most of my work. In most cases, I use Sharpener Pro to sharpen the image before printing. You may choose to select a smaller Kaleidoscope dimension in the dialogue box, as it will give you more options for a variety of kaleidoscopes.

When you like a kaleidoscope, save it to your desktop as a Photoshop file. Once you have your kaleidoscope image from Painter saved on your desktop, open it in Photoshop. (Note: Drag and drop your image into Photoshop to open it; if you double click on the image, it will open up in Painter.)

Open Photoshop's Layers palette. Turn off the background (click on the eyeball on the left) so you may see the kaleidoscope more clearly and will be able to crop it more easily and correctly.

You can, at this point, turn the background eyeball on and the kaleidoscope eyeball off to see what part of the image Painter used to create the kaleidoscope. It sometimes helps in understanding the process and to see how the image was created. Now you can flatten the image.

Sharpen the kaleidoscope, if necessary, and save it as a PSD, TIFF, or JPEG file.

Figure 3-68
Collaged image of Roman City

I used a collaged image, "Roman City," which has a burned-edge effect, applied with Auto FX Photo/Graphic Edges 7 software, for my beginning image.

Figure 3-69
Cross Kaleidoscope

"The Roman City" collage image is 7" × 10.3" 600 ppi. This image has a width of 6000 pixels and height of 4054 pixels. To obtain the cross kaleidoscope, I used the pixel option in Painter of 4000 × 4000.

After saving my cross kaleidoscope to my desktop from Painter, I opened the kaleidoscope in Photoshop and desaturated some of the color with the Hue/Saturation Tool. This made the cross kaleidoscope stand out a bit more.

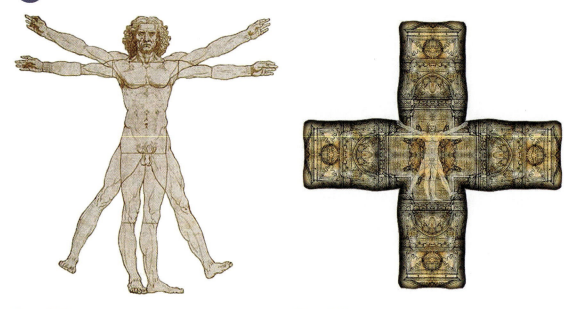

Figure 3-70
da Vinci's "Vitruvian Man"

Figure 3-71
"Vitruvian Man" added to cross

Next, I took Leonardo da Vinci's "The Vitruvian Man" (copyright free), resized it to around 2 × 2 at 300 ppi (Figure 3-70), and dragged it over on top of the cross kaleidoscope.

I then blended the "Vitruvian Man" image into the cross kaleidoscope image by using the Luminosity blend mode found in Layers.

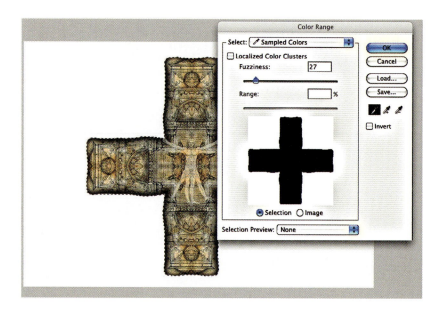

Figure 3-72
White background selected

With the kaleidoscope image finished, I flattened the image and then went to the menu for Select > Color Range. I used the Eyedropper to select the white background.

Figure 3-73
Images joined

I then *inversed* (not inverted) the selection (Command + Shift + i) to select the cross image only. Next, I used the Move Tool in the toolbox to drag the kaleidoscope image (cross image with "Vitruvian Man" image blended into it) into the "Roman City" collage image and centered it. I used the Luminosity blend mode again to blend the images and make them more integrated.

Figure 3-74
Color added

I liked this image but thought the white background surrounding the image could be more exciting, so I decided to fill in the white background with color. After flattening the image (I always save the layered image first with an "L" in the name), I selected the color first by double-clicking on the foreground color box in the toolbox and used the Eyedropper to select a color from inside the image. I chose the deep red tone.

Figure 3-75
Color range

Next, I selected the white space surrounding the image by going to the menu; under Select I scrolled down to Color Range. I used the Eyedropper Tool to select a white background with a fuzziness range of around 27%. I then clicked on OK.

Figure 3-76
Collage filled

After the white area was selected, I went to Edit > Fill. In the dialogue box I chose "foreground color" to fill the space at 100%. Remember, you can always go to Edit > Fade if you prefer a paler color.

Figure 3-77
Black-and-white version

I liked the final image but continued to play a bit more, The next three images are other ideas for my final images. I converted the color image to black and white with Nik filters found in the Nik software.

Figure 3-78
Sepia version

I took the black-and-white image and navigated to Image > Adjust > Color Balance. I added a +23 for the red channel and a −27 for the yellow channel to give me a rich brown tone.

Finally, I went back to Figure 3-72 and chose the kaleidoscope cross layer and converted it a into a black-and-white image.

As you can see, the creative variations are endless and open up a whole new venue for your work. Have fun and enjoy the process as well as your unique final images.

Figure 3-79
Final "Vitruvian Man" collaged together

Martin Addison

Martin Addison

Worcester, United Kingdom
martin@painterforphotographers.co.uk
www.painterforphotographers.co.uk
www.martinanddoreen.co.uk

Equipment

Computers: Various PCs, which seem to require updating on a regular basic and always more storage and faster processors!

Scanners: EPSON® flatbed and Nikon™ Super Coolscan 4000 for the occasional slide. Neither of them is used much now since all my capture is digital.

Printers: Epson Stylus® Photo R2400 and R2880 principally

Software: Adobe® Photoshop® for all general imaging requirements and Corel® Painter™ for anything requiring a painterly element. Adobe® Photoshop® Lightroom® for cataloguing and fast processing.

Favorite Papers: I use a range of papers by PermaJet®. Three papers in their fine art range stand out: Artists (210 g) which looks like a traditional watercolor paper; Museum (310 g), which is a slightly textured off-white art paper, and Papyrus (300 g), which has a rough surface, ideal for pastel pictures. For pictures that need more impact and stronger colors, I love the Fibre Base Gloss (295 g) and Fibre Base Royal (325 g) papers, which replicate the traditional darkroom papers and are ideal for both monochrome and color images.

Color Management System: All of my computers, monitors, and printers are professionally color profiled.

Cataloguing and Archiving: I have a simple filing system based on folders numbered with year/month/date and the subject. Combined with keywords added in Lightroom, this allows fast access to the images when I need them. Archives are stored on hard drives and DVDs.

About the Artist

Education: My photographic background has been self taught, starting as an enthusiastic amateur photographer in my teenage years. The medium was then primarily color slides, which also included many years of creating and presenting multi-projector audiovisual programs. Prints were initially in monochrome and later in color using the Cibachrome® process. It was with a set of multiple printed images on Cibachrome paper that I obtained my Fellowship of the Royal Photographic Society in 1995. I started working digitally about 15 years ago, learning Photoshop and Painter at about the same time. Over the years, I have run a number of residential and evening courses in Creative Seeing, Photoshop, and Painter, in addition to individual tutoring. Painter has become a particular focus for me in recent years which has resulted in the publication of three instructional books on how to use Painter with photographs as the source. My latest book, *Painter 11 for Photographers,* was published in 2009 and is heavily illustrated to show the techniques and methods required to master the program. The book also contains a DVD with video tutorials.

Current Job: My work background has been in retail management, from which I have recently retired. This has allowed me to devote more time to photography and painting.

Artistic Inspiration: My inspiration comes from everything around me and in particular the natural world. One of my favorite photographers is Freeman Patterson, whose writing and photography continue to inspire whenever I revisit his many books. I have always been interested in creating pictures that intrigue, sometimes using close-up techniques to explore subjects in depth. In the camera, I use multiple exposures to add texture and I extended this concept when I started color printing from slides, which gave me the opportunity to combine pictures through multiple printing. Working digitally in both Photoshop and Painter gives me the freedom to create pictures that exist only in my mind.

Creative Process

This picture of magnolia blossoms was created in Painter using the cloning process. Being a photographer rather than a painter, I use photographs as the source for all my pictures. Magnolias are such beautiful flowers; the pure colors and delicate tones never cease to attract me every year. These flowers were fully opened by the time I photographed them, and some were starting to go over so I decided to combine two photographs to make a more satisfactory composition.

When you are combining more than one photograph in Painter it is important to plan where each element will be placed in the final composition to avoid running into problems of placement once the painting has commenced. What you need to remember is that, when Painter is cloning from another document, it lines up the top left corners for reference, so if you want something to appear on the right, you may have to offset the picture.

You can download the original files from my website to work through the tutorial.

Figure 3-80
Original photograph

Figure 3-81
Original photograph

Preparation

The first stage is to assemble the two photographs into one new document. Open the two original files: Magnolia A and Magnolia B. With Magnolia A active, start by lifting the picture onto a layer. Select the Layer Adjuster tool, Select > All, then click in the picture area to move the contents of the canvas to a layer.

This image needs to be on the right-hand side and the other picture on the left so you need to add some extra canvas to the left. Click on the Canvas layer to make it active, then Canvas > Canvas Size. The picture is 2700 pixels across, so add 1000 pixels to the left; this is an estimate and if necessary more can be added later.

Now the other picture needs to be copied into this image so they can be lined up. Make the other picture active, Select > All, then click the Layer Adjuster Tool and drag the picture into the other document. Watch for the outline of the picture to confirm that it is being copied.

Move it into position, and reduce the layer Opacity to make it easier.

Overlap the two pictures; the petal in the center is not very attractive, so cover it with the other picture. When the pictures are in position crop off any excess white area at the edges.

There are two ways to go from here. You could save this as a multilayered file and clone from the individual layers. Alternatively, you could create two separate documents, which is the procedure described here.

Turn off the layer visibility of the top layer. Drop all the layers: Layers palette menu > Drop All. This will flatten the picture, ignoring the layer that is not visible. Now, File > Save As > Magnolia A.

Undo the previous step so you have the layers back again. Reveal the top layer and hide the bottom layer. Drop all, and File > Save As > Magnolia B. Now we have the two images from which we can clone. Close all the images.

Figure 3-82
Photographs prepared for cloning

Figure 3-83
Photographs prepared for cloning

Cloning Preparation

Open the two files you have saved (Magnolia A and Magnolia B). Make a new document; this should be the same size as the files we have just saved. To check the size, open one of the files and Canvas > Resize; note the dimensions. Create a new document: File > New. Enter the width and height you just noted and a resolution of 300 pixels per inch.

Figure 3-84
Blended background

Cloning

Select the Pastels > Square X-Soft Pastel brush, which is a lovely brush to use for flowers. Return the brush to the default settings.

In the Colors palette, click the Clone Color option. Choose brush size 137 and Opacity 7%.

Now it's time to connect this new image file with one of the original photographs. Go to File > Clone Source and select Magnolia A. Turn the Tracing Paper on and clone the entire picture very lightly with this soft-textured brush, avoiding the hard edge on the left. Change the clone source to the Magnolia B original: File > Clone Source > Magnolia B. Paint the remainder of the picture from this source, avoiding the hard edge once again.

Reduce the Resat slider to zero, and blend the entire picture to create a delicate color wash for the background. When the Resat slider is at zero, the brush picks up no color from the photograph and therefore changes to a blender. This is a useful tip to remember as it works with most brushes in Painter.

Figure 3-85
Bringing in the detail

Figure 3-86
Magnolia detail

Make the brush size 30, Opacity 46%, and Resat 60%, and clone the flower petals, following the lines of the picture and paying particular attention to the changes in color or tone. Enlarge the picture on screen to follow the detail more closely.

Swap the clone source again to paint the other flower.

Change to brush size 30, Opacity 20%, and Resat 0. Gently blend parts of the picture to integrate the more detailed areas with the soft background. Change to brush size 21.5, Opacity 11%, and Resat 48%. Bring back some more definite detail, the edges of the petals in particular.

Continue to bring back detail with a small brush, and then soften it with a larger bush at low Opacity and Resat values until you have finished the picture.

Combining several photographs in Painter is great fun and can produce some beautiful textures. This picture was planned at the start, but in many cases additional photographs can be added as you go along to increase the quality of the texture. Have fun!

Figure 3-87
Final magnolia painting

Alexander Kruglov (Shurelo)

Alexander Kruglov (Shurelo)

Voronezh, Russia
alek-krug@yandex.ru
http://www.shurelo.ru

Equipment
Computers: Intel® Core™ 2 Duo, 2.93 GHz
Scanner: Epson Perfection® 1200
Printer: Epson Stylus® Pro 9800
Software: Microsoft® Windows® XP, Adobe® Photoshop® (CS2),
    Corel® Painter™ Classic
Favorite Papers: EPSON® Premium Luster Photo Paper

About the Artist
It's now hard to think that not so long ago I had a very different life.
I worked as a leading expert at a large petrochemical industry but
had to retire on the insistent advice of the doctors. By that time I had
already earned my pension and did not risk anything seriously. And,
though I had various ways to go, I suddenly opted for the one that
finally brought me to the pages of this book. Maybe I awakened in
myself that little boy who went to an art school or just remembered
a piece of advice I once heard: "If your hobby becomes your job, you
don't work a minute." A few years before, I had taken an interest in
Photoshop software, devoting all the spare time I had to it. I was lucky
to get a book cover design in a Moscow editorial. Later I illustrated
a Russian–French magazine for women and edited the digital art section in a magazine on digital photography.

Creative Process
It's typical of us humans to keep in memory moments of life similarly
to how we keep photos in a family album. Some of these "photos"

fade, and we finally come to not distinguishing them at all. Others get rid of small insignificant details, thus becoming brighter and more expressive. I have such a memory of a rainy and hazy autumn day, an old garden, apples lying in pools under the trees. I was a little boy standing there with a big apple in my hand. Many years have passed since, but when it is raining I feel the taste of apples mixed with raindrops. Maybe that is why I still enjoy walking in the rain. In one of such walks an old house caught my eye. I knew it very well since I was a child. It was ready for demolition and reminded me of an apple core. For lots of years it had given comfort to all of its tenants and several generations had lived there, but it finally faced the autumn of its life, too. I decided to tell its story.

Since I started working in Photoshop, I have faced the problem of getting detailed photographic images of high definition. I bought a digital camera and learned to make photos. Nowadays, I almost always have either a reflex camera or a small digital camera, which is easy to put in my pocket. I take pictures of different objects, not only those necessary for my current work but also for future projects. I take photos of these objects from different angles and try to do it without bright lighting so that it should be easy to fit them into collages. When I started publishing my works on the Internet, I began receiving offers from amateur and even professional models to take part in my projects. I have photographed them at a studio and quickly collected a database of different types, now approaching 10,000 photos.

Figure 3-88
Apple core

I started my work with taking an apple and making a core of it. Then I put this "masterpiece" on a white sheet of paper and photographed it. With the image in my computer, I highlighted the outline. Normally I make a pencil sketch before starting to work at the PC and

Figure 3-89
Added apple components

then scan the sketch and build up my composition on it. This time I limited myself to the apple core only.

I filled in the outline with fragments of ruins and constructional elements I had in my photo database, using a wide variety of transformation tools. Moreover, I added a part sticking out of the center of the apple core. I used a tube instead of a handle. I cut it off of a photo of machinery. I paid attention to the fact that the house that provided the basis for this work had part of the window frames newly painted. The occupants wanted to somewhat renew their house at the last moment and this influenced me to "paint" the roof of my house. Then I added dimensions and shades with the Burn Tool and Dodge Tool.

Figure 3-90
Chimney and blowing leaves

To reinforce the Fall mood, instead of smoke I added some autumn leaves.

Figure 3-91
Background created

Having finished with the main subject, I took up the background, making a new canvas for it. Then I chose a photo of an autumn sky and some pictures of pools, trees, and a shabby house, as well as some clouds photographed from a high altitude. I joined all these photos with a help of layer masks, using different blend modes.

Then I just had to join these images and emphasize the foreground. For this I added a photo of a stray dog, drinking water from a pool. I shot it during that walk when I got the idea to make an apple-core house. I added some fallen leaves and reflections in the water. To make the reflection of the house I used the apple core I already had.

Figure 3-92
Adding in design elements

Figure 3-93
Finished collage of the apple core house

Ad Van Bokhoven

Ad Van Bokhoven

Waalwijk, Netherlands
www.advanbokhoven.nl

Equipment
Computer: Microsoft® Windows® PC
Scanner: EPSON®
Printer: Epson Stylus® Pro 7600
Software: Corel® Painter™ X and 11, Adobe® Photoshop® Elements 6,
    Corel® Draw, Windows® Publisher, ACDSee® Pro 2
Favorite Papers: Hahnemühle German Etching Paper
Color Management System: None
Cataloging and Archiving: DVDs

About the Artist
Education: Academy for Arts and Design in Hertogenbosch, Holland
Current Job: Being a father and an artist
Artistic Inspiration: At the moment, Tom Coates and Ken Howard,
    both English painters

Creative Process

Figure 3-94
Original photo taken at the
Louvre in Paris

This is the photograph as I took it at the Louvre in Paris. I used a digital camera—nothing special, just a Canon® Ixus 60, 6 megapixels.

Figure 3-95
Boosting the color and contrast

Before painting I worked up the photograph and gave it some more color and contrast. You may exaggerate here; just give it a boost: Saturation +++, Contrast +++.

Figure 3-96
Simplifying the painting

In this stage, I simplified the picture a lot. It is important to get fewer details and colors.

I use the Painter Auto Painting palette. Scribble different sizes, different rotations, different speeds—a bit of trial and error. Just have fun with it! It is fascinating to see things happen. Don't expect this auto painting to paint the complete picture. It is just to get the painterly feel.

The brush strokes I used are mostly ones I made myself with the brush control window.

It must look like you've painted the whole scene in half an hour with a too large brush and a limited color palette. A photograph has too much detail and color; a painter never uses that much.

Figure 3-97
Added color with the palette knife

Now I mainly use a home-made palette knife and some other home-made brushes with an extreme amount of grain. Notice the yellow in the sky.

I'm still painting broadly but with a bit more detail than before. The buildings behind are deliberately more vague than the foreground to get perspective in it.

My favorite brushes are the ones that have a grain, usually a canvas grain. I have a custom-made variant set of "oil brushes."

Again, I use a lot of smeary brushes and textured ones. Sometimes I clone parts of the photo into the painting which I then immediately smear and use the oil paint brush.

The whole painting must not be too detailed, as that would spoil the painterly look of it.

I deleted the man on the right, painted in some new colors (purples and blues), and gave the picture texture in some places. A canvas texture (Effects > Surface Control > Apply Surface Texture > Paper) was then applied using image luminance. At the end, I again added contrast and sharpened the picture.

Figure 3-98
Final painting at the Louvre

Karin Schminke

Karin Schminke

Kenmore, Washington
www.schminke.com

Equipment
Computers: Desktop and portable Mac® computers, HP® Windows® desktop
Scanner: Microtek ScanMaker™ 9800XL
Printers: Universal Laser Systems® PLS4.60 laser engraver, Epson Stylus® Pro 9600, HP® Designjet Z3200, HP® Photosmart Pro B9180
Software: Adobe® Creative Suite® Design Premium
Favorite Papers: Hahnemühle, rice, and handmade papers
Color Management System: X-Rite Monaco OPTIX system to calibrate my monitors
Cataloging and Archiving: Adobe® Photoshop® Lightroom®

About the Artist
Education: MA and MFA at the University of Iowa
Current Job: Full-time fine artist
Artistic Inspiration: Constructivists, color field painters, Henri Matisse, and Japanese prints
Career Highlight: Artist-in-residence at the Smithsonian American Art Museum
Gallery Representation: Walker fine art in Denver, CO; g2 Gallery in Scottsdale, AZ; The Gallery at Bainbridge Arts and Crafts on Bainbridge Island, WA; and Iowa Artisans Gallery in Iowa City, IA.

Creative Process
"Rites of Passage" provides an example of how Photoshop can be used to assist in decision making and production of fine art created in multiple steps. This piece began as a pencil on paper drawing of an idealized plant form. In Photoshop, I combined a scan of the drawing with several of my monoprints and a photo using layers and blend modes to collage the elements into a coherent composition. As with most of my art, "Rites of Passage" utilized many image layers, blend modes and adjustment layers. During production these were continually reconfigured to create files for the next step.

Figure 3-99
Original collage beginning

The original file was developed without color for production using the Professional Series PLS4.60 laser engraver from Universal Laser Systems. To laser engrave, a black-and-white image is sent to the engraver through the ULS laser engraving software that functions like a printer RIP, controlling many aspects of the image quality. But, unlike a RIP, you can interactively change settings during the engraving.

As with most of my work, I planned to use hand-applied layers of paint and texture to add visual interest, actual depth, color, and an organic sense of form. During production, these hand techniques were alternated with inkjet printing and laser engraving. Each step inspired the next, and Photoshop enabled the production to match the inspiration.

Figure 3-100
Painting black acrylic

I wanted a strongly contrasted background image that would show through in the final piece, so I prepared for the first engraving by painting a layer of black acrylic paint onto a 20 × 16-inch aluminum sheet.

Figure 3-101
First etching

In Photoshop, I choose a combination of layers to create the background image. As the black areas of the digital file represent the areas that would be engraved to reveal layers below, I used Photoshop's Invert Adjustment layer to match the projected outcome of the engraving when fine-tuning the image (with Invert Adjustment applied). A high-contrast-curve Adjustment layer also helped to preview the image as engraving results in a largely two-toned image.

Figure 3-102
Complete background engraving

After completing the etching of the black background image, I took a digital photo of the background and used it in Photoshop to experiment with color options for the next step.

Figure 3-103
Experimenting with color options

Using layers, I tried various color gradation and shape variations. I decided to use a shaped gradient corresponding to the leaves of the original drawing and with the spiral dropped out of the color.

Figure 3-104
Overprint

To prepare the engraved aluminum for printing, an inkjet precoat was applied and plastic strips taped to the edges of the aluminum to allow the image to print past the edges of the aluminum sheet to assure edge-to-edge coverage. The aluminum was then fed into an Epson Stylus Pro 9600. The image was printed using the ErgoSoft® PosterPrint RIP to finely control color and placement.

Figure 3-105
Printing

Figure 3-106
The printed aluminum

To allow the addition of more water-based acrylic media to the printed surface, the inkjet print layer was sealed with a mineral spirit varnish from Golden Artist's Colors. Then, layers of acrylic gel, metallic gold, and finally white paint were added to the panel, using a print of foreground elements for reference.

Figure 3-107
Adding gel

Figure 3-108
Gold applied

I wanted the final image to have some soft white in the negative shapes around the leaves to suggest life and to reemphasize the spiral shape. In Photoshop, studies of various white forms were placed onto layers above the photo of the printed aluminum, using the Lighten blend mode to preview the engraving results.

Figure 3-109
White forms added

An image with some soft gray left in the negative space around the plant and spiral was chosen for the final engraving.

Figure 3-110
Final engraving

The aluminum panel with the white coat of paint covering the surface was positioned into the ULS laser and the file was sent to the laser engraving software. While the file determines where the engraving will occur, the software determines the strength of the engraving. I felt it was better to be conservative in applying power to the laser as under-engraving can be fixed, while over-engraving can wipe the panel back to blank aluminum.

Figure 3-111
Laser movement is a blur but sparks show the trail of the laser

After the first engraving. I determined that I wanted to uncover a bit more of the background color, so the same file was resent to the laser with the power turned down to remove a bit more of the white surrounding the plant form.

A final coat of varnish both protected the surface and brought out the rich reds and golds beneath the surface to complete *Rites of Passage*.

Figure 3-112
Rites of Passage

Tony Sweet

Tony Sweet

Eldersburg, Maryland
www.tonysweet.com

Equipment
Computers: Mac® Pro and MacBook® Pro laptop
Scanner: Microtek ArtixScan™ M1 and Nikon™ film scanners
Printers: Epson Stylus® Pro 3800 and Epson Stylus® Pro 7900
Software: Nik Software, Lucis® Pro, Alien Skin Software
Favorite Papers: Museo®
Color Management System: X-Rite Eye-One®
Cataloging and Archiving: Catalog in Aperture®; archive on backup
  hard drives and DVDs

About the Artist
Education: Jazz musician
Current Job: Photographer, educator, workshop instructor, author
Artistic Inspiration: Everyone has something to share and inspiration
  is everywhere.
Career Highlight: Named Nikon Legend Behind the Lens
Stock Agency Representation: Getty Picture Agency

Creative Process
High dynamic range (HDR) imaging is the hot ticket these days,
and Photomatix is the current industry standard; however, although
Photomatix does a good job of compiling an image series, the final
output often lacks contrast and is a bit flat. So, postprocessing software intervention is essential to realize visually striking HDR images.

   In the following example, we will start with a standard HDR image
and go through several plug-ins and techniques to realize a final
image that is very different from the original, more illustration based
and photographically nonrepresentational.

   Any number of over- and under-exposures can be put together to
create HDR images. In this case, I used what I refer to as a standard 5
image series (−2ev, −1ev, 0ev, +1ev, +2ev). A large percentage of my
HDR images fall in this exposure range.

Figure 3-113
Five thumbnail images of the exposure sequence of images

After dragging and dropping the images into Photomatix (the easiest way), the following three boxes appear in order:

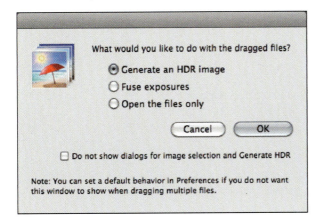

Figure 3-114
Photomatix dialogue box

I make sure that the "Generate an HDR image" is selected.

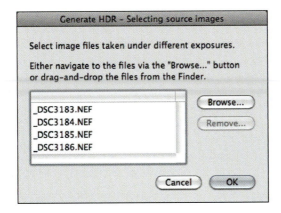

Figure 3-115
Selecting source images using Photomatix

This is a list of files you dragged and dropped. You can also browse to select images.

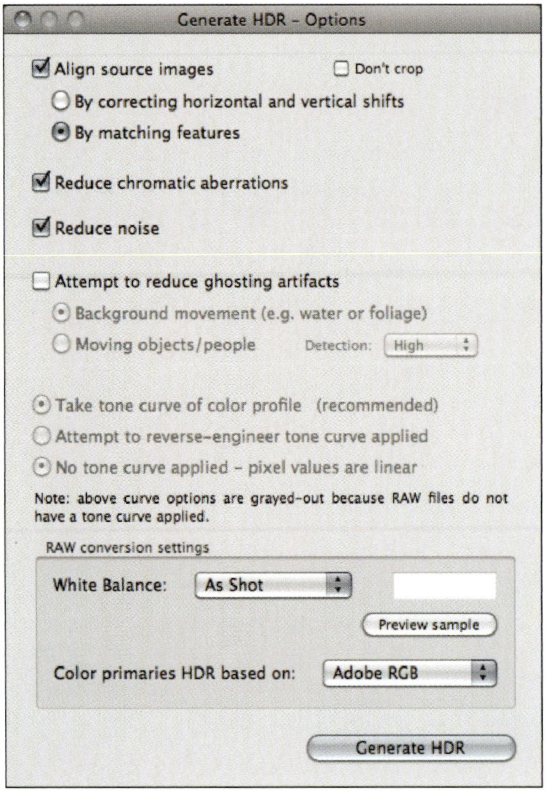

Figure 3-116
Generate HDR using Photomatix

Figure 3-117
HDR RAW file, pre-tone-mapped

I make sure that "Align source images" is checked and that the "By matching features" is selected. I don't think it matters which of the two options is chosen.

I check "Reduce chromatic aberrations."

I check "Reduce noise."

I leave the white balance "as shot" and make sure that the "Color primaries HDR based on:" is set to Adobe RGB. The ProPhoto setting may result in very intense color, sometimes difficult to adjust.

After pressing the "Generate HDR" button, an HDR RAW file appears. You can choose to save as HDR if you think you may go back to reprocess at a later time. This will save the time of processing from scratch.

HINT: The Tone Mapping Settings open up with the previous image settings. If you like the look or are shooting an HDR panoramic image, for example, this is a great thing. If not, press the "Reset: Default" button at the bottom of the window to start fresh.

After adjusting the settings to taste, here is the tone-mapping preview I obtained. Since I wanted to create a grittier look and go a little over the top on this image, I chose to double tone map. This is achieved by just selecting Tone Mapping again. This will double the amount of the effect.

Notice that this rendering came out a bit flat and bright (Figure 3-122). So, I tweaked the Tone Mapping Settings to darken the image

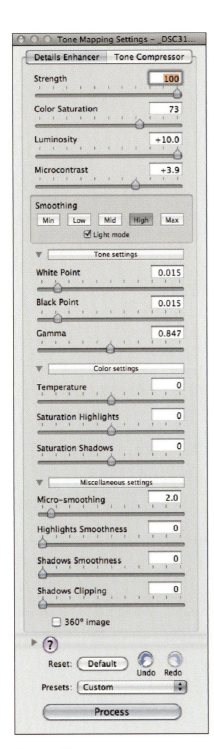

Figure 3-118
HDR settings

Figure 3-119
Tone mapping preview

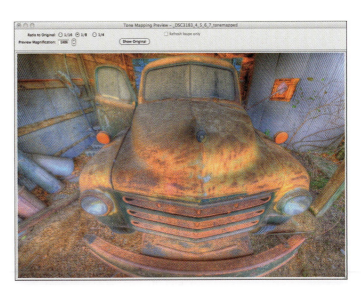

Figure 3-120
Tone mapping doubled

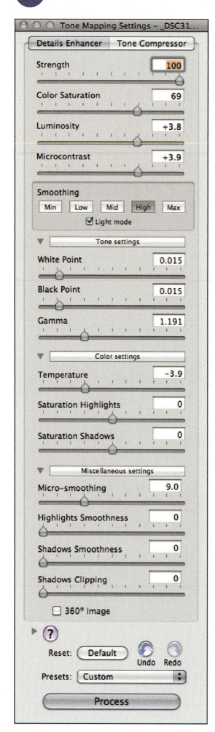

Figure 3-122
Tone mapping preview

Figure 3-123
Double-tone-mapped HDR

Figure 3-121
Tone Mapping Settings view

Figure 3-124
*Beginning in LucisPro
software*

a bit by lowering the gamma slider. Pressing the Process button completed the first stage of this process.

Now, we'll move onto multiple iterations using LucisPro software.

LucisPro is a Photoshop plug-in that enables the user to optimize an image using simple controls, or sliders, with unlimited combinations of settings. I use it mostly to bring out detail in an image, using exclusively the Enhance Detail slider. But, occasionally, and depending on the image, I'll use multiple iterations of LucisPro to render an image that is nonrepresentational. In other words, the final image is not readily recognizable as a photograph.

IMPORTANT NOTE: It's a good practice to always create a new layer when working on an effect so you have the option to blend the layers together by adjusting the opacity, if desired.

This first process increases sharpness and contrast.

Figure 3-125
LucisPro settings

As you can see, the controls are minimal and simple.

On this first iteration, the Scan Lines are set to 32, which will render the clearest image.

The next control down is "Mix with Original Image." I leave this to 100% processed. It's quicker and easier to mix the LucisPro image by adjusting the opacity in the Layers palette.

"Assign Original Image Color" can be used to compensate for the color shift that can occur when making adjustments in LucisPro, especially when working in Split Channels. I adjust this to taste. In this case, the setting of 8% allows a small bit of altered color to affect the image.

In the "Split Channels" box, I'll adjust the red, green, and blue channels to taste, but generally, if you'll notice the settings, the red channel is around the middle, the green channel is a bit higher, and the blue is quite a bit lower. I use "Split Channels" for my first LucisPro process to increase detail (sharpness) and to affect the overall color of the image, if so desired; otherwise, I'll set the "Assign Original Image Color" to 100%. The "Display Composite Image" is turned off (unchecked) when processing for detail or sharpness. This will display the channels in black-and-white mode. It's generally easier to "eyeball" sharpen in black and white, not unlike sharpening using Lab Color in Photoshop.

You can use the Preset box to save often-used settings.

"Enhance Detail" and "Smooth Detail" work in tandem or separately to effect a desired look. No rules. You have to play around here a bit. Think of this first image as a first coat of paint in the following processes.

After processing, I flattened the image and created a new layer to apply the next LucisPro iteration.

After the initial sharpening and contrast increase, this iteration begins to soften the image. The only controls used here were "Enhance Detail" and "Smooth Detail." There are no rules here, just a gradual layering of LucisPro processes, with the opacity adjusted between the previous image and the current iteration.

Figure 3-126
LucisPro settings

As you can see here, the effect is moving away from the photographic look to a more painterly or illustrative look. Notice that the "Enhance Detail" and "Smooth Detail" settings are different.

Figure 3-127
Applying Nik Software Viveza

The processing has created a very dark area on the hood, which is an issue. So, I applied Nik® Software Viveza® software to easily target and lighten that area selectively.

Figure 3-128
Silver Efex Pro

At this point, I decided to add one of my favorite moves, which is to introduce a black-and-white layer using Nik® Software Silver Efex Pro™. On the black-and-white Silver Efex Pro layer, I created a mask and painted the color back into the car, leaving the subject framed with a monochromatic background.

Figure 3-129
Going back to LucisPro again

Also, to increase the texture, I did one more LucisPro layer to lower the "Preview and Processing Scan Lines" setting to 1. I used "Enhance Detail" to bring texture (grunge) into the image.

Figure 3-130
Nik® Software Efex Pro™ Darken/Lighten Center filter

There was still something missing. The car didn't pop enough. Another favorite and often used move is to use the Darken/Lighten Center filter in Nik® Software Color Efex Pro™ (v3.0). Here, I was able to darken the edges of the frame and lighten the center (hence, the filter name), which created the almost three-dimensional look and finished the process.

For print, I'll resize and assign the paper profile, then sharpen using Nik® Software Sharpener Pro™.

Figure 3-131
Final image

Jason Seiler

Jason Seiler

Chicago, Illinois
www.jasonseiler.com
Blog site: http://www.jasonseilerillustration.blogspot.com

Equipment
Computers: Mac® Pro and Wacom® Cintiq®
Software: Autodesk® SketchBook® Pro

About the Artist
Education: American Academy of Art in Chicago
Current Job: Freelance illustrator, painting and drawing for magazine and book publications as well as character design for film
Artistic Inspiration: James Jean, Phil Hale, and Sebastian Kruger; I also love Norman Rockwell, Lucian Freud, Zorn Anders, and John Singer Sargent
Career Highlight: Working as a character designer for Tim Burton's *Alice in Wonderland*
Gallery Representation: Levy Creative Management in New York, in addition to galleries in New York and Los Angeles

Figure 3-132
Reference photo of Zach

Figure 3-133
Original sketch in Photoshop

Figure 3-134
Initial painting

These are the steps I took while painting "Red Beard." The sketch was drawn in Photoshop 133 using a small round brush, with "Shape Dynamics" clicked on to give the brush a point.

For this painting, I used Photoshop and my Wacom Cintiq; the size of the final painting is 9″ (h) × 12″ (w) at 300 dpi resolution.

Most times I start with color right away, blocking both the color and value at the same time. For this demonstration I thought it would be more helpful to break down my process and simplify my technique, making it easier to follow for both the beginner and those practiced in digital painting. I prefer to start on a non-white background, preferably a neutral gray.

When sketching with Photoshop, I sketch on a separate layer so that I have the freedom to move the sketch around or resize it with ease if needed. For this sketch, I wanted to start painting right away. All I need is a basic frame of my subject in order to start painting. The sketch is simple, basic, and to the point, yet there are no surface details. Instead, I will suggest with simple lines where I feel the eyes should be. My brush setting is usually the same with any brush that I use.

I make sure that "Other Dynamics" is clicked on and that the "Opacity Jitter" is at 0%, "Control" is set to "Pen Pressure," the "Flow Jitter" is set to 0%, and the "Control below the Flow Jitter" is off.

These settings give me the control that I prefer. I usually paint with my Opacity set to 85% to 90% and my Flow set to 100%, although this sometimes differs depending on effect.

After I'm settled with the sketch, I switch the sketch layer to "Multiply," making the layer transparent. I then create a new layer and place it under my sketch layer. This way, when I start to block in

Figure 3-135
Basic painting continues

my values, I don't lose any of my sketch lines. For the block in, I continue to use a round brush, but I click off "Shape Dynamics," leaving the brush round without the point.

When blocking in the painting, it is important to use larger brushes. There is no need to worry about or focus on the small details; instead, you want to focus your attention on the larger shapes of values or lights and darks that you see. I recommend that you squint your eyes when blocking in. Squinting your eyes while blocking in gives a slight blur to both your reference and your painting.

This will help you to see the larger shapes. It also helps to not work at full size, so I'll paint from a distance. If you decrease the window size of your reference and painting, you won't be able to see or paint much detail. Painting from a distance with larger brushes will help you cover more ground in less time.

After drawing, getting the values right is the most important thing. If the values are right, you can use almost any color and the painting will work. To properly establish the values, I first look for the darkest darks and the lightest lights. Once the darkest dark and the lightest light are established, I begin to block in a mid-value range and will go back and forth between the different values, comparing them to one another. Like the sketch, I keep it simple. You don't need more than three to four shades to block in or establish the values. Black, white, and a couple grays that fall in between will be sufficient. Once those basic shapes are laid down, I use the Eyedropper Tool to select variations within the values that I've created, giving me an even wider range of values to work from.

After a rough block in of black, whites, and grays, I create a new layer that I put on top of the first two layers. In this stage, my original sketch lines are no longer needed, so I slowly paint them out, tightening up my values, structure, and likeness. You can see in Figure 3-135 that I have begun to establish a recognizable human form, but I haven't gotten carried away with detail or spent time laboring over the exact likeness.

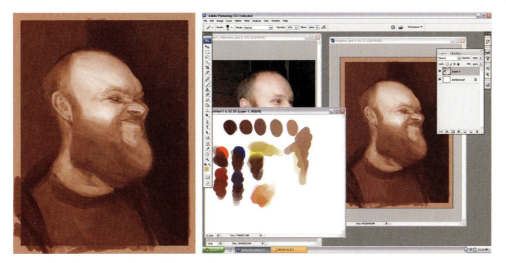

Figure 3-136
Starting to lay in color with simple color palette

I really enjoy painting with acrylics and oils, and one thing I often do with both is experiment with underpainting. I like to lay down a color with the idea that it will show through here and there throughout the painting. It also has a unique way of pulling the painting together. When painting portraits, it's fun to paint a red or red-orange underpainting.

There are greens and blues in flesh tones, and having an under-painting of opposite color adds a bit of drama and excitement to the painting. I prefer that my digital paintings look traditional and the best way to get that look is to use the same techniques that I use when painting traditionally.

Figure 3-137
Establishing color basics

After you have blocked in the black-and-white values to a point where you feel you can move on, you can flatten your layers, as you will no longer need them separated. Next, I choose the Paint Bucket Tool to create a new layer and fill it with a solid red. The exact color of red you pick doesn't really matter. I try to pick a variation of red that I see in the subject that I'm about to paint. So it can be, and is, different every time. Now I change the layer mode to Soft Light. The value painting will show through the red, and it will look as if you laid a red wash over it.

This is where the paining becomes a little more complicated. By this step, I am ready to start blocking in my painting, but first I need to create a color palette that has harmony. As I said earlier, my main priority is getting the values right. I know that if I can succeed in that, I can do just about anything with the color. After establishing the values, I can start thinking about color, focusing on warms and cools, but the values always come first. When creating a palette, I usually create a variation of red, yellow, and blue. With these three colors most colors can be created.

To create a palette, I make a new window and create a new layer. I select my Eyedropper Tool and eye drop a red color from my background. I then click my color picker and choose a few more reds based off the red that I chose and create a small grouping of flesh-like reds and browns. I do this by squinting my eyes while looking at my photo reference and then choosing color according to the values I see while squinting my eyes. When I squint at my photo reference, I see oranges, greens, blues, and violets. I create those colors and mix my red color into all of them, creating harmony. This technique is similar to the "pigment soup" technique that I sometimes use when painting with oils.

After creating the palette of colors that I will use, I begin to mix color according to temperature. For example, I know that as his forehead curves and goes away from me, the colors cool off a bit. This part of the painting can be frustrating and difficult. It can easily discourage you from continuing, but don't let the difficulty of painting bring you down. Painting digitally is so much easier than painting traditionally, as you can always undo a mistake or, if you're not sure, create a new layer to test a color on. Painting digitally is very forgiving, plus you don't have to clean any paint brushes when you're finished, and that's always a plus!

Figure 3-138

Continuing to block in color and shapes

In this stage, I still want to keep things simple and not worry yet about details. So rather than focus on individual hairs on Zach's beard, I will just focus on the overall shape of the beard.

Continuing to squint my eyes, I block in the large mass of his beard, blocking in shades and separations between darks and lights within the beard. I block in darker color behind his head; this will help to separate him from the background as well as help me establish the color in his face. I have also noticed that Zach's head shape could be developed and pushed more to enhance both humor and likeness, so I select the background color and begin to paint on top, creating a new shape to work with. Up to this point something about the likeness didn't seem right to me, and this change is what the painting needed.

Figure 3-139
Traditional painting techniques are followed

For the next few stages, I continued to work back and forth between the different values and colors. If you stay in one area for too long, you won't have surrounding color and values to compare to, so it's important to move around. Try to build up the entire painting all at once. At this point, I'm still using a large round brush for the most part, but I also like to use variations in types of brushes while blocking in my color. I will continue using a large round brush, but I also like brush #24, which is a standard Photoshop brush that has a painterly look to it. I'll paint a bit with brush #24 and then after a while I'll switch back to a large round brush. This technique helps create a more traditional look.

One of the reasons I chose to paint Zach as my subject for this demo is for the range of color in his beard and tattoos. As the painting develops, I will continue to sculpt and form the shapes of Zach's head for the sake of exaggeration, but exaggerating color can be just as important as exaggerating the features. Color can help set the mood or feeling that you may be going for. One of my goals when painting these types of portraits is to capture the person's character or essence. Memory plays a big part in doing this. What I do is try to visualize the person in my head and then capture the images that my memory holds important. In other words, what do I think of when I think of Zach? In my memory of seeing Zach in person, his beard appears to be a bright orange, but the photos I took of him didn't quite capture that. So, I used artistic freedom and painted oranges and reds that are more saturated than what my photo reference showed.

When painting from photo reference it can be easy to just copy the photo as you see it, color for color, and value for value. I don't see the point of this as I want the subject I'm painting to look more like the real person than the photo. This means that I as the artist will paint what I see but also enhance what I am seeing to make it better.

Figure 3-140
Memory is a good tool for the artist

Figure 3-141
Digital painting progress continues

As I continue to paint I decide that the background color in my photo reference is a bit too cool. It has a flat, dead look to it that I don't want in my painting, so I create a new layer on top, choose a warm green from my color picker, and paint it into the background. Turns out the color works well for me, so I flatten the layer and move on. The painting seems to be coming along. The colors and values that I have laid down are working well. The eyes, nose, and mouth are blocked in how I feel they should be, and the tattoo has also been blocked in. Now it's time to zoom in a bit and begin detailing the features.

I zoom in 50% or more depending on how tight I want to get. When I paint traditionally, I like to take a few steps back every so often to get a good feel for how the painting is coming together. I do the same when painting digitally. Every few minutes or so, I zoom out to at least 25% or smaller. This only takes a few seconds but is well worth it. Another thing that I like to do when working on the details is flip both my reference and painting either horizontal or upside down. If something is off, flipping the image will help you see flaws in your drawing and painting. For example, I have found that flipping the reference and painting upside down helps me see where I could improve the values.

As I paint on, I continue to use a round brush, but I have now decreased the size quite a bit so that I can paint in smaller details such as the creases around the eyes and small wrinkles in the skin.

This is the stage where I begin focusing on detail. I spend a lot of time on the eyes, nose, and mouth. I make corrections in the drawing of the anatomy, tightening up the structure, softening edges, and adjusting color and values.

I continue to squint my eyes, zoom the painting in and out, mix color on my palette, and paint on.

In this stage of the painting I have spent a lot of time working on the tattoo, which was particularly difficult to paint. I had to match not only the colors of the tattoos but also the values. The color and the values are affected by light and shadow. Painting the tattoos on his neck took the majority of the time that I spent on this painting.

Figure 3-142
Detail emerges

By this stage, the eyes, nose, and mouth are nearly finished. Only a little more time is needed to finish up the main features. It's now time to paint the beard. You'll notice that the beard at this stage of the painting is very basic. I have only focused on the large shapes, using only large brushes. My technique for painting realistic hair is fairly simple; it just takes time and patience.

I make a new layer on top of the other layers and choose a soft round brush; I have turned on Shape Dynamics to give the brush a point. Next, I use the Eyedropper Tool to select the darkest color, and in the color picker I change the value a tiny bit darker. I then begin to paint in small hairs into the darker areas of his beard. I select the Eraser Tool and make a light pass over the hairs I just painted. This will soften those hairs and gently blend them into the block in. I repeat this a few times, changing the color and values. Next I select

Figure 3-143
Tattoo details and progression of beard detail

the Blur Tool with the strength set to 10% and make a gentle and controlled pass over the beard hairs that were just painted. I now create a new layer on top of the first beard hair layer. I continue this process over and over again, painting little hairs, erasing them, blurring them, creating new layers, and repeating until I get to a point where I feel it looks and feels the way that I want it to. During this stage, I also paint the hair on his head as well as his eyebrow hair and eyelashes. One thing I feel I should share. When I paint hair or beards, it is not my intention to paint every little hair exactly how I see them in the reference photo. Like everything else, I am painting my impression of his beard or hair. I tend to put a lot of character and life into my hair—I paint little hairs going all over the place. Keep it simple; study what hair does and then make it more interesting.

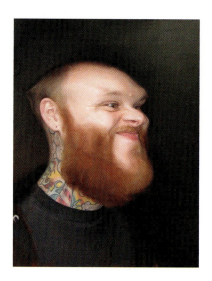

Figure 3-144
Focus on details

This is the final stage of the painting. After the hair has been painted to my taste, I finish off the painting with small details such as moles and pores in the skin, and then add a few subtle details on his jacket and shirt, like the zipper and string. You'll notice that I kept the detail to a minimum on his shirt and jacket. This is because there is so much going on with his face and neck that I didn't want anything below his face to distract or take away from that. Even the tattoo isn't as detailed as the face. The very last thing I do (and this is typical for most paintings that I do) is paint in white highlights where they are needed. This can easily be overdone, so I make mere suggestions of highlights in key places, such as on the ball of the nose and cheek, and very lightly in a few other areas on the ear.

Well, that's it. Remember to have fun. Sketch, draw, and paint from life as much as you can. Keep it simple. If you look at the design of my portrait you can see that my shapes and forms are basic and simple. When I combine strong values and color in my basic design, the final appears more complicated than it really is.

Figure 3-145
Final version of "Red Beard"

Huntington Witherill

Huntington Witherill

Monterey, California
www.huntingtonwitherill.com

Equipment
Computer: Power Mac® G5
Printer: Epson Stylus® Pro 7800
Software: Adobe® Photoshop®
Favorite Paper: Hahnemühle Photo Rag
Color Management System: ColorByte® ImagePrint
Cataloging and Archiving: FileMaker database

About the Artist
Education: Two years of college
Current Job: Self-employed fine art photographer and teacher
Career Highlight: Awarded 1999 Artist of the Year by the Center for Photographic Art, Carmel, CA
Gallery Representation: Verve Gallery of Photography, Santa Fe, NM; Mowen Solinsky Gallery, Nevada City, CA

Creative Process

Figure 3-146
Original photograph (© 2009 Huntington Witherill)

For the series "Photo Synthesis" I use a Canon® EOS 1DS Mark III digital camera and 24–105 mm, f/4L IS USM lens. The flowers and other botanical subjects are most often photographed using a relatively plain background. When the original camera images have been exposed and uploaded to a Macintosh® computer, they are altered and restructured using Photoshop in much the same way a painter might use a brush and palette of colors to achieve a painting. That is to say, the applied techniques are rarely repeated in the same sequence or configuration for any two given images (much as a painter would rarely use the exact same brush stroke twice). The process itself is accomplished in more of an intuitive and improvisational manner than by following a fixed or repeatable sequence of steps to achieve

Figure 3-147
First sequence (© 2009 Huntington Witherill)

a desired result. Once the original camera image has been exposed, the overall process might well be described as being more comparable to painting, or sculpture, or perhaps even jazz improvisation, than strictly to photography.

Beginning with the original camera image, and among an indeterminate variety of steps taken during the process of formulating each completed image, revisions made along the way will—by nature of their visual appearance when viewed on the computer monitor— indicate to me what the next appropriate step might be in order to further refine the overall character and composition of that particular image. Therefore, the finished artwork cannot be "previsualized." In performing all of the steps, I can't anticipate what the next

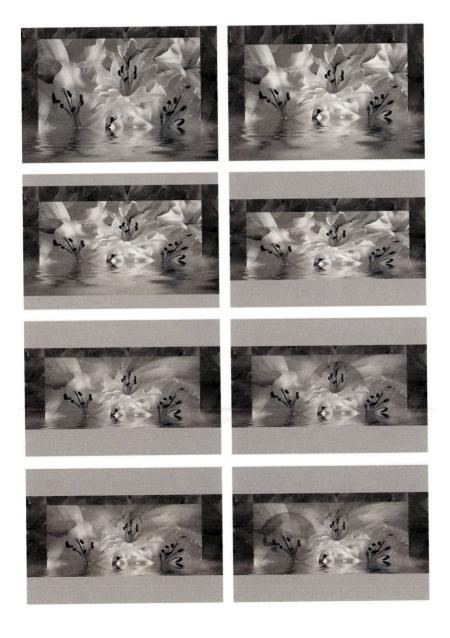

Figure 3-148
Second sequence (© 2009 Huntington Witherill)

appropriate step might be until *after* I've seen what the previous step has visually produced. Decisions are made on the fly. Each finished image is itself a product of the individual decisions being made along the way, together with an understanding of what specific controls and adjustments within the Photoshop program might best serve to accomplish each desired visual refinement. Think in terms of jazz improvisation.

Suffice it to say, if I started with exactly the same original camera image on two separate occasions, I could not hope to achieve two finished images that exhibited (even remotely) the same visual qualities. This is because I would likely make different decisions along the way, and the accumulation of those variables would then produce an entirely different result.

Some of the techniques routinely employed within the Photoshop program include masking procedures used to separate out portions of the image to alter the contrast, color, saturation, luminosity, and/or opacity of those areas. I often construct masks to segregate the edges of chosen objects within the frame so I can then alter the nature of those edges to achieve a variety of painterly effects. Frequently, areas of the image are diffused to introduce blurring into selected portions of the image (again, painting those effects back into the image through layer masks). I also create masks to alter contrast and luminosity in selected areas to achieve different types of lighting and atmospheric effects. And, the images are nearly always distorted with respect to their shape and proportion, being freely formed and reformed in a manner roughly analogous to the way in which a sculptor might mold a piece of clay.

Further, I often copy, resize, and reorient the images and then paste them on top of one another (similar to techniques used in creating a collage). Different effects can be achieved by using a variety of layer blend modes, opacity settings, and layer masks to selectively paint specific effects (and thus draw the viewer's attention) into chosen areas of the image. Though all of the techniques employed can be accomplished with the Photoshop program, the techniques themselves cannot be outlined or quantified in terms of their appropriate sequence or precise implementation. Just as with a painting, or a musical improvisation, there can be no prescribed set of procedures applied to achieve a predictably successful result.

Each finished image requires from a few hours to several days of work to complete. Also, much like a painting, one of the keys to achieving a successful result lies in determining when to intuitively stop the process and discontinue "reworking" the image. I find that I reject and subsequently discard more than 50% of the images attempted, as they eventually prove to be inferior. Finally, once the image is completed, limited-edition archival pigment ink prints are produced using an Epson Stylus Pro 7800 printer, K-3 UltraChrome™ inks, and 100% rag content fine art papers. This combination allows me to achieve a print with the desired look and feel while also serving to ensure each print's longevity.

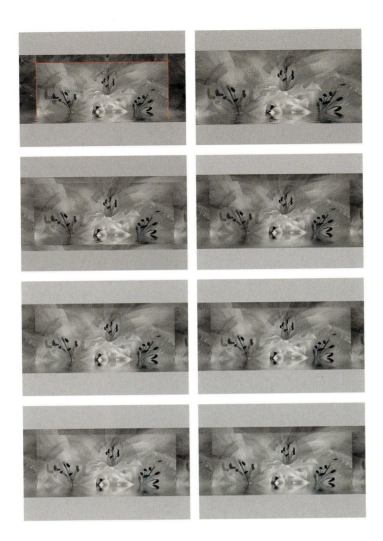

Figure 3-149
Third sequence (© 2009 Huntington Witherill)

Figure 3-150
Final of Photo Synthesis image (© 2009 Huntington Witherill)

Cynthia Brody and Thomas Morris

Cynthia Brody and Thomas Morris

Moraga, California
www.cynthiabrodyart.com
www.thomasmorrisdesign.com

Equipment
Computers: Power Mac® G5, Mac® OS X, 236 GB hard drive, 2 GB RAM, Apple® Cinema display (1920 × 1200)
Printer: Epson Stylus® Pro 1280
Software: Adobe® Creative Suite® 1 with Photoshop® 8
Favorite Papers: A variety of stock, but favoring a heavy, matte white, archival paper stock for art quality output
Color Management System: No additional considerations other than those programmed into the working software
Cataloging and Archiving: All original work on desktop of G5 machine, with backup to a 250-GB external hard drive for archiving

About the Artists
Cynthia Brody is a psychotherapist and fine artist working mostly in mixed media. Her collage style has proven to translate easily into Photoshop as she generally works with photographic images for their visual texture, combining them to create surreal stories and impressions. What she finds exciting about this style of work is the ability to bring together unrelated images in a way that seems believable and recognizable although neither is actually true. She looks for images that can be utilized for their shape, color, or texture as something else. When successful, it is only upon closer inspection that the familiar object or landscape is revealed to be something else entirely. For example, an icon that appears to be a classical female image turns out to be comprised of diverse photos of cathedral roofs, moth wings, and furniture parts, all tied together with paint. Although she enjoys painting, she finds that combining seemingly unrelated collage elements into a cohesive story with fantastic elements brings humor as well as expansiveness to the creative process. Each piece presents a puzzle for the viewer to solve. More comes forward the longer a piece is studied,

which allows one to enter the story. She has done this three dimensionally and now accomplishes it via Photoshop as well. Much of her work focuses on images of women and their self-identification and roles in society. Cynthia brings to her work her interest in the human psyche with its complexities and ironies. She has been creating art for 35 years and practicing as a family therapist in the San Francisco Bay area since 1994. She is also contributing editor of *Bittersweet Legacy: Creative Responses to the Holocaust*, a collection of art, poetry, and stories, and has curated related gallery and museum exhibitions.

Thomas Morris has been a graphic designer and creative entrepreneur for over 40 years, beginning his career designing, handlettering, and printing his own rock posters for promoters in the San Francisco Bay area. To prepare his art for offset printing, he needed to acquire expertise in lithographic platemaking, which in turn demanded a working knowledge of the process darkroom. The skill sets from years of classic (paste-up) layout work were easily transferred to digital programs like QuarkXpress®. Most all of the darkroom techniques needed in using light and exposure to create special effects filmwork for offset printing were easily transferred over to the first issues of Photoshop. Thomas committed totally to digital design in the late 1980s, streamlining his career to computer-driven design and pre-production for print. He worked as an art director in San Francisco, furthering his experience in a high-demand, creative design and production environment using Photoshop, Illustrator, and QuarkXpress. Thomas has continually upgraded his Mac-based workstation, and for the past 10 years has again been doing contract freelance corporate design and marketing using the original Adobe Creative Suite of products. Thomas has collaborated over the years with his creative partner and wife, Cynthia, and was her "hands-on" facilitator, helping her to execute her ideas in the completion of the art for this book.

Creative Process

The inspiration for this piece began with the experience of sharing a favorite redwood forest with Cynthia's 3-year-old granddaughter. She stood her on the giant redwood and told her to stay there until she got a camera. When she got back the child was gazing out into the surroundings in a way that seemed to suggest a greater understanding and appreciation for the beauty than one would have imagined. Cynthia immediately took the picture (with an iPhone®!) and it became her favorite shot of her granddaughter. In creating this project Cynthia started with that image and chose to go further with the idea of a child coming upon a world filled with wonder. The "trees" are sea anemones, which were photographed within their water-filled tanks at the Monterey Bay Aquarium.

She was intrigued at their resemblance to wind-blown trees and knew at some point they would be used as such. She wanted not only to create a story in which the child comes upon the fantastic in nature but also to represent that there is history in everything. The ghosted images of children from a hundred years ago (collected from antique shops) have shared this world before her.

We opened an original PSD file, choosing 13 × 19 inches at 150 dpi in RGB (sheet size of our archival print paper and maximum size for printing on our printer). We opened the original photo and dragged

Figure 3-151

Screen shot of all original asset files: (top left) photo of child taken in a redwood park; (top right) two scanned archival photos from collection gathered from antique shops, etc.; (bottom) three photos taken at the Monterey Aquarium through the glass

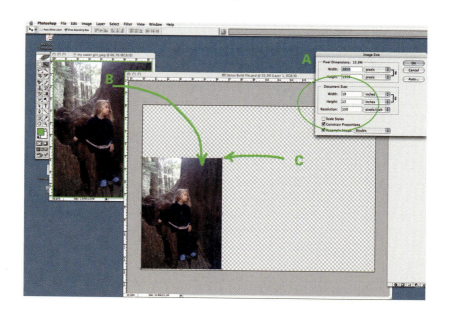

Figure 3-152

Beginning to build the canvas

and dropped it onto the blank canvas and then grabbed the image edge to resize it proportionately.

We used the Rectangle Tool (0 pixel feather) to select a section of the tree and cropped and pasted the selection onto a new layer. We next used Edit > Transform > Scale to distort the canvas. That layer was then duplicated, and we used the Curves Tool to increase

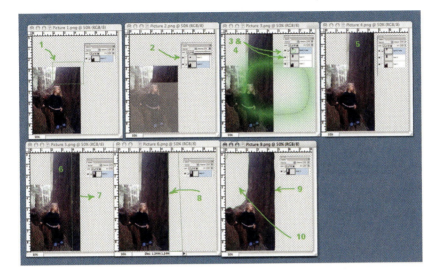

Figure 3-153
Building the "tree" art

contrast. Then, using the Oval Tool , we set a 200 pixel feather (see green halo for visual reference only) and hit Delete to soften the contrast change. All layers were merged. We used the Rectangle Tool (0 pixel feather) and expanded the side of the tree slightly. Using the pen tool, we drew an irregular edge on the tree, selected the path at 3 pixel alias, and then deleted this area. The Lasso Tool (2 pixel feather) was used to draw out the entire area to the left of the tree composition (holding down the Shift key for easy, additive steps) and we then deleted the area.

We dragged and dropped each of the three original anemone images into position on the working canvas. We placed each on layers behind the girl in tree art. Edit > Transform > Scale was used to access handles for easy resizing, making sure to hold down the Shift key to avoid distortion.

We used combinations of the Rectangle Tool and Oval/Circle Tool (200 pixel feather). You need to experiment with this setting, as the effect is determined by your canvas size and chosen dpi setting. We dragged the Selection Tool from outside the image frame and located areas for a soft, gradual delete effect. The Delete key was used to make this area softly disappear, transitioning smoothly into the next layer; repeated deletes continued to softly remove more area. We moved back and forth through the various layers until the desired morphed background composition was complete

We used the Pen Tool (2 pixel feather) to quickly isolate the desired area for altering. We used combinations of Adjustment Layer settings

Figure 3-154
Developing the composition

Figure 3-155
Morphing the backgrounds

Figure 3-156
Revising coloring of girl's outfit

Figure 3-157
*Adding the archival images
into the background*

(Curves, Color Balance, etc.) to change the outfit to the desired effect. We isolated the shoes and used the Lasso Tool at 2 pixels to change the color. Also, when the color changes were completed, we made a separate layer and used the soft brush set at 50% Opacity to paint details into the folds and shadows and merged down onto this layer when we were completely satisfied.

For "Family," we used the Pen Tool (3 pixel feather) to quickly isolate several of the children. We dragged and dropped each part of the selection onto separate layers over the background. A good deal of time was spent on each of these placements. Then, using the Oval Tool (36 pixel feather), we gradually made portions of each image disappear. We also went into each of the figures (when finally positioned) to add some color into each face while carefully removing some of the confusing composition elements on the background layers. The last step was adjusting Opacity to the final desired effect (between 50 and 60%).

For "Children," we selected and copied the rectangular area (held in the clipboard memory). We then went into the right-side anemone layer and made a separate layer of a selected area of the "tree trunk" (magic wand at 24 pixels, then 2 pixel feather). Under the Edit menu, we selected "Paste in Place" to drop in the girl image. It took several steps to achieve the final effect—for example, pulling the image handle down to distort the length, using the Oval Tool (36 pixel feather) to make the bottom of the image disappear, and dropping the Opacity.

Shown in two columns is an enlarged view of the complete Layers palette. Several areas of the background were selected using the Oval Tool at 36 pixels and set on separate layers for additional work, such as adding some color highlights and emphasis, to complete the piece.

Figure 3-158
Several additional final touches

Figure 3-159
Completed artwork

Mike Thompson

Mike Thompson

Beltsville, Maryland
www.mikeartworks.com

Equipment
Computers: Power Mac® G5, 2.66 GHz, Intel® Core™ 2
Scanner: Epson Perfection® 1660 Photo
Printer: Epson® Stylus® Photo 2200
Software: Adobe® Photoshop® Creative Suite® 4 and Corel®
Painter™ 11
Favorite Papers: EPSON® art papers
Color Management System: None
Cataloging and Archiving: Apple® Time Machine with regular DVD
backups

About the Artist
Education: Graphic Arts degree, University of Maryland, College Park
Current Job: Freelance Illustrator
Artistic Inspiration: Some of my favorite digital artists now are Bobby
Chiu, Svetlin Velinov, Jason Seiler, and Jon Foster. I have many
more, but these guys jumped to mind first.
Career Highlight: I starred in a national Coke® commercial and was
featured in an Infiniti campaign
Gallery Representation: David Goldman Agency in New York

Creative Process
My painting of Michael Cera, titled "SuperBad," was actually created as
part of a pitch for the movie "Youth Revolt." The client wanted to per-
suade the studio to use an illustrated poster for this film rather than the
usual photographed one sheet. The direction I was given was to keep
the art vibrant and make sure that Cera looked as nerdy as possible.
They wanted a *MAD Magazine* type of look minus the distortion.

Figure 3-160
Original mock-up

Figure 3-161
Photograph

This is the original mock-up that the client sent in their brief. The photo will be replaced with my painting.

Figure 3-162
First sketch

Figure 3-163
Including torso

Using photos included in the brief as reference, I began my drawing. I always start with the face since I find that most interesting. Normally, I would work up a series of thumbnail sketches first; however, the client knew exactly what they wanted so it wasn't necessary.

After I get the general likeness in his face I moved on to draw the rest of his body. Next the line drawing was scanned into my computer and cleaned up in Photoshop.

Figure 3-164
Creating gradient background

Figure 3-165
Sketch added to background

In Photoshop, I created a document that was 100% of the presentation size at 200 dpi (Figure 3-164). I chose a fairly vibrant blue and filled my background. I knew I wanted a halo effect around the actor's head so I chose a lighter blue and created a radial gradient.

I opened my scanned line drawing in a separate document, then copied and pasted it on a new layer above the background color (Figure 3-165). The Blend mode of the pencil layer was set to Multiply and the Opacity was dropped to 60%.

A third layer was then created and placed between the background and line layers. This was where I began blocking in my shirt color. I always work the same way when creating an illustration. By keeping my clean drawing very tight and painting on layers below it, I am able to work the piece like a "paint-by-numbers" set (Figure 3-166).

Figure 3-166
Adding the shirt

Figure 3-167
Adding contours

Once the shape of his t-shirt had been defined, I selected the "Lock Transparent Pixels" icon on the Layers palette. I chose a darker yellow tone and began to rough in some folds (Figure 3-167).

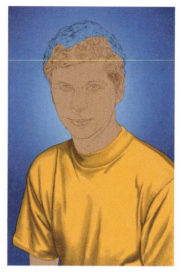

Figure 3-168
Adding skin tones

Figure 3-169
Moving into Painter

I quickly moved on and repeated the process, creating two new layers for the skin tones.

At this point, I was happy with everything and decided I was done with Photoshop for now. I saved the file and opened it in Painter. Using the Fine Detail Airbrush, I refined the glow on my background layer. I painted lighter tones of blue near the edge of his face to add more punch.

Now the fun part! After mixing a palette of flesh tones, I started blocking in the face. I always work my shadows first and save my lighter tones and hot whites for last.

Figure 3-170
Blocking in the flesh tones

Figure 3-171
Refining work in a new layer

When I was comfortable with the direction the face was taking, I created a new layer. This layer was placed above the line drawing and will be used to do my refining. I broke my own rule by getting ahead of myself and finishing the eyes. I generally don't like to work sections of my painting unevenly. Painting an illustration in sections always causes me to lose sight of my likeness and waste a tremendous amount of time.

Figure 3-172
Using the Scratchboard Tool and the Just Add Water blender

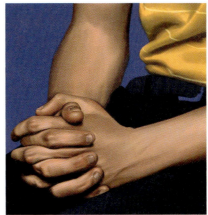

Figure 3-173
Hand detail

Luckily I could just turn off the visibility on that detail layer and get back to working the piece as a whole. I switched from the airbrush to a modified Scratchboard Tool and the Just Add Water blender. I find

Figure 3-174
Highlights added

Figure 3-175
Hair details added

that the Scratchboard Tool gives a nice random texture that works well with skin. Because of this, these are two of my favorite tools.

Now that the overall level of detail was uniform, I could add my highlights. I put a bit of extra time into the hands but I think it was worth it. For me, hands are very easy to screw up. If the lighting is wrong on one finger the whole piece can feel off. Although I was pretty happy with the final render of the hands, the client ultimately decided to use a closer crop and they weren't needed.

Almost done now. I always paint hair last because it is so time consuming. It's easy for me to lose my place here, so I need to pay special attention to my reference.

Figure 3-176
Tonal changes made to the hair

Figure 3-177
Color correction in Photoshop

Hair is one place that I don't mind letting my pencil lines show. I find that leaving some construction lines, especially around the temples, seems to add to the illusion of realism. When I stepped back, I noticed that the tone of his hair was too orange. I'm happy with everything else so I drop all my layers and create a new one set to "color." Selecting a desaturated blue, I painted over the hair. That layer's opacity was reduced until I got more of a hazel tone and then I dropped the layer. After adding a light-blue rim light, I bumped up the resolution to 300 dpi and saved it.

One last time I opened the file in Photoshop to do a bit of color correction before sending it to the client.

This is how the art was used on the finished movie poster. The only revision that Dimension films asked for was to change his shirt color.

Total time spent on this project was about 8 days—well worth it considering I have always been an avid movie fan and love the old illustrated posters!

Figure 3-178
Completed "SuperBad"

Alex Jansson

Alex Jansson

Gothenburg, Sweden
www.alexanderjansson.com

Equipment
Computers: Dell™ Studio, Dell™ Inspiron™, Wacom® Intuos3 tablet
Scanner: CanoScan® 3000
Software: Adobe® Photoshop®, Corel® Painter™, and Blender
Favorite Papers: I like all types of papers as long as it is white
Color Management System: None

About the Artist
Education: Art high school, New Domen School of Arts in Gothenburg with a BA in 3D animation.

Current Job: Freelancer; I mostly do book illustrations, covers, and designs

Artistic Inspiration: My all-time favorite artist is Gustav Klimt; the moods of his landscape paintings will always inspire me. The one artist that got me into experimenting with digital art is Dave McKean. His creativity is just amazing, and his art is very important for the development of digital art and especially the digital mixed-media genre. At the moment, a Russian artist named Vasili Zorin really inspires me. His use of color and detail is among the best I've ever seen.

Career Highlight: When I did a huge and epic piece for the New York City Ballet's production of "The Nutcracker"

Gallery Representation: Shannon Associates, New York; 115 Digital Art Gallery, Bucharest, Romania

Creative Process
The piece I've chosen for this feature is a frame from my graphic novel with the working title *Ramone Bosco*. In this scene, the main character, Ramone, and his friends Volta and Hum are facing the "court gate," or the "annoying gate," as many prefer to call it. The court gate is inhabited by weird and crazy beings that lead silly and confusing discussions of whether or not you will get permission to pass. The discussions can go on forever … most annoying and frustrating when you're in a hurry.

The idea is to depict a surreal and strange place. The gate should appear threatening, yet strange and a bit funny.

"The Court Gate" consists of photographic elements, three-dimensional renderings, and painted objects.

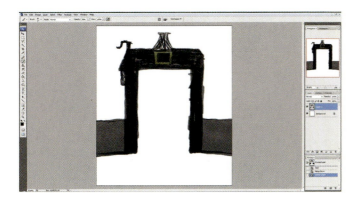

Figure 3-179
Sketch

I usually start with a document size of around 10 × 10 inches or 30 × 30 cm. Over the years, I've noticed that particular size runs smoothly without any disturbing lag when using many layers in combination with a performance-limited computer.

I start out with a really quick and simple sketch to capture the overall idea and just to get the picture in my head out on paper or the screen before it might float away into oblivion. In the sketch, I map out the composition and the balance between the foundation shapes.

When I'm out traveling, I keep small sketchbooks and use lead pencils. At home in my studio I use my Wacom Intuos3. It might be old, and new versions may be better and faster, but I love my Intuos3. My only upgrade has been from an A5 size to A5 wide to better match my monitor.

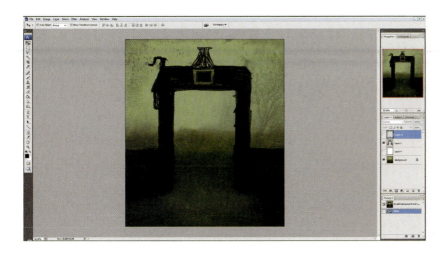

Figure 3-180
Add background

Figure 3-181
Add background

Immediately after the quick sketch I like to add a background image. It's very important for me to capture the mood I'm looking for as quickly as possible. Background images usually contain mixed and blended photographs and painted textures. Over the years I've created many background images that I use as a foundation or "skeleton" in my pieces.

The background I used in this piece originated from landscape photographs I've taken and blended with textures painted in oil or acrylics. The background image also has the green hue that is almost an obsession in my work.

Figure 3-182
Adding the characters

By adding the background some of the mood is set. I added small details to the sketch and subtle textures to the background image.

During this formative stage, I created 3D models of all of the main characters (Ramone, Volta, and Hum) and used the models as references when I created the frames of the graphic novel.

I posed the characters in the desired positions and then made a simple rendering in 3D software (I usually use Blender). This render is a Targa file with an alpha channel without any background. I copied the render into the main picture and used the Blur Tool to smooth the edges.

I then began to add photographic objects and elements. I prefer to use only my own photographs. Pictures of roofs, rusty walls, branches, lanterns, and bushes were copied into the main work area and the Magic Wand Tool and the Eraser Tool were used to mask out the images. At first I just played around with the positions and tried to keep up with the composition.

I am constantly drawing weird beings and creatures. When I am about to use them in my digital work I prefer to scan the pages from the sketch-

Figure 3-183
Adding photographic elements

Figure 3-184
Painting the court

books and revise and modify them in Photoshop or Painter, but in this particular piece I decided to draw and paint the weird beings of "The Court" directly in Photoshop. I had no exact ideas of how they would look. My intention was to improvise and let them come to life as I drew.

I created a new layer and began to paint. Being the old traditional painter that I am, I like to use Photoshop the way I paint. No advanced settings, brushes, or effects are used—just a common hard brush with the opacity turned down to around 10 to 30%. The flow is always set to 100%.

The next step was one of the most exciting: adding more textures and experimenting with blend modes. To me it is like adding varnish

Figure 3-185

Adding more textures and using blend modes

to an oil painting. In this stage, I can control the mood, expression, and outcome, making it stronger and adding depth.

Using blend modes is a big part of my digital work flow, and the ones I prefer to use are Multiply, Soft Light, Overlay, and Hard Light. The blend modes are still a bit of a mystery to me, and the most exciting thing about working with these modes is that I never know what's going to come out of it. Some textures work better than others in blend modes. Sometimes the ones I've created and really liked have not worked at all; sometimes the simplest ones work in an almost perfect way.

The texture images are also very important to me, and I love to create and experiment to obtain new and exciting ones. I really recommend experimenting with creating your own textures. Take macro shots and close-ups of every surface, material, or object that interests you. To make the photographic objects work and smoothly run into the rest of the image, I often use a combination of blend modes and duplications.

One thing with digital art is that it, in my opinion, it often gets a stiff feel and comes out too clean and synthetic. I want my work to have an organic feel. One thing I miss when working in digital media is the natural resistance on the surface when using a lot of paint on, for example, a canvas. To get there in the computer, I must make the digital surface dirty, giving it the feeling of being worn and weathered.

Having made the overall feeling more distinct, I continued to paint and modify the members of the court. The old man with the beard became a girl, and the guy in the upper right window got more solid features. I also added more details, like the umbrella, the guy with the

Figure 3-186
More painting and texture experimentation

red hat, and the noose, and the left window was given a mysterious inhabitant with a big grin.

Even more textures were added. This was a good time to stop and tell myself that this may be enough and that the picture may be ready. I often tend to keep on adding blend modes with textures until the picture become a kitschy grease that is just too much of everything.

Figure 3-187
Dodge, burn, blur, and finalizing

The next step is the finalization. I was quite satisfied with the overall expression and ready for the final touches. I flattened the image, and my computer sighed in relief. I personally don't like hard edges, so at the end of the process and after flattening all layers, I use the Blur Tool to smooth almost all of the edges. The final touches also included subtle uses of the Dodge Tool and Burn Tool to smooth the shadows and highlights and to balance the brightness and contrast of the shapes.

The artwork may be finished, but did it end up as it first appeared in my mind? No, it never does. I think that is what keeps me going.

Figure 3-188
Final artwork

Bruno Mallart

Bruno Mallart

Bonnelles, France
www.brunomallart.com

Equipment
Computer: Mac® Pro Quad-core, 2.66 GHz, LaCie™ 526 display
Scanner: Epson Perfection® 3200 Photo
Printers: Epson Stylus® Photo R2880 A3+
Software: Adobe® Creative Suite® 3
Favorite Paper: Hahnemühle German Etching Paper (310 g)
Color Management System: LaCie™ blue eye pro
Cataloging and Archiving: My hard drive and two external backups
    stored in two different places

About the Artist
Education: ESAG Paris (Superior School of Graphic Arts)
Current Job: Illustrator
Artistic Inspiration: I'm a fan of Saul Steinberg's work.
Gallery Representation: David Goldman Agency, New York; France
    Illustrations; Stock Illustration Source stock agency.

Creative Process
I wanted to create an image to use as an invitation for an exhibition of
my digital creations. I wanted a graphic arts theme with a zany and
humorous vision, like most of my work.

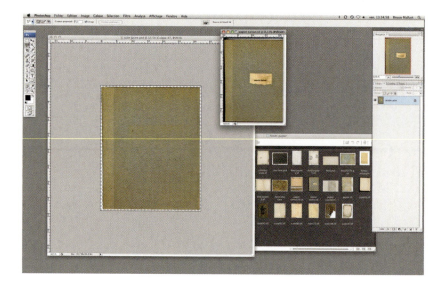

Figure 3-189
Scans

I started with a scan of an old sketch book cover that was in my library of images (my "bank") on my hard drive. I selected it with the Polygonal Lasso Tool and Eraser Tool, zooming a lot to have very precise irregular edges. I cut off the central label on the cover with a simple copy and paste. As we can see in the figure, I didn't need a perfect retouch as it was going to be hidden by the subject.

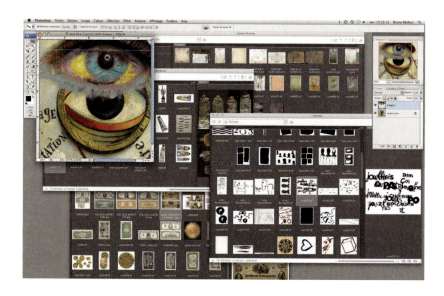

Figure 3-190
My bank of library of images

I don't use Photoshop to draw or paint. I use it to make collages, retouch, transform shapes, and perform many more actions that permit this diabolic tool! I start always from traditional drawings, paintings, and documents that I scan and store in my hard drive. I can use and reuse them when appropriate. Also, I often save, in my "images details" folder, parts of an illustration used during the creative process (backgrounds, figures, heads, objects, etc.) so I can reuse them in a new image, transforming them again or not. I'm the champion of recycling. You can often find in my images parts from an older piece of art.

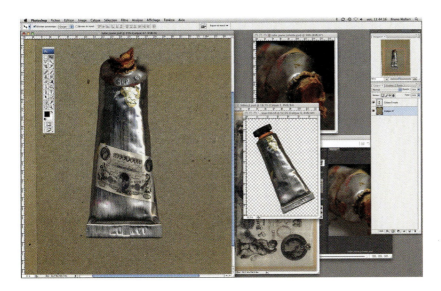

Figure 3-191
The "body" develops

I often use anthropromorphism in my work. In this image, I decided to use (due to the subject) an oil paint tube as the body. The tube as it appears is made with three different images. To give the effect of roundness, I used the Transform Tool. To create shadow and light, I used the Dodge Tool and Burn Tool.

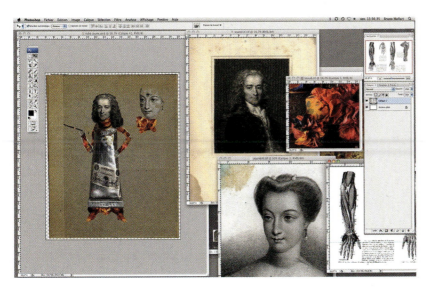

Figure 3-192
Heads materialize

I didn't have any precise idea for the head. In my portrait folder, in my library of images, I had scans of old etchings that I wanted to use at some time in the future. I mixed two etching portraits, a man and a woman, and trimmed them with the Eraser Tool and the Polygonal Lasso Tool. I worked on two superimposed layers. To make sure the two portraits had the same gray tint, I went to Image > Adjust > Variations.

Figure 3-193
Recycling previous work

Next, I searched in my image library to find anything that would fit for arms, fabric, accessories, etc. To illustrate what I said before concerning recycling: the handbag for this "graphic arts woman" comes from another image ("photo camera man") that I had already created.

All small graphic handwritings were scanned. It is impossible to clip little handwritten letters that were initially written on white paper and integrate them in a dark background like this. The solution is to use the Multiply blend mode on that layer. It darkens the stroke but the white background totally disappears.

Figure 3-194
Shadow work

Making the shadow is a little bit more complex. First, I selected the entire figure, then I filled it with black on a new layer. I modified this black shape with the Transform command to create a shadow behind the character. To create a good shadow effect, I changed the black color to a textured gray from a gouache artwork. I copied the shadow layer and used the Multiply blend mode. Further, I erased some parts in the two shadow layers to achieve exactly what I wanted.

Figure 3-195
Completed artwork

Cliff Cramp

Cliff Cramp

SoCal, California
cliff@cliffcramp.com
www.cliffcramp.com

Equipment
Computers: iMac®, Mac® OS X; Wacom® Intuos4 tablet
Printer: Epson Stylus® Photo R2880 A3+
Favorite Paper: Hahnemühle German Etching Paper (310 g)
Color Management System: LaCie™ Blue Eye Pro
Cataloging and Archiving: My hard drive and two external backups
  stored in two different places

About the Artist
Cliff Cramp's illustration work spans a wide range of genres in the entertainment industry, including background painting for animation, storyboard and visual development art for feature films, CD and DVD cover art, editorial and book illustration, colorist for comic books, and illustrations for games. His art has been exhibited in many international juried competitions. In 2000, a studio fire destroyed more than ten years of artwork. After the fire, Cliff switched to digital media for his illustration assignments, with Painter and Photoshop becoming his programs of choice. He has achieved award-winning status on CGSociety, the largest online community of professional illustrators using digital media. Cliff continues his freelance career while serving as area coordinator for the illustration program at California State University, Fullerton, where he conducts illustration courses in traditional and digital media. Cliff's artistic influences include John Singer Sargent, Howard Pyle, Harvey Dunn, N.C. Wyeth, James Montgomery Flagg, and Dean Cornwell. His contemporary influences are too numerous to list. The common thread to his influences is story. Any photo, film, painting, illustration, or book that has a great story generally has an impact on him with regard to being a visual storyteller. He enjoys old things: old cars, which he likes to tinker on; old houses, which he would like to live in some day; old furniture, which he likes to restore; and elderly people, whom he enjoys talking with. He lives with his wonderful wife and two energetic boys in sunny Southern California.

Creative Process

Story is the focus of my art, whether it is a simple character design or a more complex narrative. The task in this painting, "The Great Race," was to create an image around the concept of *a journey beginning*. When the concept is specific and the subject matter is open, such as in this case, I create the narrative centered on subjects that my children and I enjoy. I come up with a back story to the narrative in order to make the illustration more visually interesting. It is a fanciful father-and-son fictional story that takes place in the Austin/Longbridge Factory in England during the early 1960s. The main characters are mice. Austin, named after the Austin Mini, is the smallest boy to parents Alistair and Bridget. Austin, much like his father, has a keen fascination with the machines made in the factory. When he announces that he wants to drive race cars just like the humans, he is met with ridicule by the community but is supported by his family, particularly by Alistair. Austin's imagination allows him to figure out a way to accomplish his goal. I'm currently developing this story as a picture book.

Figure 3-196
Beginnings

I used the digital process to create the entire image. My drawing is usually very rough: a road map to the final painting while developing the compositional elements first. Detail comes much later. I work general to specific. The composition is the most important element at the early stage of the illustration. The image will not be successful no matter how well the image is painted if the composition doesn't work. With "The Great Race," I went for a triangular design in order to keep the viewer moving around the image. The focal point will be developed more fully at a later stage using value and color. I draw the image with the Airbrush medium in Painter using the Digital Airbrush brush. The rough value is laid in with digital watercolor using the Simple Water brush.

A digital watercolor (Simple Water brush) glaze of color is laid in over the value study. I am developing the focal point more at this

Figure 3-197

stage of the illustration. A primary color application is used for the cars. I tint the blue and shade the red, leaving the yellow car more saturated. It is important that value and color are emphasized in the focal point because of the small area of the illustration that it occupies. A consistent temperature of light and shadow is also considered at this early stage. It is vitally important that I stay general in my application at this point. In order to not be tempted to start painting more detail, I don't zoom into the image for quite some time. It is at this point that I decide whether a painting is worth pursuing further. The digital process allows me to get the image to this point quickly. It is dumped if it is not working and another attempt can be made so not too much time is wasted painting a dud. I use the digital medium for my color keys even when I paint in traditional media. It is important to note that while I work in Painter that I paint on a single layer. I only use layers for experimentation and developing an atmospheric effect.

Figure 3-198

The decision to take the painting further is made and now I can slow down a bit and start to develop the detail. It is at this point that I move into the opaque media in Painter. These are some of my personal favorites. I use the Digital Airbrush and Detail Airbrush when softening value and color transitions. I use the Soft Airbrush for atmosphere. The media that I most often use during the early stages of detailing the painting are Acrylic (Wet Acrylic brush), Oil (Smeary Flat brush), and Artist Oils (Wet brush). I'll use the Blender (Just Add Water) to soften some of the brush strokes.

Figure 3-199

I continue to develop detail while strengthening the narrative. It is important that I do not lose the focal point as I get closer to completion.

Figure 3-200

When the illustration is completed in Painter, I bring the image into Photoshop to do my final color and value adjustments.

Figure 3-201
Final illustration for "The Great Race"

Claudia Salguero

Claudia Salguero

Ottawa, Ontario, Canada
www.claudiasalguero.com
claudia_salguero.art@rogers.com

Equipment
Computers: MacBook® Pro with Mac® OS X
Printer: HP® Designjet Z2100
Favorite Papers: HP® Professional Matte Canvas, Hahnemühle Textured Fine Art
Cataloging and Archiving: My work is divided into "Commissions" (portraits, landscapes, commercial) and "Own Creations" (urban scapes, dance, music). I have back-ups on two different hard drives and I burn my images onto DVDs. I keep all the creative process of an image in the RIFF files. I save any time I get to an important stage of the process, and I save my final images in high- and low-resolution TIFF and JPEG files for e-mail and online needs. Each step saved has layers, and each layer has a name and a description of the tool used. Under the same classifications, I always have in my laptop the last RIFF version and a JPEG version of the final image of each one of my creations.

About the Artist
Current Job: Professional photographer and fine art photography creator; my background is that of a graphic designer, professional photographer, and visual artist
Artistic Inspiration: The free mind and use of color of Joan Miro; the determination of my daughter Manuela, a visual artist student; and the open mind as artist and entrepreneur of Jeremy Sutton
Career Highlight: Being recognized as Painter Master and sponsored by HP in Canada since 2007

Gallery Representation: Foyer Gallery City of Ottawa

Creative Process

Figure 3-202
Three original photos from client

This is a commissioned portrait I created from three digital pictures I received via e-mail from my client.

Figure 3-203
Composition planned

I defined the format and size of the final image—in this case, 22″ × 28″. The three pictures were resized to the final size and the resolution set at 150 dpi, which is the minimum resolution for digital printing.

Figure 3-204
Proceeding with movement

I masked and cropped the images into independent layers and worked in the composition. Even if there are changes during the creation of the artwork (as in this case, where I started with the idea of a skateboarding street scene), it is important to have a good idea of the composition at the beginning to minimize future problems, especially with resolution.

At this point I could have cloned the images into layers in a new file but I decided to "repaint" them to distort them with Jeremy Faves 2.0 Big Wet Luscious brush (size, 149; Opacity, 16; Pull, 100; Jitter, 0). This brush distorts the image with a wet and interesting texture. It looks to me like color applied onto a concrete wall with a damp cloth, which is perfect for this urban image. These third-party brushes are available from Jeremy Sutton.

Figure 3-205
Before and after face painting

By using the brush in the same direction, especially in the borders of the image, I gave the illusion of speed to the movement of the skateboarder.

The face was distorted with the same tool, but in this case following its shapes and volumes. Lights and shadows, whites and blacks, were added, carefully increasing the contrast and giving life to the face and

Figure 3-206
Graffiti used for background effect

especially to the eye. It is very important to add middle tones to the eye as well as a white spot. The freckles were added carefully spot by spot after loading the brush with the different tones in the face.

For the background I used graffiti. Nothing would work better for this image. I stretched it and filled bottom and top with black to

Figure 3-207
Collaged painting progresses

be able to fade the image into it and achieve a nice contrast with the images. I also gave some depth of field to the composition by applying Motion Blur to the graffiti.

I then reduced the size of the face, added some light to it, and erased a bit of the top in order to separate that image from the kid. I added lights and shadows to the kid with the same tool I used at the beginning: Jeremy Faves 2.0 Big Wet Luscious brush.

Finally, before printing, I added 2.5 inches to each side for the stretcher bars. The borders of the image were distorted with Distortion > Grainy Distorto 10 and the canvas stretched so the borders were visible on the sides of the frame. I also increased the sharpness by 5% using Effects > Focus > Sharpen.

Figure 3-208
Completed painting of Matt

Janet Stoppee

Janet Stoppee

Washington, Virginia
www.m2media.com

Equipment

Computers: 17″ MacBook® Pro, dual displays (LaCie™ and Wacom® Cintiq®), Wacom® Intuos4 tablet

Scanners: Epson Stylus® CX7400, Nikon™ Super Coolscan 9000 ED

Printer: Epson Stylus® Pro 4800

Software: Adobe® Acrobat® and Reader® 9; Adobe® Creative Suite® 5: AfterEffects® CS5, Bridge CS5, Dreamweaver® CS5, Encore® CS5, Fireworks® CS5, Flash Catalyst™ CS5, Flash® Professional CS5, Illustrator® CS5, InDesign® CS5, OnLocation™ CS5, Photoshop® CS5, Premier® Pro CS5, Soundbooth® CS5; Microsoft® Word; Corel® Painter™ 11; Microsoft® Excel®; Apple® QuickTime®; Apple® Keynote, Pages, and Numbers

Favorite Papers: Never met a great print medium that I didn't like!

Color Management System: LaCie™ Blue Eye Pro

Cataloging and Archiving: LaCie™ server

About the Artist

Current Job: Senior Vice President/Chief Creative Officer, M² Media Studios, Inc.

Artistic Inspiration: For digital painting (in alphabetical order): Martin Addison, Sue Bloom, John Derry, Kat Gilbert, Don L. Jolley, Richard Noble, Tim Shelbourne, Jeremy Sutton, and Cher Threinen-Pendarvis

Career Highlight: Painting in Photoshop and Illustrator CS5 from our own photos has brought me great joy and inspiration.

After college I began in visual communications as an art director at advertising agencies and design firms. Once I began working for The Stoppee Photographic Group, illustrating the book *The Photographer's Guide to Using Light*, in 1985, I became involved in the just emerging world of computers in the studio and its impact on a fledgling multimedia environment. I was among the first to adopt the Wacom tablet, Painter, Photoshop, Illustrator, and PageMaker. As the studio became M2 Media Studios, Inc., I found myself working in video, three-dimensional, animation, and interactive media. When the Nikon D2x digital single-lens reflex camera became widely available, I found myself behind the camera once again, rather than directing photographers in how to bring my vision to life. This led to a book I coauthored with my husband, Brian Stoppee, *Stoppees' Guide to Photography and Light,* and the recently released *The Photographer's Lighting Toolbox.* With 19 years of Painter in my background, making the jump to painting in Photoshop was not an easy one to embrace at first; however, as soon as I began to work with the paint engines of Photoshop and Illustrator I discovered that there was no going back. Never before had I felt the energy of what I paint than I did in these programs due to the responsiveness of the brush. Painting in a digital medium felt like it was truly the natural media I had experienced in my earlier years of working with acrylic paint. Projects that used to take me two or three days I can now finish in a matter of hours, not only resulting in an increase in my productivity but also giving the paintings more of a gratifying flow. My move to Photoshop and Illustrator for painting was opportunely timed, as our website, m2media.com, launched on the same day as the Adobe CS5 announcement (April 12, 2010). The site offers a special Online Learning section where I can help others to learn what it is that I'm doing with these apps and all things relative to image making. It also ties in nicely with our touring seminar series.

The Creative Process

Though I enjoy creating illustrations from my own photos, my collaborations with photographer Mike Pocklington goes back to my first day at The Stoppee Photographic Group. One of Mike's last big projects was to photograph in Italy for *The Photographer's Lighting Toolbox.* As a tribute to Mike, for this book I've chosen one of his

Figure 3-209
Before and after photo corrections

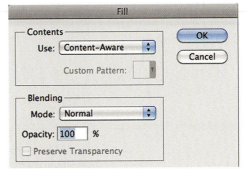

Figure 3-210
Content Fill Aware dialogue box

photos from that trip, all of which I did the Photoshop postproduction work on after his death. I have always been inspired by Mike's eye for light, color, and composition. Like myself, Mike was always quick to be the first to embrace new technologies for the creative community.

What works beautifully as a photo does not always literally translate into an illustration. A little further Photoshop postproduction work is often necessary. Photoshop CS5's introduction of Content-Aware Fill has made this process all the more simple. I removed the distracting elements from the photo, such as the intercom box next to the door, a vent, a rock protruding from the wall, and some elements of the rain gutter. This was as easy as using the Magic Wand Tool to encircle an offending visual and filling the area in the same way this has always been done in Photoshop (Edit > Fill); however, in CS5 the dialogue box allows you to select Content-Aware, under Fill, and Photoshop does all of the rest for you. Some photographers may want to laboriously rework these retouching details but I find that for the style of illustration that I use, such intense attention to refinement is not needed. I did enhance some of the flower blossoms with the Rubber Stamp Tool to assist in the color composition, placing blossoms where they were missing.

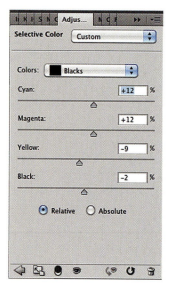

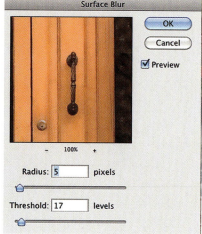

Figure 3-211
Further adjustments and modifications

Figure 3-212
Door receives a surface blur

To create a great photographic reference, further modifications are needed if the most desirable painting is to be achieved. I start with Photoshop's Adjustments panel and choose Selective Color. For this photo, I adjusted the blacks, blues, and reds.

Part of what convinced me to paint in Photoshop was that the resulting image looks very much like traditional media rather than something that is too photo like. To achieve this here, I diminished some of the photographic details with the Filter > Blur > Surface Blur feature. Choosing the Preview checkbox allows me to see the effect on the entire image as I make adjustments to the Radius and Threshold.

Figure 3-213
*Using John Derry's Actions
for Photoshop CS5*

M2 was one of the first studios to buy Painter 1.0. Soon after that app shipped, John Derry became part of the Painter's development team. After 19 years of working with Painter, I appreciated how John created a means of working with Photoshop CS5 in a manner similar to how I always worked with Painter's cloning feature, something John made even better for Photoshop by creating Actions of his own. The Actions do an excellent job of taking an existing non-layered image and creating a base version of the image set to a lesser opacity

Figure 3-214
Layered effects

for use as a guide layer when painting. It creates three cloning layers: Underpainting, Intermediate Strokes, and Detail. This is in the same package as John's fabulous set of brushes and textures. Of course, you can adjust any of these once the Actions sets up everything for you.

I work with two displays. This allows me to paint with a Wacom Intuos4 tablet and the calibrated LaCie display while observing the original photo on my 17" MacBook Pro. I take John's layers a step further by doing two underpainting layers, one for broad strokes (first) and another for medium ones (second). This is done with Texture off so all that I'm doing is blocking in paint.

Figure 3-215
Details added

Next I worked in the details with Texture on using John Derry's brushes. I jumped back and forth between the intermediate and detail layers.

For the final refinements, which make the image pop, I used John's Restoring brush on a new layer. This pulls the finest detail out of the reference photo. Though I did not use this technique for this painting, I sometimes hand-draw minor strokes without the Blender brush.

Figure 3-216
Final digital painting

II

Step-by-Step Painting

4 *Painting in Photoshop®*
with Your Photos

The concept of painting digitally is a strange one to most people. Using the mouse to paint is like drawing with a bar of soap in some ways. Digital tablets and styli seem to be more natural implements to use with digital art tools. They offer the wonderful ability to experience the impact of touch and the strength of a stroke. Their pressure sensitivity allows for a powerful laydown of color or a thin, wispy veil of color. This alone recommends them. If you do not have a tablet and stylus, however, don't despair. All of the following techniques can be performed with a traditional mouse.

When asked about why he photographed, the famous photographer Henri Cartier-Bresson said simply "that it was quicker than drawing." In his modesty he was suggesting the incredible immediacy of photography. His work was both intuitive and disciplined. His photography was not casual. Composition was paramount and, of course, his renowned "decisive moment." All of this is to say that, as a photographer, you responded to an impulse to make your photograph. That impulse was recorded on film or digital media.

I often feel the need to dig into the image still further. In my wet darkroom days, that meant learning and using a vast array of alternative processes. Some of those techniques allowed me to further manipulate the captured image into the one I saw in my mind's eye. The extraordinary range of possibilities in the digital art arena is truly amazing. In this chapter, I'll share with you some of my favorite techniques of digital painting in Photoshop. Photoshop alone can offer a far greater range of artistic potential than most users realize.

Take a look at your contact sheets, trays of slides, or file browser. The time has come to select an image to which you would like to give a painterly rendition. Some images will speak to you more than others. Follow your intuition and select from your heart. Of course, that is not to ignore the basic principles of design, composition, color, line, etc.

It is often necessary to clean up a photo to ready it for the painting. Perhaps there was debris on the street, power lines over a bucolic rural landscape, or an unnecessary element in the photo that distracts from the central impact. Look for these problem areas and correct them in Photoshop before starting to "paint." Preparation of the photograph will often include use of the Clone Stamp Tool, Healing Brush, Patch Tool, layer adjustments, and more. These are vital preliminaries that need to be executed with skill before starting the painting. Compare it, if you will, with the traditional preparation of a canvas done by a painter in advance of painting. The canvas needs to be sealed, gessoed, and made ready to receive paint. These time-consuming traditional painting steps ensure that the painting has a greater chance of archival survival.

> We do not see things as they are. We see things as we are.
>
> —*The Talmud*

Once you have eliminated the distracting elements and feel comfortable with the contrast and saturation of your image, it is time to decide how you will execute the digital painting. Most Photoshop users don't get further than running a single filter on the image. Using a watercolor filter on the image does not make it a watercolor painting. Oh, that art were indeed that easy! Art is often seen best in its subtlety. Just think how van Gogh's paintings would have looked if his brush strokes were always uniform in size and directionality. You want something that is unique to you and your sensibilities. Passing your image through a filter, lock, stock, and barrel, will yield an image that lacks your touch and imagination. The rendering, or mark making, should truly be your own. How can we achieve this kind of individuality in Photoshop using the tools it has to offer? Let's take a look in this chapter.

As I was writing this edition, the latest version of Photoshop debuted (Photoshop CS5). It opens up all sorts of new possibilities for digital painting with the introduction of the Mixer Brush Tool. This one tool alone is worth the upgrade. I'll detail some techniques with this new tool at the end of this chapter. All of the other techniques detailed here will work in previous versions of Photoshop and in the new CS5. This gives you the best of all worlds, no matter what version you are currently using.

How to Use Photoshop Filters and the History Brush Tool to Create a Digital Painting

Filters are the first place that many photographers go to for an artistic rendition of their photograph. Photoshop offers many, many options for your artistic interpretation. One of my favorite methods involves the History Brush Tool. What a wonderful tool!

Figure 4-1
Original photograph of a Roman café table

This photograph was a grab shot as I walked the streets of Rome. I liked the neutral tones and the simple arrangement of café chairs and table. The bouquet of daisies was an added plus.

Figure 4-2
Cigarette butt that needs to be removed before we begin

Correct any flaws that exist in the original photo
To make Figure 4-1 ready for painting, I first needed to become the street sweeper or maid for the establishment. There was a piece of debris under the table and a stray cigarette butt nearby, both of which were captured in this image.

A simple minute or two with the Clone Stamp Tool cleaned up the sidewalk for our ensuing painting. Look around for any other distracting elements. Does the image need to be cropped? Does the color need any alteration? Use a critical eye when analyzing the image at this stage of the process. The success of the end product may well depend on this crucial first step.

This technique relies on the ability of Photoshop to make a history state that can be revisited as necessary to complete the painting. In order to show the effect of the filter on the image, I've included a close-up view of the daisies on the table with each step. Let's begin.

Figure 4-3
*Filter > Brush
Strokes > Crosshatch*

> Every artist was first an amateur.
>
> —RALPH WALDO EMERSON,
> *Letters and Social Aims:
> Progress of Culture* (1876)

Apply the Brush Strokes > Crosshatch filter
Make a copy of this history state by clicking on the camera located at the bottom of the History palette
Name the history state
The Brush Strokes filter Crosshatch was applied to the image using a Stroke Length of 14, a Sharpness of 7, and Strength of 1. I then took a snapshot of the image with that filter applied. Use the little camera at the bottom of the History palette. The snap of this current history state will appear under the snap of the original image in the History palette, as it looked when the file was opened. Take the time now to name that history state "Crosshatch." Simply double-click on the name and retype its title. As we add more history states, this naming convention will become more important as we search for the intended filter effect. Now return to the original image, walking backward in your History palette.

Apply the Artistic > Cutout filter
Make a copy of this history state by clicking on the camera located at the bottom of the History palette
Name the history state
The next step is to repeat the process but using the Artistic filter Cutout, with the number of levels set at 6, Edge Simplicity set at 6, and Edge Fidelity set at 2. Although I give the particular settings that I used on the image, please experiment with the sliders to create the effect that you want for your image. Make a snapshot of this history state and again return to the original image, as it was opened.

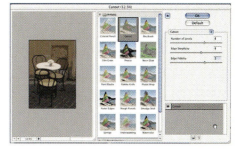

Figure 4-4
Filter > Artistic > Cutout

Figure 4-5
Filter > Artistic > Dry Brush

Apply the Artistic > Dry Brush filter
Make a copy of this history state by clicking on the camera located at the bottom of the History palette
Name the history state
The next filter that was applied was the Artistic Filter known as Dry Brush. I set the Brush Size at 2, the Brush Detail at 8, and the Texture at 1. I took a snapshot of this filter effect and returned to the original image in the History palette.

As you can see by now, we are accumulating various filter effects with our snapshots of each particular effect. Please take the time to name each effect to make things easier later. We will eventually be using these history states to paint from and it will be important to discern which one was dry brush or watercolor.

Figure 4-6
Filter > Artistic > Rough Pastels

Apply the Artistic > Rough Pastels filter
Make a copy of this history state by clicking on the camera located at the bottom of the History palette
Name the history state

The next filter employed was the Artistic filter Rough Pastels. This is a good one for showing brush strokes and texture. The settings used were Stroke Length 11, Stroke Detail 7, Texture > Sandstone, Scaling 100%, Relief 20, and Light from the Top. There is a variety of textures that you can use, including canvas, brick, sandstone, and burlap. The Rough Pastels filter allows a color to be carried through another color mass with a stroke effect. That can be very nice for a painterly feel. Pastel artists often use a sanded colored board to draw on. The sand actually saws off the soft chalk, capturing the particles of chalk, giving a gritty kind of look. This filter can mimic that look well. Again, take a snapshot in the History palette, rename that history state, and then return to the original image.

Figure 4-7
Filter > Artistic > Underpainting

Apply the Artistic > Underpainting filter
Make a copy of this history state by clicking on the camera located at the bottom of the History palette
Name the history state

The next Artistic filter, Underpainting, is a great one to loosely map out the colors that will be used. Underpainting is a technique used by painters to block in where the major color masses will be in the painting. It is used for composition placement and establishing color tonal areas. This technique has been used for centuries and was the basis of the finished painting that follows. It is virtually the foundation that the completed work is built on, especially in oil painting. You will notice a blurry kind of effect in this digital version of underpainting. This is not a filter that will render crisp details, but instead loose color masses. The settings on this filter were set to Brush Size 6, Texture Coverage 16, Texture > Sandstone, Scaling 100%, Relief 4, and Light from the Top. Take a snapshot and name it, again returning to the original image.

Art after all is but an extension of language to the expression of sensations too subtle for words.
—ROBERT HENRI,
The Art Spirit (1923)

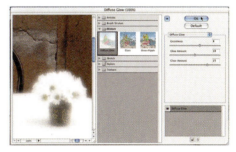

Figure 4-8
Filter > Distort > Diffuse Glow

Apply the Distort > Diffuse Glow filter
Make a copy of this history state by clicking on the camera located at the bottom of the History palette
Name the history state

The next filter comes from a different category, Distort, and its name is Diffuse Glow. This filter gives a halo effect and blurs the image. I often use this filter to help simulate an infrared effect. The settings used were Graininess 6, Glow Amount 10, and Clear Amount 15. It offers a soft, rather romantic effect that can also be used for dreamy portraits. Again, take a snapshot, name this new history state, and return to the original image.

Figure 4-9
Filter > Sketch > Graphic Pen

Apply the Sketch > Graphic Pen filter
Make a copy of this history state by clicking on the camera located at the bottom of the History palette
Name the history state

The next filter, Graphic Pen, can be found under the filter category called Sketch. Graphic Pen yields a nice sketch effect created by a directional mark. The settings were set to Stroke Length 15, Light/Dark Balance 50, and Stroke Direction coming from the right side diagonally. By itself, this filter can make a nice illustration from a photograph for perhaps a newsletter, magazine, or annual report, but we will use its mark making effect here in our digital painting. Take a snapshot, rename the layer, and return again to your original image.

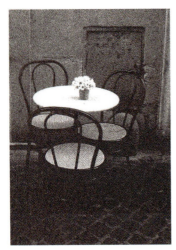

Figure 4-10
Filter > Texture > Grain > Stippled

Apply the Texture > Grain > Stippled filter
Make a copy of this history state by clicking on the camera located at the bottom of the History palette
Name the history state
Another sketch-like filter is the one under Texture called Grain > Stippled. You will notice that under Grain, there are a lot of options for making marks. The Stippled option provides the effect an illustrator would achieve using a very fine pen point to create an illustration from thousands of dots of ink. The settings were set at Intensity of 40, Contrast of 50, and Grain Type to Stippled. Again, take a snapshot of the effect, name it properly, and return to your original for one last filter.

Figure 4-11
Filter > Stylize > Find Edges

Apply the Stylize > Find Edges filter
Make a copy of this history state by clicking on the camera located at the bottom of the History palette
Name the history state
The Find Edges filter is located under Filter > Stylize. It looks for differences in contrast along edges. There are no sliders to adjust. The effect is automatic, but you can fade it as much as you would like. To fade any filter, simply go to Edit > Fade > (whatever the name of the filter was). Again, and finally, take a snapshot, name the layer, and return to the original layer. We are now ready to "paint" from our history state wells.

We will be using the history states that we created from each filter we applied. To the left of the snapshot of that remembered history state is a "well." When we want to apply some Rough Pastels to our image, we will dip our History Brush Tool into the well beside the snapshot of Rough Pastels.

I recommend that you set your opacity on the History Brush Tool to a low amount (5–20%); this gives a more subtle effect that can be intensified by simply brushing over an area again and again.

Art is the stored honey of the human soul, gathered on wings of misery and travail.
—THEODORE DREISER,
  Life, Art and America
  (1917)

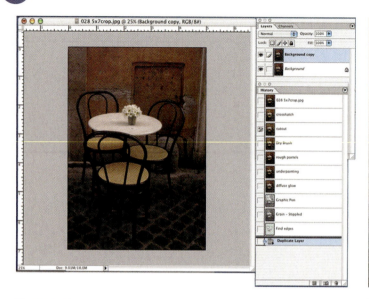

Figure 4-12
The stack of previous history states made from the use of filters

Figure 4-13
The digital painting starts to evolve, using the History Brush Tool to apply strokes derived from various filter effects

Using the History Brush Tool, dip into the "well" of the history state you want to use

Use a low opacity for subtlety

Grab that History Brush Tool and, with a low opacity setting, brush light applications from the History palette. Place the History Brush Tool in the well to the left of that snapshot, and brush away.

I wanted to place an irregular edge on this piece and chose an eraser technique. It is so easy.

Add an inch all the way around the image by going to Image > Canvas Size and adding the extra space

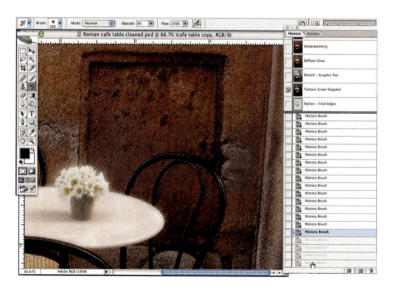

Figure 4-14
Light, transparent applications of various filters are applied with the History Brush Tool

Erase around the edge with an irregular, textural brush

There are a lot of crazy brushes. We traditionally use a hard-edge brush or a soft-edge brush, but many more are available. There are

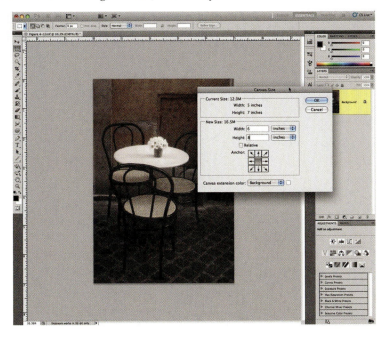

Figure 4-15
Canvas was added around the completed image

brushes that resemble bristle brushes and give an irregular, scratchy kind of effect. They are wonderful for scratching away at the edges of an image, and the effect is distressed and more interesting. Try some of these irregular brushes for painterly edges using the Eraser. Here, I used a brush made later in Chapter 11 (Figures 11-31 and 11-32).

I paint as I feel like painting; to hell with all the studies. An artist has to be a spontaneist.
—ÉDOUARD MANET,
 in *The World of Manet*, by
 Pierre Schneider (1968)

Figure 4-16
An eraser was used on the edges with an irregular brush shape

Figure 4-17
Finished artwork with irregular edges: "Roman Café Table"

Using the Art History Brush Tool to Create a Digital Painting

The Art History Brush Tool is generally underutilized by most Photoshop users. It is a little quirky, but lots of fun. As always, select a photograph on which you would like to apply a painterly effect.

Correction of Flaws

If the image requires any correction prior to working, please do that first. In my example, I increased the contrast a bit in Curves before starting.

Figure 4-18
*Original photo that was
captured digitally*

Figure 4-19
*A little boost in contrast
made in Curves*

Increase contrast in Curves
Flatten the Layers
Save and close the file
Reopen the file
Add a new layer and fill it with white
Using the Art History Brush Tool requires adding another layer above
the photograph and filling it with white. Think of this layer as your
sheet of watercolor paper, where you will deposit the paint.

Figure 4-20
A new layer was added on top and filled with white

In order for this technique to work, you must close and reopen the file if you have altered it in any way, like we did with the Curves adjustment. It looks to the opening history state for its information.

Figure 4-21
Art History Brush Tool and the Dab method

Select the Art History Brush Tool and the Dab method to paint the image

Select the Art History Brush Tool. It is nested with the History Brush Tool and can be easily identified by the distinctive curly-cue top on the brush icon. The modifiers for this tool are, of course, in the upper menu bar. There are lots of different brush strokes (see Figure 4-29).

I selected one of my favorites, the Dab method. Start brushing on your white layer and see what effect you can achieve. I used a brush size of 32 for this example. The bigger the brush you use, the less detailed your image will be. Conversely, the tinier the brush you use, the more detail you will achieve. The choice is yours.

Painting is just like making an after-dinner speech. If you want to be remembered, say one thing and stop. … Have the ability to see largely.
—Charles Hawthorne, in *Hawthorne on Painting* (1938)

Figure 4-22
White layer opacity lowered

Lower the opacity—it is like using tracing paper!

It sure would be nice to see where you are painting in relationship to the photograph. No problem. Just lower the opacity of the white layer to see through to the photograph beneath.

Continue brushing the dabs of color on the white layer

Continual brushing using the Dab method yielded the image shown in Figure 4-23. I decided not to brush the green area outside the flower. Only a small bit of green was used to establish the outside edges of the flower.

Set the blend mode to Lighten

In the Lighten blend mode, the white area of the upper painted layer will be ignored, but the colored areas will interact with the photograph

Figure 4-23
*Flower made from Dab stroke
with Art History Brush Tool*

Figure 4-24
Blend mode set to Lighten

beneath it, yielding a bit more detail. Figure 4-24 shows the Lighten mode utilized for the current blend mode. Experiment with various blend modes.

Figure 4-25
Tight Short stroke used with the Art History Brush Tool

Art History Brush Tool > Tight Short stroke was explored for effect
Just to satisfy my curiosity, I also tried the Tight Short stroke with the Art History Brush Tool. I still preferred the Dab method on this flower, but it was worth the try.

Apply the Artistic > Sponge filter
I seem never to be satisfied with a result and I am always asking "what if" questions. In response to that urge, on this piece I applied Filter > Artistic > Sponge on the Dab layer. I liked the variegated gray spotting in the background. I returned the blend mode to normal. If you don't like the variegated splotching background, it would be easy to remove it with the History Brush Tool set to a previous white layer. I think the sponge effect added some texture that was interesting.

This interpretation is a little reminiscent of the pointillism era in painting. That movement, led by Georges Seurat, featured the application of paint in a dabbing style. The eye blended the various colors together. A similar effect can be achieved in Painter®. We will explore that later in Chapter 5.

Try the various brush offerings in the Art History Brush Tool repertoire. Remember that you can vary the amount of detail by changing

A great work of art is like a great shock.
—ALEXEJ VON JAWLENSKY, IN *DAS KUNSTWERK II* (1948)

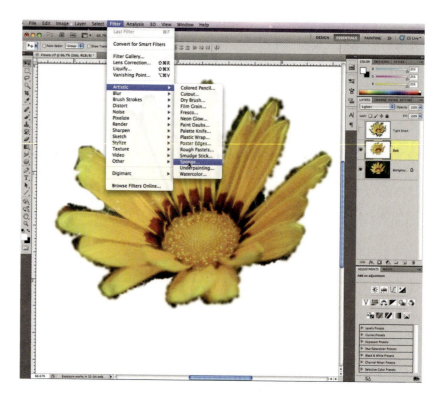

Figure 4-26
*Filter > Artistic > Sponge
used on the Dab version*

Figure 4-27
*History Brush Tool used to
produce a light shadowed
area under the flower*

Figure 4-28
Completed flower using the Art History Brush Tool method of brushwork

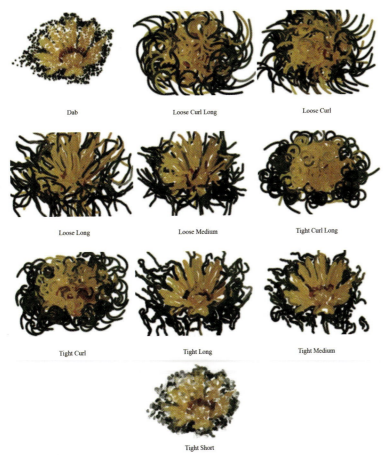

Dab	Loose Curl Long	Loose Curl
Loose Long	Loose Medium	Tight Curl Long
Tight Curl	Tight Long	Tight Medium
	Tight Short	

Figure 4-29
Types of Art History Brush Tool strokes

the size of the brush. For purposes of illustration here, the brush size was 70 on all of the examples in Figure 4-29. And, of course, there is no reason that you can't combine various brush strokes all in the same piece by simply changing the stroke selected.

Figure 4-30
Art History Brush Tool painting of sunflowers

Using the Pattern Stamp to Create a Digital Painting

Pattern Stamp for a painting? You must be kidding. No. This may seem like a crazy way to make a painting, but it works. Bear with me on this one. The first order of business is, as usual, to get your photograph ready to make a painting.

Figure 4-31
Original photo and a saturated version

The saturation was boosted on the original image

The photograph was given a bit more pep with a saturation increase, using a Hue/Saturation adjustment layer.

Figure 4-32
Define the Pattern

Figure 4-33
Name the pattern, which is your photo

Choose the Pattern Stamp Tool. Go to Edit > Define Pattern. Identify the current open photo, and click OK

The next step seems bizarre, but try it. Choose the Pattern Stamp Tool that is bundled with the Clone Stamp Tool. Go to Edit and then to Define Pattern. A dialogue box will appear. In the window the current open image will appear along with its name. Click OK. You will notice that the photograph now appears as an option in the pattern options available in the top menu bar. That indicates that when the Pattern Stamp Tool is selected and the desired pattern is selected, you will be pulling the color information from the original photograph.

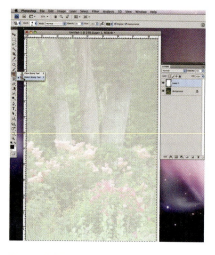

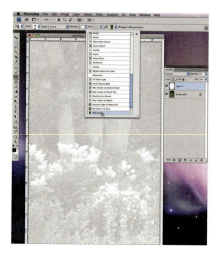

Figure 4-34
Add a new layer, filled with white

Figure 4-35
A scanned piece of white canvas board used as a pattern

Create a new layer and place it on top of your original photo. Edit > Fill with white, but any color will work.

Select your Pattern Stamp Tool, and be sure that the newly created pattern is the one featured in the menu bar at the top of the panel.

If we select a regular brush from the options available to use in the Brush palette, we would simply be making a clone of the original image. We want more than that. We want a painterly effect, like the look achieved with a real brush loaded with wet paint. So, we need to experiment a little. As you can see in Figure 4-36, I selected a brush that gave me a pastel-like effect. I also checked the boxes for Aligned and Impressionist on the modifiers for the Pattern Stamp Tool.

Begin to paint with the Pattern Stamp Brush, using the original photograph as your selected pattern. You will get a scratchy, pastel on rough paper effect.

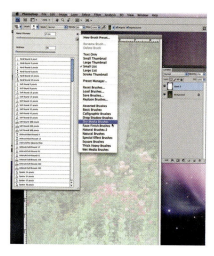

Figure 4-36
Dry Media Brushes library selected

Figure 4-37
The brush selected was Pastel on Charcoal Paper

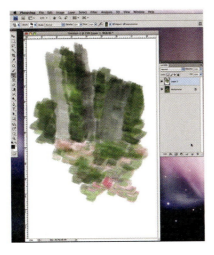

Figure 4-38
Beginning to lay down color

Continue painting, building up color and varying the size of your brush and the opacity

Continue to build up your brush strokes. You will see that it will build up in the color effect after repeated applications. I like the messy edges, but that is your artistic choice.

Figure 4-39
Initial underpainting

Figure 4-40
Add a mask to bring a slight amount of the original photo back

A mask was added to the painted layer. Painting with a light opacity of black on the mask allows some suggestion of the original photo to show through. I allowed a bit of the bark texture and some leaf and flower details to show.

Figure 4-41
Canvas texture added

Scan a piece of white canvas board

Now for another marvelous trick using the pattern stamp. Using the flatbed scanner, I scanned a piece of white canvas-covered board. You know, the kind of board sold to amateur oil painters who don't want to stretch canvas over stretcher strips. It is a cheap and easy way to secure a "ground" to paint on. They are usually pre-gessoed, so the artist can jump right into the painting. Save the scan as a separate file or use it as a new pattern, as we did with the photo.

In this example I placed the scanned canvas image above the painted photo and set the blending mode to Multiply, making the white areas disappear. When the white areas are gone, all that remains is the tone-filled areas, showing the bumpy nature of the canvas. You are going to be able to use this scanned piece of board over and over, every time you want a canvas texture to appear on your paintings.

Figure 4-42
Pattern Fill selected

HINT: Once you learn this great technique you can imagine scanning burlap and other textured surfaces to use in a similar fashion.

I proceeded to use the canvas to create a new pattern to draw from, just as we did with the lighthouse. This pattern will stay in my Pattern Stamp brush options every time I open Photoshop.

Figure 4-43
Heavy Weave selected from pattern options

Figure 4-44
Heavy Weave pattern

If you don't want to scan a canvas panel, don't worry. Photoshop is coming to the rescue. There are many pattern libraries to choose from that feature a variety of texture patterns. To illustrate, I have selected the Heavy Weave pattern and increased the scale percentage to 364%. Again, the blend mode was set to Multiply.

You can click on the pattern fill layer and change the pattern selected at any time. We've used Heavy Weave and Fibers 1 patterns in this example.

It needs a certain purity of spirit to be an artist of any sort.
—D.H. LAWRENCE, "Making Pictures," in *Assorted Articles* (1928)

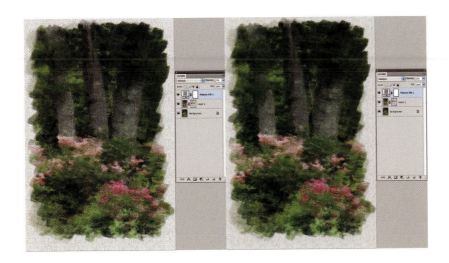

Figure 4-45
Heavy Weave pattern on the left and Fibers 1 pattern on the right

Figure 4-46
Completed painting of "Pat's Garden" using the Fibers 1 pattern for texture

Another Pattern Stamp Painting

I cropped and straightened the photo a bit in preparation for painting.

The Pattern Stamp Tool, located with its cousin the Clone Stamp Tool, is an underutilized tool. It is most often grabbed by mistake, and it lays down a pattern of strange bubble shapes (the default pattern).

Photoshop is loaded with lots of libraries of assorted patterns, from canvas to burlap to grass. We can add patterns to the existing libraries.

Figure 4-47
Original photo of Venice at night

If we use the entire photo as a new pattern, we then have a great cloning source from which we can pull color information.

Figure 4-48
Creating a pattern

Select All
Edit > Define Pattern
Add a new layer and fill it with a color for your paper
I added a layer of a buff colored paper to serve as my piece of pastel paper. Any color, including white, will work. Choose a textured brush. Again, my favorite brush is the Pastel on Charcoal Paper brush. Use the Pattern Stamp Tool, equipped with that type of texture. Using a moderate size brush apply a loose underpainting of color placement.

Figure 4-49
*Basic underpainting using
the Pattern Stamp Tool*

Figure 4-50
*Refining the painting with a
smaller brush*

Continue to make your brush smaller in diameter, refining the painting more. Occasionally I'll lower the opacity of the painted layer to identify shapes from the original photo for reference. However, if you leave that layer more transparent, it is hard to distinguish what the painted layer looks like in actuality. So, only take a glimpse at it from time to time.

Figure 4-51
*Layer mask added to bring
in detail*

Painting from a photo is always a push–pull concept. By that, I mean that you want it to look painterly, but you still want a few details showing. The balance is in deciding where to leave the image loose and painterly and where to tighten it up with a few details. To allow a few details to show through from the original photograph, I applied a layer mask. Painting with black, at a low opacity, on the layer mask will reveal a bit of detail from the photo below.

Figure 4-52
Added layer of accent colors

To continue the painterly feel, I added another layer. On that layer I painted directly with color to accent the existing colors, enriching the overall piece. For illustration purposes here I've added a disposable layer of white so you might more clearly see exactly the accent colors that were added. That white layer was discarded later.

Figure 4-53
Completed Pattern Stamp Painting

Using the Art History Brush Tool and Emboss Filter to Create a Textured Digital Painting

Figure 4-54
Original digital photograph with poor lighting

I am always amazed at how much detail exists in a photograph that is over- or underexposed with a digital camera. The bouquet of mixed flowers in Figure 4-47 was dimly lit by window light. One of my favorite blend mode techniques is to duplicate the layer and set the blend mode to Screen to lighten a photo that is too dark. I'm going to assume that you will have some photographs that are not perfectly exposed. The legendary master, Ansel Adams, burned and dodged with his wonderful negatives. Chances are that we, too, will need to do a little work on our digital negatives. Here is a great technique for improving that photograph before we begin to paint.

Figure 4-55
Blend modes and masking used to correct exposure

You can never do too much drawing.
—TINTORETTO,
  in *Tintoretto*, by Evelyn March Phillipps (1911)

Copy the layer and set the blend mode to Screen
This brightens the image. It virtually looks like you turned the flash on, rendering more detail in the shadows. It can, however, blow out your highlights at the same time.

Figure 4-56
Photo corrected and cropped—almost ready to begin painting

Add a layer mask to create the proper lighting

The left side of the photograph was now too light. Using the Screen blend mode technique for lightening a dark photograph is a great trick, but it works globally across the entire photograph. In most instances, you only need a portion of the image to be rendered lighter in tone. This calls for masking. Using a mask will hold the desired highlights in place but will open up the areas that are too dark. I always tell my students that, "Masking is your friend." A mask allows you to really burn and dodge with a great deal of control. This technique has much more control than using the Burn Tool and Dodge Tool that are available to you in the Photoshop toolbox.

Figure 4-57
Saturation beefed up for more color

Crop photo for composition

The photograph has been cropped and the exposure manipulated to give an image that can be used in a painting.

Increase color saturation, using Hue/Saturation adjustment layer

Rich, saturated color is desirable in some paintings. For this example, I increased the saturation through an adjustment. I then flattened the layers, and the image is ready to be painted. Save the image.

Create a new layer and fill it with a color. Brown was used on this example

The old masters' style of oil painting was to paint on a colored ground. The canvas or board was sealed with various chemical agents, such as rabbit skin glue or white lead, and then covered with a pigmented layer. This allowed the artist to paint in the highlights and shadows and work toward a middle tone, using the colored ground as that middle tone. Today, most artists choose to gesso their canvas to seal it. If they are working in the style of the old masters, they may then apply a layer of color. This layer is usually made from some paint and a painting medium. I often use a brown or gray color for my pigmented layer, which is applied on top of the dry gesso. In order to replicate that effect digitally, I created a new layer (Edit > Fill) and filled it with a brown tone, thus producing my ground. I reduced the opacity of that layer so I could see through to the photograph beneath.

Figure 4-58
Underpainting on brown layer with the Dab Art History Brush Tool

Select the Art History Brush Tool (Dab brush strokes) and paint in image

Choose a rough, textured brush from the brush options available

To create a simple underpainting, roughing in the color tone masses, I painted with the Art History Brush Tool using the Dab brush option. The brush type selected was Pastel on Charcoal Paper, found in the Dry Media Brushes library. This maps out the basic colors and forms. It is rough, but a good technique. This is a good place to step back and analyze the composition. Are there any apparent changes that should be made now? If not, proceed.

The Pastel on Charcoal Paper brush skips on the surface, leaving vacant areas, mimicking the true effect of that kind of art material. You are not limited to the commonly used brushes, even when you are in the Art History Brush Tool category. So become daring. Go for a brush that mimics texture.

Lower the brush size to achieve more detail

More details are needed now. I lowered the size of the brush to bring in some details. The smaller the brush is, the more details are shown. The larger the brush is, the looser the paint effect will be.

Examine closely, inch-by-inch, for corrections now

It's time to stop and look at the painting and slowly examine it in a detailed and thorough way. I usually zoom into the painting and carefully go over each part of it, section by section, for additions, deletions, and corrections. Your painterly effort is almost complete at this point.

Fine art is that in which the hand, the head, and the heart of man go together.
—John Ruskin,
The Two Paths (Lectures on Art in Its Application to Decoration and Manufacture) (1859)

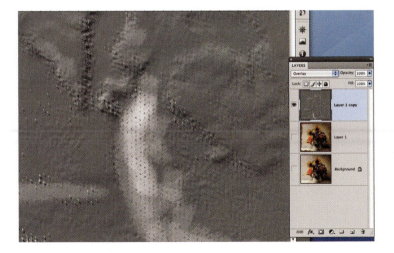

Figure 4-59
More detailed effect with smaller brush

Figure 4-60
Duplicated, desaturated Emboss layer

Duplicate the layer and set the blend mode to Overlay

The next step is to duplicate the painted layer by simply dragging that layer to the new layer icon. Now set the blend mode on this new layer to Overlay Mode. It will look really strange, with colors that border on neon, glow-in-the dark, bizarre shades. Relax, we are only partially there.

Desaturate this duplicate layer and use Filter > Emboss

Use Image > Adjustments > Desaturate to remove the color from the duplicate layer. To achieve the texture of an application of opaque paint, like oil paint, the next step is to use Filter > Stylize > Emboss. The effect will be determined by how you move the sliders. They predict the thickness of the paint effect. To isolate the effect, you may wish to turn off the visibility of the other layers to concentrate on fine-tuning the effect.

With all the layers turned on, zoom in to check out the embossed effect on your painting
Brush light gray for a lightened effect

To increase the textural effect, I used the earlier Chalk brush to brush light gray on the desaturated layer in areas where I wanted a little lightening and a textural feel.

Figure 4-61
More detail added using the History Brush Tool

Using a small History Brush Tool, add a little bit more detail

When an image is originally opened, the History palette stores a copy of what it looked like. Using a small-diameter History Brush Tool (not the Art History Brush Tool), brush on a little detail at a low opacity. That brings a bit of the detail from the original image back into the artwork. You can do this on the existing layer, as I've done here, or you can place it on a separate layer.

These close-ups reveal the paint stroke effect and the application of an embossed thickness and texture to exaggerate the brush strokes. It is wise to go over the entire painting, section by section, looking at minute detail. This close examination will show you areas that might need more work.

Figure 4-62
Close-up of embossed area

Brown Edge Effect

This version allows the brown canvas ground to be seen along the edges and peeking through the paint strokes in areas that were not covered by color. You may decide that this is the final version.

Figure 4-63
Close-up

White Edge Effect: Paint with White Using the Chalk Brush

If you want a white edge that still looks painterly, try painting with that Chalk brush again with the normal Brush Tool selected and the color white. Figure 4-56 shows this white chalk edge effect.

Figure 4-64
Completed piece

Photo Illustration Using the Find Edges Filter

Figure 4-65
Original photo shot in Venice on gondola ride

Use a photo with good edge contrast

The next example is an interesting way to make a photo illustration. Select a photo with some edge detail. Here, I am using a photo that I took while on a gondola ride in Venice (Figure 4-57).

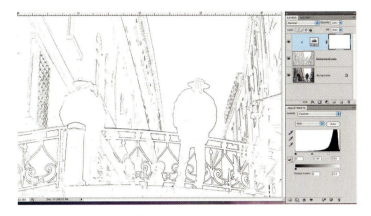

Figure 4-66
Find Edges filter layer created and modified

Copy the layer
Apply Filter > Stylize > Find Edges
Apply Image > Adjustments > Desaturate
Use Adjust > Levels to remove small unwanted particles
Copy the layer by simply dragging the layer to the new layer icon at the bottom of the layer palette. On that new layer apply Filter > Stylize > Find Edges. I really like the effect that this filter gives, but often there are mid-tone areas that look like the windshield of your car when it has been sprayed with dirty water by a passing car. These areas just give a messy gray or colored texture. To remove them and crisp up the contrast, go to Image > Adjust > Desaturate first to remove any color. Use a levels adjustment layer to pull the sliders in until you like the effect. This clears out the unwanted gray areas.

Use the History Brush Tool, at low opacity, to brush back some of the original photo's color image
Now we can color back into this area using the History Brush Tool. Set the opacity low and gradually stroke the color from your original back into the illustration. Leave some areas empty of color to enhance this interesting effect. This would be a great technique for illustrations in newsletters, annual reports, and magazines, but don't rule out the use of this style when making images that are more fine-art oriented.

The beautiful, like customs, like ideas, undergoes every sort of metamorphosis.
—EUGENE DELACROIX, *The Journal of Eugene Delacroix,* translated by Walter Pach (1937)

Figure 4-67
Completed Find Edges illustration

A Glorious Use for the Glowing Edges Filter as an Oil Painting Tool

Figure 4-68

Original scan of a
ranunculus blossom

This project involves the use of a crazy filter called the Glowing Edges filter. This filter puzzled me for quite a while. As I experimented with a variety of filters and tried the Glowing Edges filter, the background went black and the edges of the photo became neon, glowing colors. I couldn't imagine what I could really use it for.

I needed to think beyond the apparent effect and understand what the filter was really doing and how I could use it to benefit my work. I eventually realized that I could invert the black to white. I could also desaturate those crazy colors to a black-and-white line drawing. Ah-ha! The light went on. The benefit to using this filter as opposed to its cousin, the Stylize > Find Edges filter, is the ability to move sliders and control the quality of the line drawing that it creates.

Instead of a photograph on this project, I am working with a scan made from a cut flower on my scanner. I simply love using the scanner as a camera. Yes, it has a shallow depth of field, but it is absolutely wonderful for minute detail. When ranunculus were in bloom in the spring, I literally made hundreds of scans, using different groups, arrangements, and colors of flowers. The ranunculus lends itself to this kind of scanning as most of the petals are on the same focal plane.

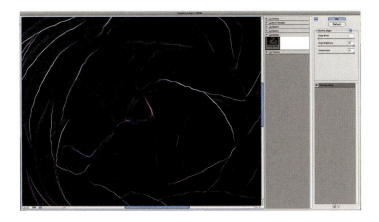

Figure 4-69
Glowing Edges filter

Duplicate the background layer
Use Filter > Stylize > Glowing Edges
The Edge Width was set to 1 (very narrow at 1 or 2 is recommended). This will be your pencil sketch line later. The Brightness was set to 20 and will be your dark pencil line later. The Smoothness was set to 15.

Figure 4-70
Invert and desaturate the duplicate layer

Use Image > Adjustments > Invert
Use Image > Adjustments > Desaturate
Now to turn that crazy filter into a line drawing. By inverting and desaturating, I have created a very nice line drawing. The software was working on the contrast of those edges.

Figure 4-71
Using Multiply blend mode

Use the Multiply blend mode

The Multiply blend mode makes white disappear. By switching to the Multiply blend mode, I can apply only the line drawing on top of the photo.

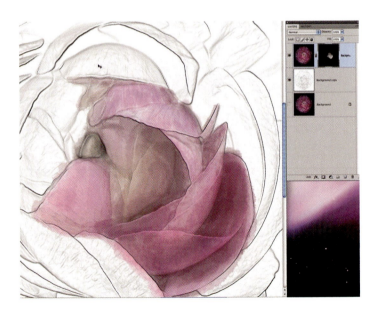

Figure 4-72
Begin to paint

Duplicate the background layer and place it on top of the stack
Apply a Layer > Layer Mask > Hide All mask
Choose a brush. I used the Oil Medium Brush Wet Edges
Begin to paint with white on the Hide All mask

The Hide All mask conceals the recent duplicate background. I will reveal it slowly, using white on the black layer mask. The opacity of the brush was set between 25 and 30%. The Oil Medium Brush Wet Edges builds up light layers of color with a ragged edge. When you stroke over a previous stroke, the color intensifies.

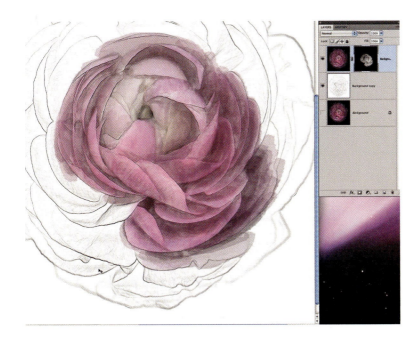

Figure 4-73
Continue to expand your painting

Figure 4-74
Completed flower portion of painted image

Figure 4-75
Create a background

Add a new layer and paint a background
I used several cool colors and the same oil brush to rough in a multi-colored background, overlapping the flower a bit.

Add a layer mask and paint with black on the mask to refine the edges

Figure 4-76
Add a layer mask to refine the flower edges

The painted flower layer was duplicated to intensify the color saturation.

Figure 4-77
Impasto oil effect is added

Add a New Layer
Set the blend mode to Multiply
Add a layer effect of Bevel and Emboss
Paint with white on this new layer
To add texture to our flower, a Bevel and Emboss layer effect was added. Set the blend mode to Multiply, making the color of pure white disappear. As you paint with white, only the shaded or embossed areas will show. This technique will give you the illusion of depth, mimicking the thickness of oil paints.

Figure 4-78
Completed impasto oil painting

Edge Effects for FREE!

Imagine painterly edges in Photoshop that you can create without buying a program. There are many edge effects software programs available today. They range from wildly funky edges to painterly edges to faux photographic edges. The prices range broadly, also. These effects are quick and generally easy to apply to your images but they can be expensive. Let's explore a few free ways to make interesting edge effects.

Scanner Edge Effects

Your scanner can be a wonderful assistant in building a library of edge effects. There is no limit to the variety of edges you can create with this method.

Materials:

- White artist's paper (experiment with rough cold press watercolor paper and smooth hot press paper)

- Black ink
- Artist's brush (I like a wide Japanese brush)
- Scanner

Figure 4-79
Ink-coated paper

Brush ink on good-quality, thick, artist paper. Leave rough edges

With a ruler and a pencil I map out the proportion of a 35 mm negative, with a very light pencil mark. This is a rough guideline to assist me in making a black rectangle. I brush the ink on the paper using the guidelines as a template. I intentionally make the edges rough, showing the brush strokes. Let this dry. If the black area has sections that are not dense with black, it may require a second coat of ink.

Scan this black rectangle. Save it and give it a name that indicates the nature of this template (e.g., rough edges on watercolor paper, thin wispy brushy strokes). Develop a whole library of different brush edges that you can use on your work.

Now, how do you use these edges? Open a photo or digital painting to which you would like to add an edge effect. Open the scanned edge effect.

A painter spends his life in despair trying to paint the beauty he sees—in so doing he approaches more beauty.
—CHARLES HAWTHORNE,
in *Hawthorne on Painting* (1938)

Figure 4-80
Bring the ink/paper scan on top of the photo

Copy the edge effect template onto the layer above the photo
Combine the ink-coated paper scan and photograph
Set your blend mode to Screen
This produces the desired edge effect. In my example, the scale of the edge template had to be adjusted to fit the photo beneath.

Figure 4-81
Transform the ink-painted area to fit the underlying photo

Instead of trying to reproduce exactly what I have before my eyes, I use color more arbitrarily, in order to express myself more forcibly.
—Vincent van Gogh,
Further Letters of Vincent van Gogh to His Brother, 1886–1889 (1929)

Choose Edit > Free Transform and pull the bounding box edges to make the edge effect fit the photo
I stretched mine to fit the proportions of the underlying photograph.

Figure 4-82
Screen blend mode creates the brushed edge effect

Set the blend mode to Screen

Figure 4-83
Image > Adjustments >
Invert

Figure 4-84
Inverted ink layer
Image > Adjustments >
Invert

How would you like to double the usefulness of your edge effect? Try this trick. On the edge effect layer, go to Image > Adjustments > Invert. What was white will turn black, and vice versa.

Change your blend mode to Multiply
Your outside edge is now black!

Two for one! One edge effect template will allow you to make two different edge effects.

Do you want to try for three? Once you understand what can be accomplished with the use of blending modes, all sorts of possibilities open up. Let's duplicate the edge effect template layer. Simply drag that layer to the new layer icon at the bottom of the layer palette.

Duplicate the ink-painted layer
Set blend mode to Screen
Image > Adjustments > Invert
Free Transform to change the size of the bottom ink-painted layer just slightly
Change the blend mode on the new layer to Screen. Invert the black and white areas on the new layer, by again going to Image > Adjustments > Invert. The next step will give us a bit of a three-dimensional effect, similar to a drop shadow. Using the Free Transform command, simply pull the edges of this layer a little bigger than the layer above it.

Voilà! Three edge effects from one edge template. The possibilities are endless. Experiment. Try different kinds of brushes on a variety of paper textures. Each template will be unique to you, as each brush stroke will be different. It's fun, practical, and economical.

Color is raw material indispensable to life, like water and fire.
—FERNAND LEGER,
  in *Modern Art 1890–1918,*
  by Jean Clay (1978)

Figure 4-85
Duplicate the ink-painted layer

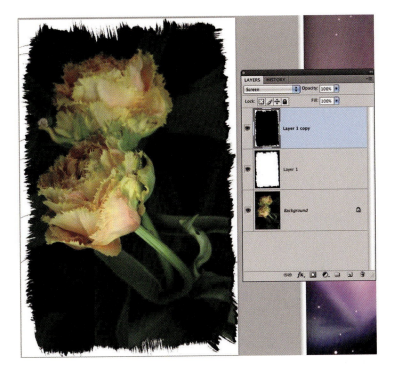

Figure 4-86
Offset layers to create shadow

Film/Photo Edges

Let's use that scanner again and scan in a Polaroid® transfer image. The edges on this type of process are unique. They give a telltale reminder to the viewer of how the image was made. The Polaroid gel that oozes out along the edges during this process leaves a trace of color that is identifiable as a Polaroid transfer. We can mimic that effect through scanning and transforming.

Figure 4-87
Original Polaroid transfers

Polaroid Transfer Edges

Figure 4-87 shows two separate Polaroid transfers. Each has a unique border that is a result of this process. Notice also the softness of the image and a texture that resembles grain.

Figure 4-88
Erasing Polaroid transfers

Use a Rough brush to erase the actual Polaroid transfer image
I want only the outside edge of the scanned transfer. With the eraser set to a Rough brush (number 60), I erased the inside of the transfer.

Only the edges remain. Transfers that are hollow can be kept in a library of edge effects to use on later projects.

Figure 4-89
Empty Polaroid transfer edges

Figure 4-90
*Photograph and Polaroid
edge are joined*

Join the Polaroid edge and the photograph. You will probably need to use Free Transform to get the proportions just right. If I am trying to truly mimic a Polaroid transfer, the photograph is too sharp.

Figure 4-91
Gaussian Blur and Noise

Figure 4-92
Scanned film edge

Apply Filter > Blur > Gaussian Blur
Apply Filter > Noise
To continue along with the concept of creating a faux Polaroid transfer, I can run two filters on the photograph layer. I first use a light application of Filter > Blur > Gaussian Blur, followed by Filter > Noise. The filter applications move the image closer to looking like a real Polaroid transfer.

Film Edge Effects

Occasionally, you will see a photo that has, as its frame, the edge of a piece of film. This seems to be a popular edge in recent years. We can mimic this effect, also.

Lay a strip of film on your flatbed scanner and scan it. Save that file. Take a portion of that filmstrip and copy it into its own document. For this example (Figure 4-92), I've shown you the scan on the right, and on the left I have inverted the image. Either way will work. Your own taste will determine which version you like best.

Good composition is like a suspension bridge; each line adds strength and takes none away.
—ROBERT HENRI,
The Art Spirit (1923)

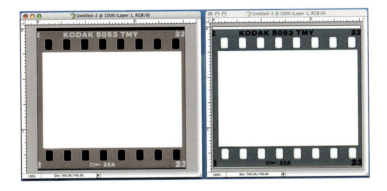

Figure 4-93
Film edges

Figure 4-94
Film edges and photos combined

In Figure 4-94, I've inserted a photograph under the layer of the film edging. Again, either one would work. It's a matter of taste.

You can take this a step further by selecting the film edging (I used the Magic Wand Tool) and darkening it. Darkening is done easily with either an adjustment in Curves or Levels. I also cropped the film edge down a little. This gives a contemporary feel to the edge effect.

Figure 4-95
Edge effect of a film negative

There is absolutely no limit to the number of edge effects that you can make, creating a library of edges that you can use well into the future. The bonus is that they are all unique to only your work.

I would encourage you to explore the painting possibilities within Photoshop. Try combining some of the techniques shown in this chapter using filters and the Pattern Stamp Tool, Art History Brush Tool, and History Brush Tool. Try some of the more irregular brushes. In Chapter 12 you will discover how to make your own unique brushes.

New Photoshop Mixer Brush Tool

Now, onto this new tool available in Photoshop CS5, the Mixer Brush Tool. I should mention that to get the full effect of this new tool I would really recommend using a pressure-sensitive tablet. This brush allows you to pick up color from underlying layers, mix colors, and apply paint in a truly painterly fashion. You are going to love it!

Figure 4-96
Preparing to paint

As in all painting projects it is essential to ready yourself for the project. If you need to increase the saturation, clean up the photo with the Clone Brush Tool, or change the color balance, do these tasks before embarking on the painting. I've also added additional canvas on the sides of the photo to use as a scratch space and a mixing palette area. I will eventually crop that area away, but it can be very useful during the panting process for blending colors and creating a place to pick up paint.

Add an additional layer and select the Mixer Brush Tool, located with the standard brush. The icon for the new Mixer Brush Tool has a drop of liquid beside it.

Figure 4-97
Applying large brush stroke underpainting

I selected the Round Fan Stiff Thin Bristles brush. You can get a preview of what the brush stroke will look like in the Brushes palette (available from the Window menu). I'm painting on the new transparent layer. The cloning information is being pulled from the original image. I renamed the background layer so I could lower the opacity on the original image. If you leave the background layer at 100% opacity, it can be distracting in that it does not allow you to see clearly what you are painting.

The various settings for the Mixer Brush Tool are detailed here. If you turn off the control that manages loading your brush with the current color after each stroke, you have enabled cloning. That is an important concept for creating a painting from a photograph.

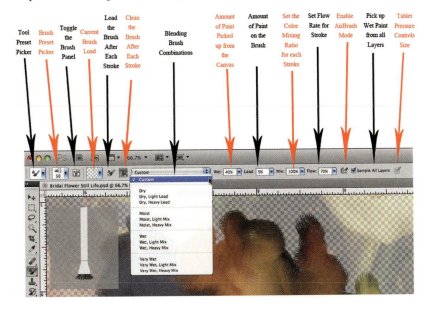

Figure 4-98
Chart illustrating the various settings for the Mixer Brush Tool

The Blending brush combinations give you a variety of brush loads, from a dry brush to a very wet one. There are so many options here. You just need to jump in and experiment. Be open to a few surprises.

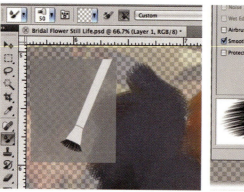

Figure 4-99
Bristle brush preview

You can turn on and off an actual preview of how your brush is working. It can be very revealing. For some people, the preview is distracting. The choice is yours. You toggle the preview with the button at the bottom of the Brush palette.

Figure 4-100
Painting progressing with more detail

Now, back to our painting. I have established a loose underpainting. This brush has reached down and pulled the color information from the original. The bigger the brush, the looser the painting will be.

I owe the next technique to Tim Shelbourne, who discovered that if you place the original layer on top of your stack you can still pull the color information but also bring back detail. Lower the opacity of the original photo layer (now on top) to 1% or greater. Create a new layer and place it in the middle of the stack. Switch to a different mixer brush, one that is dryer. I used the dry light load version. I painted in selected places, not everywhere, to bring some detail back. You can work this way, changing from a loose application to a dry application of paint, varying your brush type and load, for quite a while.

Figure 4-101
Mixer area on extended canvas

If you want to load your brush with multiple colors from your painting, you can turn off the clone color, switching to load the brush color, and click on the option key to select an area that has several colors. I then deposited it on my extra canvas margins. You can also use this area to mix colors. You can now dip into this area, like working from a real palette with real paints, loading your brush with several colors, for a more naturalistic effect. This area will be cropped later, so there is no lasting effect from creating this mixing area.

To recap, I have the original photo at the top of the stack with a very low opacity (generally 1 to 2%), the loose and wet painting layer at the bottom of the stack, and finally the middle layer, where I used a dry mixer brush to restore detail.

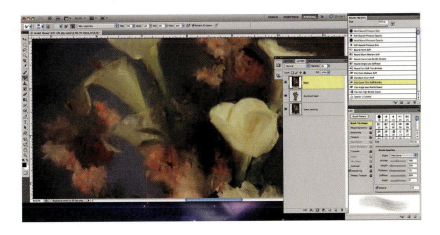

Figure 4-102
Layers displayed

View this illustration from the top left corner, moving clockwise.

Upper left corner is the original photo.

Upper right corner is the loose, wet mixer brush layer.

Lower right corner is the layer where I used a dry mixer brush to restore a few details.

Lower left corner is the addition of a few low-opacity color strokes (mostly the traditional Pastel on Charcoal Paper brush) for accent areas.

I like to add some finishing touches and often pile on another layer to add these strokes nondestructively. On a new transparent layer, I select colors from the painting using the Color Picker. Hold down on the Option key to select. The new color ring is surrounded by neutral gray to aid you in seeing the selected color with minimal color influences.

Figure 4-105
Expanded color choices in the same color family

Using the selected color as a starting spot, I usually proceed to select a more saturated or brighter shade to use for my accent strokes. If you are on a Mac and are using the Color Picker, click on Command + Control + Option to bring up the expanded color chart. If you are on a Windows machine, use Alt + Shift + right click.

For this painting, I used the regular Pastel on Charcoal Paper brush found in the Dry Media Brushes library. It is, perhaps, my favorite brush. It has texture bumpiness already embedded in. Using it at a light opacity (20% or less), I deposit some more color to liven up a painting. I frequently change colors and work throughout the painting, adding these finishing strokes. If the strokes need any blending in, revert back to the cloning version of the new Mixer Brush Tool, with Sample All Layers checked.

Figure 4-106
Completed painting

Using John Derry's Third-Party Brushes

I've decided to include John Derry's third-party brushes here in this chapter instead of Chapter 9. I think anyone really intent on making digital paintings in Photoshop should consider purchasing these inexpensive and wonderful brushes. John has engineered the shape and characteristics of many brushes for you, eliminating the time required to create these brushes on your own. They may be found at johnsartistsbrushes.com. John is a pioneer in digital painting in both Painter and Photoshop and is one of our featured artists in Chapter 3.

The original photo was shot in mid-coast Maine. In preparation for the painting, the saturation was boosted, using a Hue/Saturation adjustment layer.

Figure 4-107
Original photo

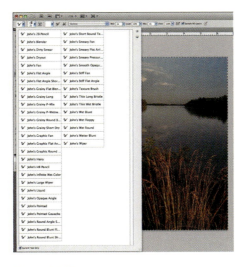

Figure 4-108
Tool presets

John's Artists' Brushes are found in your Tool Presets menu. Their names give a good indication of their effects. Blenders do not apply color; they blend the underlying colors. Smeary brushes apply color but also blend with underlying colors. Dirty brushes contaminate the brush color with blended colors. Short brushes have a quick dry-out on the stroke. Dry brushes do not replenish their color. Floppy brushes have long hairs, and the brush stroke varies significantly with pressure. Opaque brushes apply color at 100% opacity. Brush shapes vary from blunt to angled to fan to curved and pointed. There is much to explore here, so let's get started.

Figure 4-109
Beginning of digital painting using John's Blender

Click on the Background layer name and rename it Base. If it is called Background you cannot lower the opacity. Lower the opacity of that Base layer to 1–50%. Add a new layer. The first Mixer Brush I've chosen is John's Blender. It gives a soft, yet significant lay down of color.

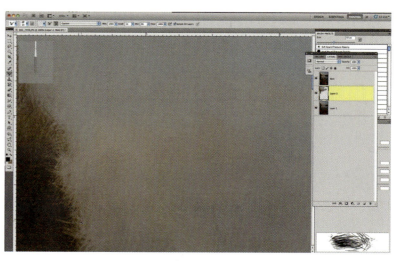

Figure 4-110
First painted layer using only John's Blender

Figure 4-111
John's Hairy brush adds a textural and painterly component

Using John's Blender brush over the whole image results in a very soft and burry application of the fundamental colors in the photo.

John's Hairy brush was used on another layer. This layer was placed under the Base layer but above the blurry, Blender layer. This brush has a great effect when the size of the brush is increased. This large brush may noticeably slow down the processing time. Be patient.

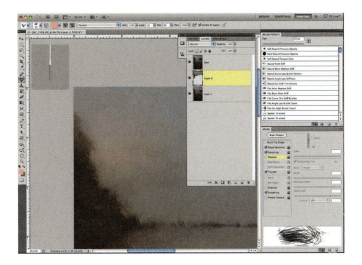

Figure 4-112
Peach tint added to the sky

Continuing with the Hairy brush, the brush was loaded with a soft peach tone and used lightly on the sky to increase the sunset feel.

Figure 4-113
Finished painting

The painting was finished using a Dry Load Mixer brush on the bottom portion of the painting, revealing the reeds in the foreground.

Be sure to check out Janet Stoppee's contribution in Chapter 3, where she uses these brushes.

Figure 4-114
Water lily painted with Mixer Brush Tool

Figure 4-115
"Reluctant Angel" painted with Mixer Brush Tool

There are so many possibilities now available for digitally painting in Photoshop. I expect that these techniques will expand and the market for more third-party painting tools will prosper as more budding artists and photographers try their hand at digital painting.

5

Painting in Painter™

Artists often have a variety of art supplies in their studio spaces. My studio contains oil painting supplies, watercolors, gouache, pastels, charcoals, colored pencils, inks, encaustic paints, oil sticks, dry pigments, and more. There are brushes galore. They each have special uses. My expensive sable brushes are only for my watercolors. There are natural bristle and plastic bristle brushes for oil painting. My large map case holds drawers full of different papers in various textures and colors. Although many artists specialize in a particular medium, such as watercolors, they often have dabbled at using other media over the years.

Wouldn't it be wonderful to have all those tools, and more, at your fingertips? Wouldn't it be wonderful to never spend time washing and cleaning up your brushes and gear? It is possible to use these tools in their digital version with the software called Painter. Painter began as a great little black-and-white program, called Sketcher, that came in a

If one hasn't a horse, one is one's own horse.

—Vincent van Gogh, *Further Letters of Vincent van Gogh to His Brother, 1886–1889* (1929)

cigar box type of packaging. In time, it was packaged in a paint can and was marketed as Painter. It has had several owners over the years, but it has been owned by Corel® for several years. Although many digital artists use the variety of art media available in Painter without using photographs, we will not address those applications. Our task in this chapter centers on how photographers can use the digital art materials available in Painter. Be prepared to be amazed by the realistic effects those art materials will lend to your work. Another pleasant side effect of using these digital art materials is the lack of fumes and odors associated with some art materials. You will not be digging pigment out of your fingernails or wiping paint off your hands and clothes. Hooray!

Painter uses several traditional file formats, including PSD, TIFF, and JPEG. What may surprise you will be the native format of Painter called RIFF. You won't see that format in any other program. It is particular to Painter. If you are going to use your file in another program, such as Photoshop, just be sure to save it in a file format accepted by the other program. This native painter format of RIFF allows you to keep a watercolor "wet" over a prolonged period of time. In real life, if you are painting and your long-lost college roommate calls from 3000 miles away, necessitating an extended phone call, your painting will have dried out on your return. If you had been painting digitally and saved the file in the RIFF format, you could return to the "wet" paper two weeks later. Also, with digital watercolors in Painter, you can instantly "dry" your painting to apply another medium, such as pastels, on top of your painting. This is an artist's dream come true.

As a photographer, you will want to prepare your photograph before bringing it into Painter. I usually do any cropping, image adjustments (such as rubber stamping to remove objectionable areas), and contrast, tonal, or color adjustments, etc., in Photoshop. After all, Photoshop is the photo manipulation program; let's use it for what it does best. In fact, the primary question that I ask repeatedly is "What program will be best for the task at hand?" I often go back and forth between Photoshop and Painter, according to the job I need to do. It is just common sense. The look of the Painter interface has improved in recent versions. In the past, the tools consumed so much of the screen real estate that there was barely room to work. It has a much more practical and streamlined look now. But, of course, you will still not want all of the windows and palettes open at once. If you are comfortable with the Photoshop layout, then you will find the Painter interface similar in design and that it reinforces your instinctual impulse as you reach for a tool.

Our example, of 18-month-old Anne, is shown here in its refinement before it was brought into Painter to create a painting. The original capture on the left was taken on a playground in the shade. It certainly had its deficits, but the honest expression and look reeled me in. The middle image was cropped, lightened, and brightened. The image on the far right involved using the Clone Stamp Tool to remove the stray lock of hair. Anne's eyes were enlarged a fraction by using the Liquify filter. A right shoulder area was constructed, using the Clone Stamp Tool. Next, the image was rendered in Lucis Pro 6.0. Notice the increased contrast.

I prefer drawing to talking. Drawing is faster, and allows less room for lies.
— LE CORBUSIER, *Time Magazine* (May 5, 1961)

Figure 5-1
*Refining a photo in
preparation for painting*

Painter is a wonderful asset to photographers who desire to make their work more painterly. It is good for portraits, photo illustrations, still lifes, landscapes, and much more. We will explore a few of those applications in this chapter. If you need to brush up on your Painter skills or you are a novice at Painter, please refer to Chapter 13, which explains essential skills.

Figure 5-2
Photo and Clone

Simple Cloning Techniques

File > Open (choose the photo you want to use)
File > Clone
Now, on to working with photographs in Painter. Go to File > Open (just like you do in Photoshop), and select the file you want to open. You now have your photograph in Painter. The first step is to clone your photograph. This preserves the original. We never work on the

The artist expresses only what he has within himself, not what he sees with his eyes.
—ALEXEJ VON JAWLENSKY, in
Das Kunstwerk II (1948)

original. Simply go to File > Clone. A clone of the original image will appear with the name Clone of … (whatever the name of the original image was).

Select > All
Delete

The next step seems counterintuitive. Choose Select > All and hit the Delete key. You have just eliminated the clone, right? Wrong! The upper right-hand corner of the image has a button for tracing paper. You can toggle the tracing paper on and off, revealing and concealing your original image. Another technique is to simply use Quick Clone. The result is the same but faster.

Select the Clone Tool
Select the cloning icon ("rubber stamp") in the Color Picker

Select the cloning icon. HINT: It looks like a rubber stamp. There are tons of different types of brushes and different art media that can be used in cloning. My personal favorites include the Impressionist Cloner, Chalk Cloner, and Watercolor Cloner. The vibrant Color Picker needs to be disabled to pull from the colors of the original cloned image. Just toggle the "rubber stamp" icon, located next to the foreground and background blocks, in the lower left-hand corner of the Colors palette. If the Color Picker palette is enabled, it will pull from the current color selected. When the Clone color option is activated, the color wheel will appear grayed down. Simply click on or off the "rubber stamp" icon to activate or deactivate the Clone color option or the Color Picker option.

Figure 5-3
Pastel Cloning begins with Tracing Paper "on"

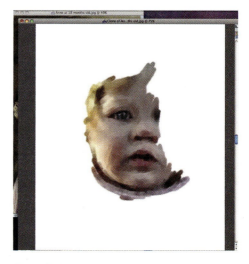

Figure 5-4
Pastel Cloning with Tracing Paper "off"

Choose Chalk Cloner from the various Cloner variants
Begin to brush the Chalk Cloner onto the "blank" clone
For this example, I chose the Chalk Cloner. I used a large brush and roughed in the cloned colors. This provides an underpainting indicating the shapes and approximate colors. The larger your brush, the rougher the image and less accurate the colors. The large brush pulls from a large selected area on the original image and averages out the approximate color from all the pixels selected. A smaller brush will give you more detail and more accurate color. Our image is very rough, painterly, and smudgy now.

It is important to use Tracing Paper in order to see the placement of the photo elements. But, it is equally important to turn Tracing Paper off frequently to truly see the quality of your painting. Tracing Paper can be misleading, letting you think there are details on the painting that are not really there.

Calamity is a time of great opportunity.
—CHINESE PROVERB

Figure 5-5
Close-up of refined portrait, using the smaller brush

Use a smaller brush for more detail
Next, I wanted to firm up the painting a bit so I selected a smaller brush. Working with the smaller brush brought in more detail. The strokes were made in the direction of the object (e.g., sweater pattern and locks of hair). Make your brush stroke on the painting just as your hand would do if it were following the contour of the object that you are painting.

Art is an ideal within the four corners of an image.
—BENEDETTA CROCE,
Aesthetic as Science of Expression and General Linguistic (1909)

Use the Straight Cloner at a very low opacity (1–3%)
At this point in the process, I usually like to bring back some of the detail from the original image, so I chose the Straight Cloner. This brought the exact photo up. That, however, was way too much. I would have been merely restoring the image to its photographic beginnings. I wanted just a hint of the details. The opacity was set very low, at 2%, and I added strokes, as if adding a light transparent veil over the original, only in the areas where more detail was desired.

Michelangelo's energy
terrified me; I felt a
sentiment I could not
express; on seeing the
beauties of Raphael I was
moved to tears and the
pencil fell from my hand.
— JEAN-HONORÉ
    FRAGONARD,
personal notes on a visit
to Italy in 1752, in *Letters
of the Great Artists*, by
Richard Friedenthal
(1963)

Chalk Cloner reapplied to areas that are too photographic

If you bring back too much detailed photographic information, just go back to the Chalk Cloner and again stroke on those loose colors. Try doing that at a very low opacity. This is helpful if a diffusion effect is needed over any area that is too sharp.

It was time to stop, step back, and assess the progress to this point. What did the painting need?

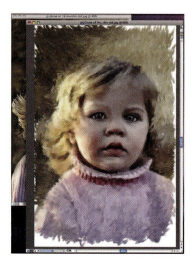

Figure 5-6
*Impressionist Cloner is
applied to the background*

Apply some Impressionist Cloner

I love the scattering of brush strokes available with the Impressionist Cloner. I used it, especially in the background. It also creates a brushed edge. I wanted these new brush strokes to blend in with the previous chalk marks, so I used the Chalk Cloner at 39% opacity in areas, slightly concealing these new impressionist strokes and blending them into the whole composition.

Figure 5-7
Close-up inspection

The end of the process was near. This was an excellent time to step back and assess the image so far. What did it need? Did the edges need help? Did it need more detail somewhere or, perhaps, less detail somewhere? Did I need to add more color or, conversely, tone down any existing color? You need to be your own harshest critic, and try to have an objective eye for needy areas.

Figure 5-8
Effects > Surface Control > Apply Surface Texture > French Watercolor Paper

Apply Surface Texture > French Watercolor Paper

Painter gives you the ability to use your drawing implements on textured surfaces. If a brush name includes the word "Grainy" it will interact with a textured surface. But, wait, it doesn't end there. You can add the texture after the painting is completed. Just use the Apply Surface command. I used the French Watercolor Paper choice and moved the amount slider low to make the effect subtle.

A painter paints a picture with the same feeling as that with which a criminal commits a crime.

—EDGAR DEGAS,
The Notebooks of Edgar Degas, translated by Theodore Reff (1976)

Figure 5-9
Paper texture applied

Figure 5-10
Completed portrait of Anne

If I didn't start painting, I
would have raised chickens.
—ANNA M. MOSES,
*Grandma Moses: My Life's
History* (1952)

Print and assess the proof

After the corrections were made, a proof was pulled. The image was printed and again evaluated for color, quality of brush strokes, etc. The final image was printed on a heavy inkjet watercolor paper.

Painted portraits are challenging work. You don't want the image to be photographic in nature. You really want a painting. Figure 5-11 illustrates a digital painting I made of a friend. Every portion of this large work has been painted. Most of the work was done in Painter. Many various brushes were used, including cloning ones, pastels, and gouache paint. Although I can make a passable piece in an hour or two, this painting took the better part of a weekend to achieve the look that I wanted. Digital painting is not done in an instant. Time is needed for the discernment and study that are necessary throughout the art-making process. Give yourself the gift of time and patience to see yourself through to a satisfying conclusion and pleasing piece of art.

Figure 5-11
Painted portrait of "Scott"

The wonderful responsiveness of the chalks and pastels make them some of my favorite tools. The colors are true to your selection, and the ability to have the paper surface interact with the pastels is a wonderful textural element. The digital painting of a statue in a small

Figure 5-12
Les Bastides de Jordan, France

village in Provence, France (Figure 5-12) was made with these techniques, as was the painting of a vase and stairs shown in Figure 5-13, which also began as a slide taken in France.

Impressionist Cloner

An artist should paint as if in the presence of God.

—MICHELANGELO, in *Michelangelo's Theory of Art,* by Robert J. Clements (1961)

Another favorite cloning tool is the Impressionist Cloner. The shape of this brush leaves a mark that is similar to a grain of rice. You can make the size of that mark vary by enlarging or shrinking the brush size. For this exercise I thought it would be fun to use a photo that has the feel of a painting from the era of impressionism. Figure 5-118 was taken at a Civil War re-enactment. There were lots of people, trucks, food tents, etc., in the original photograph. The distracting elements were removed in Photoshop, primarily using the Clone Stamp Tool.

Figure 5-13
Les Baux, France

Figure 5-14
Photo corrected in Photoshop

Figure 5-15
Photo clone created

File > Clone
Select Clone and Delete
The image was cloned (File > Clone). The clone was selected and deleted. Tracing Paper was turned on, for our visual orientation.

Figure 5-16
Chalk Cloner applied for an underpainting

Cloner > Chalk
Before I begin with the Impressionist Cloner, I like to rough in the painting with large, loose areas of color. A different cloning technique was used for this. I chose the Chalk brush with the Tapered Large Chalk variant (brush size 66.6). The cloning option needs to be selected on the

Colors palette. Chalk gives an initial laydown of color. It also allows the texture of the selected paper to show through. Basic Paper was selected for this image. This initial coloring with chalk avoided lots of bare spots that would have appeared if I had begun right away with the Impressionist Cloner. The Impressionist Cloner, used alone, will yield bare spots, unless there is extensive repeated use over an area. We can avoid that problem by supplying a solid laydown of color with the Chalk Cloner before moving on to the Impressionist Cloner.

Figure 5-17
Impressionist Cloner applied

Use Impressionist Cloner brush

Once the entire painting had a good underpainting of color it was time to use the Impressionist Cloner. A brush size of 19 was used over the entire painting. In Figure 5-17, you can see the texture of the previous step with chalk and paper and the beginnings of the Impressionist Cloner in the upper left-hand corner.

Painting must be impulsive to be worthwhile; an aesthetic excitement.
—Charles Hawthorne,
    in *Hawthorne on Painting*
    (1938)

Figure 5-18
Large, chunky Impressionist effect

The entire painting got an application of the Impressionist Cloner. Any areas of blank paper that would have peeked out were covered by the first layer of chalk underpainting. At this point the painting was loose, with large marks from the cloner.

Figure 5-19
Smaller brush used for more detail

More detail was definitely needed on the women and their dresses and parasols. The size of the Impressionist Cloner brush was lowered to 4.8. Compare the woman on the left in Figure 5-19 with the figure on the right. A smaller brush size was used on the woman on the left which yielded more detail.

Figure 5-20
Smaller brush used throughout in selected areas

The smaller brush size was used on both women and in occasional spots throughout the painting.

Use Straight Cloner at a very low opacity to restore some detail
For some finishing touches, the Straight Cloner was used with a 2% opacity to bring back a little of the grasses in the foreground and more definition to the parasols. It's not a Monet, but it gives a bit of the flavor of that era.

Why talk when you can paint?
—MILTON AVERY,
in *Milton Avery,* by Barbara Haskell (1982)

Figure 5-21
"Parasols" with tiny touches of Straight Cloner applied

Other paintings made with this Impressionist Cloner technique are shown in Figures 5-22, 5-23, and 5-24. The sky in Figure 5-24 was purposely made to resemble the sky in Vincent van Gogh's "Starry Night." The original slide was shot with a medium-format slide film in a sunflower field at dawn, near van Gogh's residence in the south of France. The sky treatment was a bit of an homage to the way van Gogh applied those marvelous marks of color on his canvas. The foreground of the sunflowers relied a bit more on the Chalk Cloner and Straight Cloner brushes.

Every time I paint, I throw myself into the water in order to learn how to swim.
—ÉDOUARD MANET,
in *The World of Manet, 1832–1883,* by Pierre Schneider (1968)

Figure 5-22
Lavender Field, France

Figure 5-23
Arles Lane, France

Figure 5-24
Van Gogh's Sunflower Field, St. Remy, France

Pastel Cloning

Figure 5-25
Original Roman sculpture photo

File > Clone

The next example of cloning relies on the custom brush function that is so powerful in Painter. This technique delivers an effect like a chalk drawing on a rough, colored, charcoal paper surface. Open your photograph as usual in Painter and clone the image.

Figure 5-26
Color-toned base paper

Delete the cloned image
Pick a color
Effects > Fill > Current Color at 100% opacity

The cloned image was selected and deleted. A color from the Color Picker was selected for our charcoal paper. Try looking at your original photo and make a color decision that complements the image. Opposites on the color wheel are frequently good possible choices. Go to Effects > Fill > Current Color at 100% opacity. This will create the colored charcoal paper.

Figure 5-27
Brush Creator

Window > Show Brush Creator
Choose modifiers

The next step in this process is to create a special brush. Go to Window > Show Brush Creator. This brings up a fairly large menu. There are lots of ways that you could modify a brush and plan how it will react with the surface on which it draws. I picked the Chalk brush with the Dull Grainy Chalk variant. The modifiers that I selected were:

- Dab Type—Circular
- Stroke Type—Singular
- Method—Cover
- Subcategory—Grainy Hard Cover
- Opacity—30%
- Grain—10%

You will find that the possibilities for variations are virtually endless. Experiment!

Figure 5-28
Dull Grainy Chalk used at 30% opacity

The Tracing Paper icon was turned on, and an application of the Dull Grainy Chalk variant was used. Because the opacity was set to 30%, it was possible to build up color with many strokes or allow some areas to be more thinly painted. The paper type selected for this image was the Italian Watercolor Paper—a good selection since the photo is of a fountain in Rome.

Painting begins with outlining key areas.

I think I'm beginning to learn something about it.

—PIERRE-AUGUSTE RENOIR, his last words about painting at age 78, in *Renoir, An Intimate Record,* by Ambroise Vollard (1930)

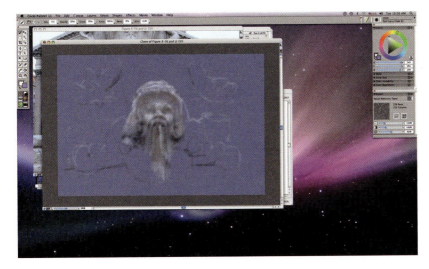

Figure 5-29

Use the Tracing Paper feature to paint over the outlines of the photo. Turn Tracing Paper off once the outlines are established.

I generally use the Tracing Paper feature to map out the contours of the photograph (see Figure 5-29) and then turn Tracing Paper off. I like to really see the effect the strokes are having on the painting. If the photograph is still visible, it can distract me and I'm less able to see the quality of the marks that I am making. I occasionally turn Tracing Paper on and off to check with the information available in the original work.

Figure 5-30
Assess your work

Most of the painting is done with Tracing Paper turned off. This is the honest version of what you are creating. After the application of chalk is completed, it is a good time to, again, step back and analyze the painting. What are its strengths? What are its shortcomings? What does it need?

Figure 5-31
Straight Cloner used for detail

Figure 5-32
Final version

Use the Straight Cloner for areas needing more detail (2% opacity)
A little more detail was needed on the smaller aspects of the photo. The Straight Cloner was used sparingly at only 2% opacity to bring a little more clarity to the final touches on this piece.

The final painting retains a chalk drawing feel and enough detail to carry the image successfully.

Other images made with this technique are shown in Figures 5-33, 5-34, and 5-35.

Painting is the grandchild of nature. It is related to God.

—REMBRANDT,
   in *Rembrandt Drawings*,
   by Paul Némo, as
   translated by David
   Macrae (1975)

Figure 5-33

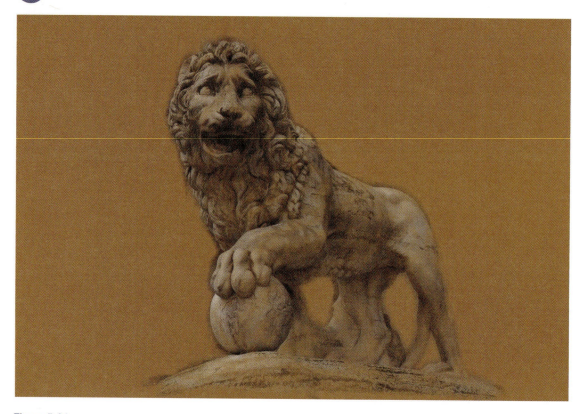

Figure 5-34

Figure 5-35

Oil Paint Cloning

Figure 5-36
Original photo, taken in Venice

One of the wonderful techniques available to you in Painter is the ability to apply paint that has a thickness, like oil paints. A thick application of paint is often called *impasto*. In the next example, I used a photograph that I had taken in Venice (Figure 5-36). The nature of the image led me to believe that it might be a good image to work from using the Wet Oil Cloner. The brick work, which was showing the passage of time, would work well with a thick brush stroke of paint.

Figure 5-37
Wet Oil Cloner selected

Create a clone (File > Clone)
Select and delete the clone
Select Cloner brush > Wet Oil Cloner
The image was cloned, selected, and deleted, as I have done in previous examples. The Cloner brush was selected and the Wet Oil Cloner variant was the type of brush used. A size 10 brush was applied for

preliminary brushwork. That size was great for dragging in horizontal strokes over the brick area. You will notice that a previous laydown of color will smear into the next stroke, if overlapped. That is just the way real oil paints interact when painting. The cloner is pulling the color information from the underlying photograph. The larger the brush, the more color samples that are selected and averaged for the color application. A smaller brush will always yield more detail and accurate color sampling, as per the photograph.

Figure 5-38
Use Tracing Paper to establish outlines

Use the Tracing Paper feature to establish key areas
Turn Tracing Paper off to see the real painting and the marks that you are making
It is occasionally helpful to use the Tracing Paper feature as you paint to see where you are on the original image. I like to rough out the outlines of areas using Tracing Paper and then turn Tracing Paper off.

Figure 5-39
Straight Cloner applied lightly for detail

With Tracing Paper turned off, I can more clearly see the type of brush stroke I am making and how it interacts with previous strokes (directionality of the pull of the brush and the amount of color blending that is occurring as the paint smears). I can concentrate more on my mark making without the distraction of the underlying photograph.

Assess the painting
Use Straight Cloner at 2% opacity for details in selected areas
Select Oil Brush > Glazing Brush variant > lay down a light glaze

After covering the canvas with paint strokes using the Wet Oil Cloner, it was time to step back and assess the painted image. I used the Straight Cloner at 2% opacity to bring a little of the window-box foliage into view, instead of green smears. The next step was to leave the Cloning brush and go to the Oil > Glazing Brush, also set at a low opacity. I picked a rich dark brown and glazed over the shadowed areas on the left, intensifying the shadows and depth.

The content of a painting is tied up with the time, place and history. It is always related to man's beliefs and disbeliefs, to his affirmations and negations. How we believe and disbelieve is mirrored in the art of our times.
—MARK TOBEY,
in *The Artist's Voice,* by Katherine Kuh (1960)

Figure 5-40
Glazing brush used

Use the Glazing brush to deepen shadows, lighten highlights, and add detail

The Glazing brush was used with various shades of aqua, green, pink, and yellow to add some color interest in the window boxes. More flowers were added using this brush. The photograph was taken in January and the geraniums were just hanging onto life. The Cloning brush was akin to adding fertilizer to the dirt. The growing conditions improved immediately. Feel free to use your creative license.

The completed painting has the look of an oil painting. There are smears, loose blending of colors, and the appearance of a thick, impasto, paint application. There are several oil options to use and many different brushes. Experiment with thick paint. Be selective with the photograph that you choose. Not all images will look good rendered in oil paints. Some images are better suited to a delicate watercolor rendition than to a thicker, more opaque application of paint. Choose the medium to match the feel of the photograph. This image was printed on inkjet canvas.

Figure 5-41
*"Venetian Canal" completed
painting*

More Oil Painting

Figure 5-42
Oil Paint Cloner used

Use Oil Paint Cloner on the clone
I'm going to show a few more variations on the Oil Paint Cloner, since
the look of an oil painting is often an effect that many photographers
desire. In Figure 5-42 the Oil Paint Cloner was used for the first painterly effect.

Figure 5-43
Oil Paint > Glazing Round brush used

Light application of color gazing was added with the Oil Paint > Glazing Round brush

The next brush that was used was the Oil Paint > Glazing Round variation. Colors were selected from the Color Wheel and stroked lightly into the hair area. The opacity was set low to give a feel of transparency.

All the Fine Arts are different species of Poetry.
—Samuel Taylor Coleridge,
On the Principles of Genial Criticism (1814)

Figure 5-44
Highlights and shadows intensified

Highlights and shadows were intensified with the glazing brush Blender brush > Oil Blender was used on the floor area

That same glazing variation was used on the ballet skirt to add highlights and shadows. An oil blender (from the Blender brushes) was used on the wooden floor.

Figure 5-45
Completed "Ballet Dancer" painting

The finished piece (Figure 5-45) takes a snapshot of a teenager's ballet recital and turns it into a little painting, worthy of framing and displaying.

Bristle Oil Cloner

Figure 5-46
Before and after

Our next oil variation is the Bristle Oil Cloner. Think of this as a brush made of coarser hairs, similar to a boar's bristle brush, which is made from the thick, strong, stubby hair on the back of a pig. In real oil painting, a variety of brushes are available. Some are softer for more delicate blending and some are coarser for a more textured mark. In Figure 5-46, compare the original photograph on the left to the Bristle Oil Cloner painted version on the right.

Figure 5-47
Underpainting using Furry Cloner

File > Clone
Select and delete the clone
Select Cloner brush > Furry Cloner variant to create an underpainting of color
One of the techniques I use for a quick underpainting is to paint the clone with the Furry Cloner. It is an amusing cloner that makes pompom-type marks with variations of the color that were sampled in

One wants the spirit, the aroma, don't ye know? If you paint a young girl, youth should scent the room; if a thinker, thoughts should be in the air; an aroma of personality … and, with all that, it should be a picture, a pattern, an arrangement, a harmony such as only a painter could conceive.
—James Abbott McNeill Whistler, *The Gentle Art of Making Enemies* (1890)

the cloning area. It works quickly and gives a rough underpainting of color. In my work, this underpainting is almost always covered later by other brushwork. Figures 5-47 and 5-48 show a beginning view and an overall look at the Furry Cloner used on the whole painting.

Figure 5-48
Completed Furry Cloner painting

Figure 5-49
Bristle Oil Cloner with new layer added

Cloner brush > Bristle Oil Cloner used throughout the painting
Oil Painting brush > Glazing Round used for accent color glazing
Add an additional Layer for accent colors in the water
Use Glazing Round brush for accent color glazing
The Bristle Oil Cloner was used for the majority of the actual painting. That brush most closely resembled the type of brush mark that I wanted in the painting.

Figure 5-49 adds an additional layer. The color of the water and the color of the duck's tail feathers are too similar. I decided to give the water a pretty cool tone and used the additional layer set for the Colorize Composite method. The Composite methods are like blend modes in Photoshop and are located under the word "Layers" in the Layers palette.

Figure 5-50
Additional accent color layer

Figure 5-51
Close-up of accent colors

Figure 5-51 shows a close-up of the brushwork and the addition of extra colors using the Oil Paint variant Glazing Round.

Figure 5-52 shows the completed painting. Many additional colors were added with that oil glazing brush. More color was added in the duck's rear feathers to differentiate the duck from the water.

Figure 5-52
Passau, Germany, Duck

Combining a Variety of Media into One Painting

Figure 5-53
*Oil Cloner, Bristle Oil
Cloner, and Van Gogh Cloner*

File > Clone
Select and delete the clone
Cloning made with three cloners: Oil Cloner, Bristle Oil Cloner, and Van Gogh Cloner

The next oil painting (shown in Figure 5-54) was made with the Oil Cloner, Bristle Oil Cloner, and Van Gogh Cloner. Figure 5-53 shows a close-up of the loose brushwork that was applied using all three cloners.

Figure 5-54
Light glaze applied to wall

Figure 5-55
Glazing effect intensified

A glaze was brushed onto a separate layer to add color effect in specific areas

After finishing most of the painting (Figure 5-54), I wanted to warm the background wall a little with a glaze of a soft apricot color. That was applied on a separate layer and combined using the default

You will paint well
when you are able to
forget that you are
painting at all.

—Kimon Nicolaïdes,
The Natural Way to Draw
(1941)

blend mode (Figure 5-55). The effect would be like putting a gel over your lighting source in studio photography but limiting the effect to certain areas.

Figure 5-56
Completed painting

The flowers used in the digital oil paintings shown in Figures 5-56 and 5-57 were photographed the day after the wedding of my daughter, Emily. The flowers had been used in the wedding and the lace under the vase was the lace handkerchief that she carried with her bouquet that day. I wanted to make a painting using some photographs of those items as a special gift for the newlyweds. As I worked on the photography that day, a beautiful blue and black butterfly kept coming into my picture frame as I made photos. In Figure 5-56, I decided to welcome the butterfly into the composition. I decided not to question the serendipity of its presence. For that painting, I actually used all of the following brushes: Watercolor Cloner, Bristle Oil Cloner, Fine Gouache Cloner, Van Gogh Cloner, and Watercolor Run Cloner. I switched vases for Figure 5-57. This painting has a slightly different feel and more closely resembles an old Dutch still-life painting.

Figure 5-57
"Wedding Bouquet" still life completed

Figure 5-58 shows the detail of brushwork used in the painting. Notice the addition, again, of an apricot-colored glaze on the back wall. This was made with that wonderful oil Glazing Round brush.

Forget that you are
drawing or painting and
feel that you are using this
medium to reach out and
touch the model.

—Kimon Nicolaïdes,
  The Natural Way to Draw
  (1941)

Figure 5-58
Detail of painting

Adding Texture to Your Painting

Figure 5-59
Original photograph

The next still life has a Spanish flavor and incorporates the ability of Painter to render a surface texture. For this photograph, I selected items that I had brought home from a trip to Spain (a fan and a hand-tooled metal box from Toledo). The bouquet was made with red peonies.

The background was actually the fabric of a jacket, not wallpaper. Go to the fabric store and buy inexpensive remnants for interesting background colors, textures, and patterns. I probably shot over 60 versions of this still life, moving items and lighting until I found the one that was most pleasing to me, in terms of lighting, color, and composition.

Figure 5-60

File > Clone
Select and delete clone
Clone Brush > Van Gogh Cloner and Chalk Cloner
The entire painting was cloned with the Chalk Cloner and the Van Gogh Cloner. Notice the evidence of the Van Gogh Cloner in the fabric background. The Van Gogh Cloner gives wonderful strokes of color. I next used the oil cloner to give a thick, impasto brush stroke throughout the painting. That version was saved.

Duplicate the layer
Effects > Surface Control > Apply Surface Texture > Coarse Cotton Canvas
Adjust the light source
Here comes the fancy footwork, folks. I reopened that saved file and duplicated the layer. I then selected a paper texture (Coarse Cotton Canvas). Under Effects > Surface Control, I chose Apply Surface Texture. That dialogue box and the settings used are shown in Figure 5-61. Try moving the light source around. A slight adjustment has a profound effect on the texture.

Figure 5-61
Apply surface texture

Figure 5-62
Canvas texture applied

Figure 5-62 shows the canvas textural effect on the painting. It seemed a little too strong for my tastes. Here is where that duplicated layer comes in handy. The layer that had the textural effect applied was named "canvas" and was at the bottom of my layer stack.

Top layer is the cloned painting set at 65% opacity
Bottom layer is the canvas version of the painting
Layers are combined (Drop) to tone down the canvas effect
The top layer named "painting" did not have the cotton canvas texture applied. It was still the painting as I had saved it. I blended those two layers together using a 65% opacity on the painting layer, allowing some

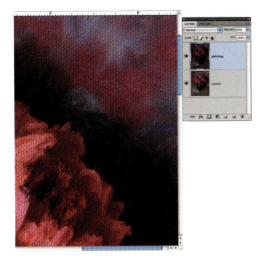

Figure 5-63
Layers combined

of the texture to be used from the bottom "canvas" layer. Those two lay-ers were condensed into one (Drop). That new version was saved with a new name that incorporated the word "texture" in its title. Be sure to use the "Save As" command to retain the original painting.

Draw lines, young man, and still more lines, both from life and from memory, and you will become a good artist.
—Jean-Auguste-
   Dominique Ingres,
   spoken to Edgar Degas
   as quoted in *Ingres,* by
   Walter Pach (1939)

Figure 5-64
Photoshop combination of Painting and Painting with Canvas

Open both paintings in Photoshop (Painting and Painting with Canvas texture)
Use a layer mask to bring out the paint strokes and eliminate the canvas texture
The canvas texture version is the top layer with the Layer Mask
The next step was made in Photoshop. Both painted files were opened. One had a canvas texture and one was rich in impasto brush strokes. I wanted both attributes combined into one painting, and here is how

I did it. I placed the canvas-textured painting on top of the impasto painting (background layer). Using a mask on the canvas painting layer, I used the brush tool to stroke black in a light opacity onto the mask. This revealed the impasto painting on the background layer.

Figure 5-65
Close-up view

Figure 5-65 illustrates the combination of the canvas texture and the thick impasto brush strokes in selected areas.

The completed painting in Figure 5-66 reveals a painting that reflects the use of canvas texture and brushwork texture in unison.

Old Masters Inspiration

Our next example began with the idea of making a still-life painting similar in feel to an old Dutch composition made in the era of Rembrandt. I simply love the shape of pears and frequently photograph and draw them. I wanted a small collection of pears with a dark background and a reflective surface for them to rest on. I couldn't find anything that matched my criteria, so I improvised. I placed the pears in a shoe box and used window light for the digital photograph.

In Photoshop, enlarge the canvas (Image > Canvas Size)
Copy the lower portion of photo and flip it
Use a mask to join the two images exactly
In Photoshop, I enlarged the canvas (Image > Canvas Size) and then copied the lower portion of the pears shown in Figure 5-68, placing it on a separate layer. I flipped the image to be a mirror image of the original pear, using Edit > Transform > Flip Vertical. To make an exacting blend, a mask was used on the new layer.

Figure 5-66
"Memories of Toledo" completed painting

Figure 5-67
Original photo of fruit in a shoe box

Figure 5-68
Reflection added

Figure 5-69
Corrected photo is ready to go into Painter

The finished photo was now ready to be transported into Painter for the actual painting process.

The secret of drawing and modeling resides in the contrasts and relationships of tone.

—PAUL CÉZANNE,
to Emil Bernard, in *Paul Cézanne, Letters,* edited by John Rewald (1941)

Figure 5-70
Van Gogh Cloner used

File > Clone
Use Van Gogh Cloner variant
In Painter, the photo was cloned, selected, and deleted (just as we have done on previous paintings). I used the Van Gogh Cloner all over the piece for the initial laydown of colors.

Figure 5-71
Oil Brush Cloner used

I never feel that it's a
waste of time to make
drawings. It is like being
in communication with
the object, with the place,
which soaks up (as a
sponge soaks up water) all
the life that once existed
there.

—ANDREW WYETH,
from *Two Worlds of
Andrew Wyeth: Kuerners
and Olsons,* Metropolitan
Museum of Art (1976)

Use Oil Brush Cloner to achieve a textural impasto effect and smooth the roughness of the Van Gogh Cloner

The next cloning tool that was used was the Oil Brush Cloner. This tool smoothed the color variations that resulted from use of the Van Gogh Cloner. The Oil Brush Cloner gives an impasto brush stroke to the surface. You will notice visible texture in the quality of the brush stroke.

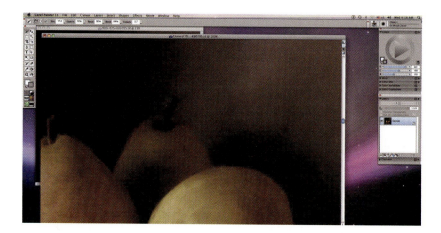

Figure 5-72
Detail

Figure 5-73
Glazing used to enhance the color

Add a new layer and use the Oil Paint > Glazing Round brush at a low opacity to enhance the color

Next, I wanted more color in the pears. Food photographers employ food stylists, who often handpaint the blush on a peach or pear in preparation for photographing the fruit for an assignment. With Painter, you become the food stylist. The touch of your digital brush will add the desired color vibrancy and appeal. A new layer was added and additional color tones were painted on the new layer using the Oil > Glazing Round Brush, set at a low opacity. The new layer was copied and the blend mode was set to Luminosity for a bit more punch in the color.

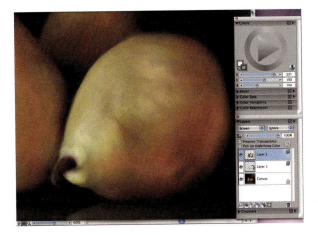

Figure 5-74
Blend mode set to Screen

Copy the glazing layer and set the blend mode to Screen
As I continued working, I tried various blend modes and then decided to switch from Luminosity to Screen on my top layer. I highly recommend getting acquainted with the blend modes in both Photoshop and Painter. The blend mode selected directs the software as to how the information on the selected layer will interact with the layer directly beneath it. Try a variety of different blend modes and see which one will best fulfill your intention as to how these layers will interact.

Figure 5-75
*Glazing in background was
added to new layer*

Add a new layer
Add color with the Oil Paint > Glazing Round brush to the upper right-hand corner of the background
My next task was to warm the color of the background in the upper right-hand corner. I placed a new layer on top of the stack. With the Oil Paint > Glazing Round brush selected, I applied a warm brown tone to that area.

An artist is a dreamer consenting to dream of the actual world.
—GEORGE SANTAYANA,
The Life of Reason (1905)

Figure 5-76

Opacity of the layer was reduced

Reduce the Opacity of the glaze layer to 67%

By keeping the background on a separate layer, you can exercise more control on that specific portion of your painting, without disturbing the other brushwork (in this example, on the pears). The opacity was reduced on this overlay from 100% to 67%. This allowed for a better integration into the painting.

Figure 5-77

Sfumato effect pioneered by da Vinci

In Figure 5-77, you can notice the soft blending of color tones in the rear of the still life. The softening of those edges corresponds to what happens with a shallow depth of field in photography. In painting terms, it resembles a technique used by Leonardo da Vinci called *sfumato*. This effect gives the appearance of looking through a veil of smoke. da Vinci used it on his famous "Mona Lisa" and other works.

Figure 5-78

Figure 5-79
Dutch still life

Drawing is describing form and the importance of it is its veracity, not the finish.
—Ned Jacob,
in *American Artist Magazine* (August, 1975)

Figures 5-78 and 5-79 illustrate our before and after on this Old World still life. I don't think many people would believe that it began in an empty sneakers box.

More still life paintings are included here. Figure 5-80 was made primarily with the Chalk Cloner.

Figure 5-80
Peonies and Lavender still life

Each year, when the peonies are in bloom, I put together at least one still life using these incredible blossoms. They have such large, showy blossoms. Figure 5-81 was made with the Chalk Cloner and the Oil Cloner. Notice the impasto texture of the Oil Brush Cloner's brush strokes.

Created for a commissioned Christmas card, the illustration shown in Figure 5-82 was made primarily with the Chalk Cloner and the Oil Brush Cloner.

Figure 5-81
Peonies still life

The Impressionist Cloner was the primary tool used for the creation of Figure 5-83, one of my favorite pieces. The brush size was varied for larger or smaller strokes.

I occasionally take on a wedding assignment for clients who want a more artistic approach to their wedding photos. The painting shown

The concern of the artist is with the discrepancy between physical fact and psychic effect.

—Josef Albers,
from *Interactions of Color*
(1953)

Figure 5-82
Sledders

Figure 5-83
Sunday Riders

Figure 5-84
Wedding Embrace, Cape May, NJ

in Figure 5-84 was made from a photograph taken at a wedding that
took place in Cape May, New Jersey, on the beach. I used the Chalk
Cloner and various watercolor cloners, including one that left telltale
spots of water.

Figure 5-85
President's House, McDaniel College

Sometimes you may find yourself struggling with an image because the software doesn't seem capable of giving you what you had imagined. This was the case with Figure 5-85. The whites that I desired did not seem pure enough in my digital painting. I tried painting and erasing, but I simply wasn't satisfied with the results. I printed the painting and looked at it with dismay. I was right. The whites simply were not white enough. I then took a real paintbrush and some opaque white watercolor paint and literally stroked real paint onto my print. As that was drying, I felt compelled to add a few details with real colored pencils. When the print was dry I scanned it back into the computer and worked on it a little more until I felt satisfied with this commission. The point to this story is that you have to use the tools that are appropriate to your task. Feel free to intermingle digital painting tools with real painting tools. You do not need to be a purist about the tools. It is the art that is important, not the tools that were used. Use what feels right. Follow your instincts.

> Don't copy. Feel the forms. Feel how much it swings, how much it slants—these are big factors. The more factors you have, the simpler will be your work.
> —THOMAS EAKINS,
> in *Thomas Eakins*, by
> Lloyd Goodrich (1987)

Photocopy-Inspired Painting

Figure 5-86
Original photograph of a priest character at a Renaissance festival

The next example sprang from a conversation I had with an artist friend, Ann Curtis. Ann is a wonderful artist and is known throughout the United States for her work at Renaissance festivals, making plaster body-cast sculptures. As most artists do, she also dabbles in other media. She showed me a few portraits that she had done with her colored pencils, working on black-and-white photocopies of photographs. They were lovely, but the poor quality of the photocopy paper meant that her creations were not going to be very long lived in archival terms. She was having such a good time with this process that I thought I could show her how she could achieve similar results digitally. The resulting prints would have a much higher archival standard. For this project I decided to use a digital photograph that I had taken at the local Renaissance festival.

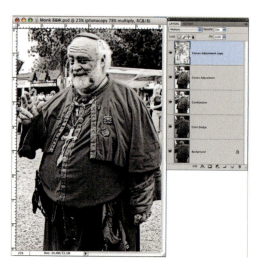

Figure 5-87
Photocopy version of the photograph

Desaturate the color photo
Copy the desaturated photo on a new layer
Use Color Dodge blend mode and combine those layers into a new layer
Duplicate the combined layer
Apply a Curves adjustment to lighten the image
Duplicate the layer and apply Filter > Photocopy
Set the Photocopy layer to 78% opacity and set on the Multiply blend mode

My first task was to convert this color photograph to the look of a black-and-white photocopy. When I thought about what a photocopy looks like, I realized that lots of mid-tones and detail in highlights and shadows are lost. I wanted to replicate that effect, so it would resemble a real photocopy. Here are the steps that I used. I desaturated the image, leaving a black-and-white rendition of the photograph. That layer was copied and the Color Dodge blend mode was applied to it. Those two layers were combined into another layer, labeled "Combination." By leaving the first two layers, I reserved my ability to go back into those layers later, if need be. The Combination layer was duplicated and a Curves adjustment was applied to it, lightening the image. That layer was duplicated and the Photocopy filter was applied to it. This new layer was then set on the Multiply blend mode and reduced to 78%.

Figure 5-88
Hand-colored version

Save
Flatten and save this flattened version (under another name)
Using the flattened version, create a new layer
Set the blend mode on the new layer to Color
This is a good point in the process to save your work. I saved both a full layered version and a flattened one. The next step is the fun, artistic one. Create a new layer and set the blend mode on it to Color. This

is your hand-coloring layer. I selected colors from the color palette and painted them onto this layer. You can be rather messy, loose, and imprecise in this step. Figure 5-88 shows the completed Photoshop piece. Figure 5-89 shows only the hand-painted layer set to Color blend mode.

Figure 5-89
Hand-colored layer only

Bring flattened colored version into Painter
File > Clone
Select all and delete

Figure 5-90
Image cloned in Painter and painted background added

Use the Chalk Cloner and Straight Cloner
Add a background using Artist Pastels and blend with Just Add Water
Mission accomplished! But, then I started thinking about what it might look like if that completed Photoshop portrait were used as the basis for a clone image in Painter. Figure 5-90 was made using the Chalk Cloner and Straight Cloner. The blue background was painted in with Artist Pastels and blended with Blender > Just Add Water.

Figure 5-91 was made with the same tools but with a difference at the beginning of the cloning process. When the portrait was cloned, and the clone was selected and deleted, the entire area was then filled with the tan color. This simulated a piece of tan charcoal paper. My little experiment yielded another way to make a photo-like illustration. In this case, it was a portrait, but this same process could be used on other subject matter.

One touch of nature makes the whole world kin.
—WILLIAM SHAKESPEARE,
   Troilus and Cressida
   (1601)

Figure 5-91
Painter version with solid background

Auto-Painting: Painting in a Hurry

Those engineers at Corel are wizards. They think of everything to help the artist out. The next technique is super easy and quick. Since Painter X they have included an Auto-Painting option. Here is a look at how it works.

Figure 5-92
Horse racer and its clone

Select a photo and clone it, as explained earlier in this chapter. Turn off Tracing Paper, creating a white layer on which to work.

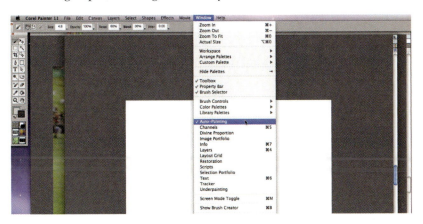

Figure 5-93
Selecting Auto-Painting

In the Window menu, select Show Underpainting > Auto-Painting.

Select Smart Stroke Brushes from our choice of brushes. Within that category, select the Acrylics Captured Bristle Brush variation. Your choices continue with what type of mark to make in the Auto-Painting and how large should the brush be. I have chosen Scribble Large with a brush set at 10.4 pixels. Press the green arrow at the lower right of the dialogue box to start the Auto-Painting. It will continue until you click again to stop it.

Figure 5-94
Selecting desired brushes

Figure 5-95
Resulting Auto-Painting

Figure 5-96
Proceeding with more detail

This Auto-Painting Brush is a great way to create a fast underpainting. You can proceed further by lowering the size of the brush, for more detail and handpainting directly onto the clone. I lowered the brush size to 4.4 and then to 2.8 to refine more detail in some sections, leaving the background area loose and painterly.

I then used the Straight Cloner with a small brush (3.6) and a very light opacity (4%) in just a few spots, such as the jockey's head and reins. Use the Straight Cloner sparingly. You do not want the original photo back, just a slight indication of critical details.

Figure 5-97
*Straight Clone added for a few
detailed touches*

Smart Stroke Painting

Figure 5-98
*Smart Stroke Painting with
Smart Settings of Casablanca
photo*

Another way to go with this tool is to check the box marked Smart
Stroke Painting, which follows the lines of the photograph and is less
random. Next, check the box marked Smart Settings. This is an automatic feature that starts out with a large brush size and then decreases
in size, yielding more detail. It will "finish" the painting on its own.
This becomes a fabulous base for a painting.

With this giant head start, it is now easy to refine the image a bit,
using the Chalk Cloner. The goal is still to have a painterly looseness
with just a bit more definition where needed.

Figure 5-99
Adding Chalk Cloner

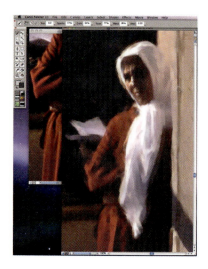

Figure 5-100
Decreased brush size for more detail

Continuing to use that Chalk Cloner, I decreased the brush size for more detail on the people and various areas throughout the image. It is like walking a tightrope to achieve the right balance between photographic detail and a loose painterly feel. You determine how loose or tight the finished image will be.

The elements of design prevail whether you are photographing, drawing, or painting. *Composition, line, color, form,* and *directionality* are still the pillars of good design. A strong photo will be a good candidate for a painting.

I have used the Acrylics Captured Bristle from the Smart Stroke Brushes for this example, but try another one from that grouping. Experiment with the different kinds of marks you can make with the Auto-Painting dialogue box. A ton of options are available to you. Try them out.

Figure 5-101
Finished digital painting of Casablanca Mosque, Morocco

Make Virtually Any Brush a Cloner

Although there are loads of cloner brushes, you can turn almost any brush into a cloner. Here is a simple example.

Figure 5-102
Beginnings of oil painting

Select a photograph. Create a clone (File > Quick Clone), and then decide what brush you would like to use from the literally hundreds of variations. Ask yourself what treatment best suits the image. For this photo of fringy looking pink poppies, I chose the category of Oils, then the Thick Oil Bristle Brush. It is a smeary brush that displays the tracks of stiff bristles and gives a shine and shadow to the brushwork.

Be sure to have the Brush Controls palette out. Here, I chose Dab Type > Bristle Spray and Stroke Type > Single. Opacity was set at 100%. Under Cloning, I checked the Clone Color box so the program would know to grab the color from the underlying photograph, not the current selected color.

Figure 5-103
Match the direction of your strokes to the subject matter

When you are working with a brush that yields an impasto or thick paint feel, be sure to focus on the direction of the brush strokes as you lay them down. They should make sense. Follow the contour of the object you are painting. Random zig-zags, which most folks are tempted to use to lay down color quickly, seldom creates the type of look you ultimately desire. Notice how portions of the stroke shine. In some areas of your work that may not be desirable. If you try painting from a different direction, you may improve that effect dramatically.

Illustrative Sketch Technique

Although this technique is not really a painting per se, it is a great sketch effect that gives the feel of an intaglio, or etching, print. It is especially good with photos that have a complicated area of detail. I chose an image of a medieval German doorway.

Figure 5-104
Applying Sketch Effect

As usual, clone the image. Copy this new layer (Select All > Edit > Copy > Paste in Place). On this new layer, use Effects > Surface Control > Sketch. Our settings were Sensitivity, 3.49; Smoothing, 1.55; Grain, 0.27; Threshold High, 23%; and Threshold Low, 100%. Watch the preview window until you achieve the look you like.

Change the composite method to Overlay. You will notice the lightened color and a gritty look, depending on your Sketch settings. I liked the look but wanted to push it further.

Figure 5-105
Overlay composite method

Figure 5-106
Duplicate that layer

I duplicated the sketch layer by right clicking. When duplicated, it retains the Overlay composite method for the newest layer. This intensifies that sketch effect and lightens the image more.

Figure 5-107
*Change composite method
to Gel*

This image was now moving toward the look of an old etching, so I intensified it by changing the newest layer's composite method to Gel. *Voilà!* This would look good printed on an off-white, rag-based paper to further emphasize the etching (or intaglio) feel.

Painting Approach with Blenders

There are so many ways to paint in Painter, it would take several volumes to catalog the possibilities. In the real art world, tools used to blend can include water, turpentine, paper-shading stumps (tortillions), and chamois. These tools can smear, blend, or water down a painting effect. Painter has a variety of blending tools, and a few of them can reach down from a new layer and pull up color information to blend it, creating a painting effect. One of the best is the Just Add Water blender.

Figure 5-108
Blending layer created

In our example of windmills in the Netherlands, I created a new blank layer above the canvas by clicking on the icon with stacks of layers at the bottom of the Layers palette. Click on the box that says Pick Up Underlying Color. Next, select Blender Tools with the Just Add Water variant. Proceed to stroke areas of the image on this new layer. If you want to see what has been deposited on the new layer, shut off the visibility of the canvas layer (as shown on the left of Figure 5-108).

Figure 5-109
Painterly rendering using a blending tool

Proceed to brush the blending tool throughout the image area, varying the size and opacity of your brush as needed. In our example, this approach worked well until I reached all the branches and twigs of the overhanging tree. Blending here created a muddy mess.

Figure 5-110
Additional layer for sky

To avoid the muddy mess that blending would create in the tree branch areas, I created another new layer and painted that portion of the image with the Real Round Bristle brush, found in the RealBristle™ Brushes category. I sampled colors from the original image to create the colors with which I painted. I then dropped all the layers together, joining them. I renamed this blender painting. By giving it a different name, I retained the original image to archive and use further.

Figure 5-111
Three files open—pay close attention

The next technique requires some attention to details. I cloned the new file, Windmill Ptg. In addition to Windmill Ptg and its clone, I also opened the original image, Windmills. When working on the clone, you need to direct the software to the image source that you want to use. I wanted the new painting for all the blending work I had done, but I also wanted the tree details from the original image.

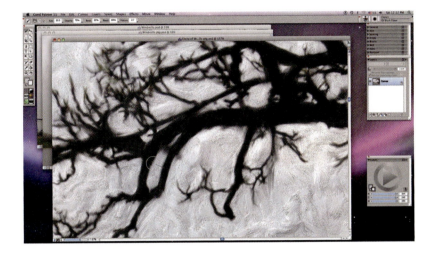

Figure 5-112
Tree is cloned using a textural brush, Oil Brush Cloner

I switched back and forth from the Blender painting of the windmills, as my source image, and the original image for the tree limbs and branches. That allowed me to retain the painterly Blender painting and introduce the limbs into the image. I chose the Oil Brush Cloner for a rough, creamy, and textural brush stroke. I could have stopped here but instead added a colored canvas border and canvas texture. I flattened the image and gave it a new name.

Figure 5-113
Coarse Cotton Canvas selected and color of that canvas

In the Paper Texture box, I selected Coarse Cotton Canvas. In the color palette, I selected a beige color. This may seem a little puzzling, but I then cloned my clone painting. I filled that new clone with the beige color (Edit > Fill). I then used the Straight Cloner to clone in the center of the painting that was recently saved. I left some border showing (see Figure 5-113) and proceeded to paint toward the edges, giving a textural brush look.

Figure 5-114
Adding Canvas texture

An interesting effect that can be achieved in Painter is to apply a texture on top of a painting. Simply go to Effects > Surface Control > Apply Surface Texture. You have many options. Paper Texture is one of the options, and within that category you can determine where the light is coming from and various qualities of the light. Here, I kept the light effect subtle, at 6%. That allowed the brush strokes to still show through.

Figure 5-115
Close-up of brush work and canvas texture

I would recommend experimenting with the Blender tools as painting tools, using this technique.

Figure 5-116
Completed Blender painting

Edges and Cloning

Figure 5-117
Doctored original photo

As a photographer, you know that some images speak to you immediately. Others take time to float to the surface of possibilities. The image shown in Figure 5-121 took a decade to be made. That long ago, with a long lens and from far away, I took a photograph of a Civil War re-enactor. I just liked how he was standing and waiting for someone. I did not ask permission or get a release from him. I never intended to use the image. The background was full of water coolers, ice chests, fellow soldiers, pick-up trucks, and more. It was simply awful. Looking through my slides years later, I stumbled onto the image of the soldier again. I decided to scan it into my computer and delete the objectionable background elements in Photoshop. Armed with that improved doctored image (Figure 5-117), I returned to the site of the annual re-enactment, where I had taken the original image. Tens of thousands of re-enactors were present. How would I ever find this one man so I could give him his photograph and get him to sign a release form? It was a long shot at best. I showed the photo around in the re-enactors' camp. Unbelievably, fellow re-enactors recognized him and directed me to his unit. I found him, gave him his photo, and secured a release from him. He was a needle in a haystack, indeed, but found.

Figure 5-118

Enlarged canvas and clone stamped background

Duplicate the image
Use Filter > Stylize > Find Edges on the duplicate layer
Set the Find Edges layer to the Darken blend mode
Add a new layer and add more handcoloring, painting with the brush tool and selecting the desired colors

Set the hand-colored layer to the Color blend mode
Enlarge the canvas (Image > Canvas Size)
Clone Stamp the image to expand the background
Select the clone-stamped area with a feathered lasso tool, and run a
Gaussian Blur filter on it to soften it

My first step in this photo illustration was to duplicate the layer. On the new layer I applied the Stylize > Find Edges filter. The edges were not sharp in the original image (due to the use of a long lens with no tripod). Using the Find Edges filter provided more edge definition. The Find Edges layer was set to the Darken blend mode. This provided a black edge around the edges that had contrast. Another layer was added and some handcoloring was applied to it using the Color blend mode. For the photo illustration, I needed more ground around our re-enactor. I expanded the canvas and clone stamped more ground in place. Those areas were selected and softened with the filter Gaussian Blur. I just wanted the color tones, no detail.

Figure 5-119
Painter Clone

Open flattened painting in Painter File > Clone
Use the Chalk Cloner, Van Gogh Cloner, and Oil Cloner
Add a new layer, set to the Gel blend mode, and paint in additional color tones

I saved the image and opened it in Painter. The image was cloned with a variety of cloners, including the Chalk Cloner, Van Gogh Cloner, and Oil Cloner. I added additional layers and applied more color directly to the clone. In most instances, the blend mode was set to Gel.

Art is the lie that tells the truth.

—Pablo Picasso,
in "Picasso Speaks,"
The Arts Magazine (May, 1923)

Figure 5-120
Layers are blended

Use Blender brushes to blend the new paint into the previous version
Various Blender brushes were used to combine the clone and the overlaying Gel layers.

The resulting illustration was achieved more than a decade after the original slide image was made. The background had been simply horrible and the image lacked sharpness. Despite those huge impediments, a pleasing image was made using the digital artistic tools of a modern era. Maybe we should go back through those old slide collections and find other candidates for revitalization using these techniques.

Figure 5-121
Completed painting

Painterly Edge Effects

One of the techniques that I love to incorporate into my digital art-work is the use of painterly edges. There are so many possibilities and so many brushes. We will explore a few here. Feel free to mix and match them as possible edge effects.

Figure 5-122
New layer filled with white and painted with the History brush in Photoshop

Open photo in Photoshop
Add a new layer and fill it with white
Use the History brush, with a rough brush type selected, to paint the photo onto the white layer

There are just tons of edge effects that are available to you. Some effects were discussed in Chapter 4. Edges are easily purchased in var-ious third-party software packages. Many are really great. Let's look at how you can achieve painterly edge effects within Photoshop and Painter.

Figure 5-122 was created solely in Photoshop. A new layer was applied over the existing photograph and filled with white. The irregular stroke was made using the History brush and selecting scratchy wide brushes (located in the lower realms of the Brush selections).

The kind of photography I like to do, capturing the moment, is very much like that break in the clouds. In a flash, a wonderful picture seems to come out of nowhere.
—Elliott Erwitt,
Between the Sexes (1994)

Figure 5-123
Art History Brush used

Experiment using the Art History Brush
In this example, I used the Dab and Tight Short variations
The next example is two different brush stroke types found in the Art History Brush selections. The left-hand portion of the image demonstrates the use of the Dab type of stroke. The right-hand portion of the image shows the Tight Short stroke. Each brush type yields a different kind of mark.

Figure 5-124
Eraser as a paint tool

Try using the Brush Tool to create a border effect
Don't rule out using the Eraser Tool or some white paint if your background color is white. In Figure 5-124, the scratchy-looking brush was filled with white and stroked onto the painting. Brush marks were made from the border into the image, mimicking the grass directionality in the photograph.

Figure 5-125
The Rough Pastels filter was the dominant effect on this piece

Duplicate the image and apply the Rough Pastels filter
Stroke white around the border

Figure 5-125 illustrates the duplication of the image and the use of the Rough Pastels filter on this duplicate layer. White was stroked onto the image around the edges.

Figure 5-126
Beginning of edge effect

It, therefore, should be
possible for even the
photographer—just as
for the creative poet
or painter—to use the
object as a stepping stone
to a realm of meaning
completely beyond itself.
—CLARENCE JOHN LAUGHLIM,
   to Daniel Masclet
   (October 19, 1953)

Fill the original photo layer with white
**Use the Magic Wand Tool to select the white edge of the top layer
and then delete it**

The bottom layer (the original image) was filled with white. I used
the Magic Wand Tool to select the white border area on the top layer.
I then deleted this selection area. There appears to be no change. But
wait ... there's more.

Figure 5-127
Edge effect develops

Choose a shadow from the Layer Style effects

A torn edge effect can now be achieved by using Layer Style effects.
I chose a shadow to be cast from the irregularly edged top layer. The
shadow falls onto the white layer beneath. Ta-da! These are the settings I used:

- Blend mode—Multiply
- Opacity—49%
- Angle—47 degrees
- Distance—8
- Spread—27
- Size—16
- Noise—23

Figure 5-128 shows this simple edge effect. It is a particularly good
edge for a photo illustration in a magazine or newsletter.

The effect shown in Figure 5-129, on colored paper, was created in
Painter.

Figure 5-128
Completed edge effect

Figure 5-129
Painter clone with a brown-tone paper

Open photo in Painter
File > Clone
Select all and fill with a color (a brick-red type of brown was used in our example)

Edge effects in Painter can vary widely as well. The beginning premise, once again, is the clone. We will look at a few examples. In Figure 5-129 the photograph of the Irish coastline and sheep has been cloned. The clone was selected and deleted. The space was filled with a shade of brown. The view on the right indicates the transparency of that brown layer, if the Tracing Paper feature is turned on.

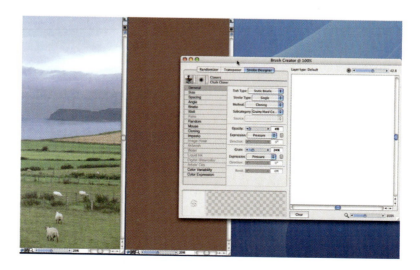

Figure 5-130
Use of Brush Creator

Window > Brush Creator

Using the Brush Creator (located in the Window options), I created a rough, bristle brush with these modifying factors:

- Dab Type—Static Bristle
- Stroke Type—Single
- Method—Cloning
- Subcategory—Grainy Hard Cover

Figure 5-131
Chalk Cloner brush used

Use the Chalk Cloner brush

I selected the Chalk Cloner brush and applied it to the brown, bumpy paper. Notice the fragmentary way the color is deposited on the higher raised surfaces of the paper. This created an uneven edge effect. The look is very much like using real chalks on rough pastel paper. Additional applications of chalk over the area yields a more solid laydown of color.

We must never forget that art is not a form of propaganda; it is a form of truth.
—JOHN F. KENNEDY, from an address at Amherst College (October 26, 1963)

Figure 5-132
Chalk Cloner used on white paper with a large brush

I recommend experimenting with other Cloner brush types. Figure 5-132 demonstrates the use of the Chalk Cloner, and I used the Van Gogh Cloner in Figure 5-133. The Impressionist Cloner also gives an interesting small, rice-like dab of paint. Experiment with many, and see what you might like.

Figure 5-133
Van Gogh Cloner

I especially like to use the Watercolor Run Cloner along edges. This brush is just fascinating. You can brush an area and then watch the color run down, depositing more color on the outside edge of where the color comes to rest. It is so wonderful at simulating gravity at work with a real water medium. Using this brush creates a Watercolor Layer that must be dried or dropped down on the layer beneath before other non-wet brushes can be used.

Figure 5-134
Watercolor Run Cloner used along the edges

A cousin to the Watercolor Run Cloner is the Watercolor Cloner. This brush applies various random sizes of little drops of paint onto the canvas. They also spread and settle out. Notice the textural effect they gave in our example.

Figure 5-135
Watercolor Cloner adds a textural feel

Figure 5-136
Watercolor Wash Cloner

I don't often use the Watercolor Wash Cloner, as the color is very dark, even with a light opacity. One way to use the Watercolor Wash Cloner, for its edge possibilities, is to cover the area, except the extreme outside edges, with another cloner. In this example, I used the Bristle Brush Cloner. That double cloner approach can yield some watercolor effect on the edges without darkening the interior of the clone.

There are always two people in every picture: the photographer and the viewer.
—ANSEL ADAMS,
   in *Playboy Magazine*
   (May, 1983)

Figure 5-137
Bristle Brush Cloner used over the Watercolor Wash Cloner

Figure 5-138
Woodcut Filter effect

Duplicate the layer
On the duplicate layer, apply Effects > Surface Control > Woodcut
Paint the outside edges with Chalk > Dull Grainy Chalk
A completely different kind of look is seen in Figure 5-138. In this example, I have duplicated the image and applied Effects > Surface Control > Woodcut. This look resembles a relief print carved from wood or linoleum blocks. After applying the woodcut look, the outside edge was painted with Chalk > Dull Grainy Chalk. The color of the chalk was selected from the colors used in the woodcut.

Figure 5-139
Oil Brush Cloner

Art after all is but an extension of language to the expression of sensations too subtle for words.

—ROBERT HENRI,
The Art Spirit (1923)

The final edge that we will explore in this chapter is the Oil Brush Cloner. This effect lends a thick, streaky, impasto feel to the edge.

Explore the realm of possibilities available in Painter or Photoshop or a combination of both programs. Your job, as the artist, is to find the brush or mark that works best for the feel and look that you have in mind for your artwork.

Figure 5-140
Completed oil effect painting

This chapter provides but a little taste of the art tools available in Painter. I have concentrated on the cloning tools, as they are the tools most likely to be used by a photographer. You are not restricted to those tools and should explore other tools in Painter and the combination of those tools with cloning tools. The possibilities are virtually without end.

6

Assembling a Collage in Photoshop®

In the digital world of fine art, the technique of collage is undoubtedly one of my favorites. It is practically without limits. Everything becomes a possible component part of your image. You are limited only by your imagination. Techniques and approaches are as varied as the medium itself. Collages can be very structured, even rigid, in their underlying substructure. They can also be loose, free, and ethereal. You can use photos from your digital camera or scanned elements. If you have not ventured into the world of digital collage you simply must dive in!

Collages are beautiful. They have the ability to combine many images and textures in a unique manner. They can have the delicacy of a butterfly's wing or the graphic nature of a wanted poster. The range is huge. We will explore various methods of assembling this type of artwork.

Collages combine a variety of images into one piece. They can combine just a couple of layers or a hundred. Each layer can be handled separately. Layers can overlap previous layers and, with transparency, reveal layers underneath. There are so many options.

The first task is to gather imagery for a collage. What is your theme? Do you want to assemble family images for a special occasion or person? A collage portraying the life of one person or their family heritage can be interesting. A collage depicting a vacation can be a variation to the traditional album. A collage of a wedding day is a splendid way to share many photos in a work of art that can be framed and displayed.

Be sure to scan images with enough information to allow you to use them large or small, as the assembly process begins. Be open with your original concept and allow the process to dictate spacing and scale decisions. Be sure to determine, at the beginning, the ultimate size of the printed piece. Will it be printed as a 12 × 16-inch piece or something smaller or larger? For something that has a good photographic quality, plan on using a resolution of 300 to 360 dpi.

Figure 6-1

Texture and color are the two most important design elements that unify a collage. Of course, other basic design elements, like scale and directionality, are also important. Select a unifying element to pull the piece together. It can be something as simple as a photo of clouds or water. A bit of texture often works well. A crumbled scrap of fabric, a rusted piece of metal, or a faded piece of wallpaper—all can be candidates for the task of uniting the entire design.

How do you want to construct this collage? Some concepts will work well with a grid structure. Guidelines can be particularly helpful in lining up these collages, since they often use many layers. Other collages will benefit from a nonlinear approach that relies on overlapping layers with transparency. The concept will dictate the best approach.

Photoshop is the ideal tool for making collages. In the past, collages were constructed by cutting and pasting images and objects together. With Photoshop, each element can reside on its own layer. That allows you maximum flexibility in arranging the various elements into the best composition.

Too many layers? It is easy to be overwhelmed by the sheer number of layers when working on a collage. To preserve your sanity, make a habit of naming each layer. Finding a tiny picture in a sea of layers takes lots of time. Named layers are easier to locate. If you are indeed drowning in too many layers, think about using layer sets to group them.

Photographs are not the only element that can be used in collages. Use your scanner as a camera and introduce other elements into your work. Try scanning a seashell, a moth wing, a leaf, a rusted key, a crumbled piece of tissue paper, etc. Scanned elements often work well as the textural layer that can unify the design. I recommend visiting your local antique mall or flea market. Interesting old postcards, magazines, fabric, lace, and more can be collected for pennies. Be sure to protect the glass of your scanner. If the object could scratch the surface of the glass, use a piece of clear acetate between the glass and your object.

Art is an outsider, a gypsy over the face of the earth.
—ROBERT HENRI,
The Art Spirit (1923)

Figure 6-2
Red begonia scan

My Scanner Is a Camera

I must confess to being a scanaholic. I scan everything. I scan leaves, flowers, feathers, fossils, rocks, insects, old letters and journals, antique currency, tin-type photos, quite literally anything. It is all fodder for inclusion in my library of digital images. In the spring, my scanner works full tilt on a variety of spring flowers: daffodils, tulips, ranunculus, lily-of-the-valley, hyacinth, lilacs, and pussy willows. In the summer, it scans peonies, dahlias, begonias, impatiens, lilies, geraniums, water lilies, and lotus blossoms. If an interesting item will fit on the glass platen of my scanner, it gets scanned.

Figure 6-3
Yellow ranunculus flower and bud

Over the years I've developed techniques to aid me in my scanning addiction. I think of the scanner as a camera with a very shallow depth of field. Depending on your type of scanner, you will probably discover that there is a bit of focus, or near focus, above the actual glass contact area. Anything beyond that area falls off into the blurry, out-of-focus area. But, that can be a really good thing, depending on what you want for an outcome.

If you simply lay a flower on the glass platen the petals may crush or flatten in an unflattering way. I prefer, in most cases, to suspend the flower above the glass using a pinching device, developed for the soldering of jewelry. Called a *third hand,* it is tweezers with a weighted base. It has a sturdy and somewhat weighty bottom that I place safely off the glass scanning area. The pinching device allows you to rotate and lower the flower until it is just off the glass surface.

Figure 6-4
Third hand holds a rose over the scanner platen

Figure 6-5
Metal rack used to suspend items to be scanned

Another contraption that I have rigged up is a black metal rack that sits above my scanner. It was built as a three-drawer, office cabinet on wheels. I bought it at a discount store and removed the casters and drawer stops. I also removed the wire mesh drawers. What remained was a wire skeleton that fit perfectly around my scanner. I can suspend items from the wire rack with transparent, monofilament fishing line and can raise and lower them to be scanned. If they are raised, they can become blurry. If they are lowered and just touch the glass surface they are tack sharp. The transparent thread becomes my *f*-stop, allowing for a fall-off of focus.

To scan using these devices, I leave the lid of the scanner open. I turn off the lights in the room and minimize any other additional light source. I often scan at night to keep it simple.

Another important tool to have nearby is a very soft, tight-weave cloth to wipe the scan platen. Be careful to never scratch the glass. When scanning flowers, you will be cleaning frequently because of dropped pollen from the flowers. It is a bit of a nuisance, but so much easier than all the corrective cloning that would need to be done in Photoshop to fix the scan.

Other techniques include painting the inside of a shoe box with black paint or lacing monofilament line across inside and suspending items in the web of thread. Some artists also drape black velvet behind the object, although covering the object with dark fabric never seems to work well for me. I usually still pick up the texture of the fabric.

Open up your imagination to all sorts of scannable materials. Go to thrift shops, antique stores, old bookshops, wholesale florists, and libraries. Try scanning maps, snippets of old magazines or musical scores, and vintage postcards. Try scanning fruit, cabbage leaves, mushrooms, and nuts. Perhaps you have an antique doll, with a haunting face. Try her out! Once you get started and became thrilled with the enormous amount of detail that you can bring into your work with scanning, your artistic vistas will explode with possibilities.

Simple Collages

Figure 6-6
Two images to combine

A good way to begin experimenting with collaging is to find two simple images that you want to combine. Our example would be two different types of animals. A trip to the zoo can yield a ton of animal images. Nature is so endlessly fascinating in its variety of animal possibilities (feathers, scales, fur, etc.). Our first example comes from photos taken in Australia, where they seem to have a monopoly on animals that appear to be put together from spare parts. Our example will just keep going on that theme of really different creatures. A lizard and an emu were both photographed in profile. They appear to be somewhat compatible.

Figure 6-7
Adding canvas and combining animals

Resize objects to the correct proportion
Add canvas, if needed

The first step was to resize the emu head to be the right scale for the lizard and its background. I placed the emu head on a new layer above the lizard and used Edit > Free Transform to scale the emu head smaller. Be sure to hold down on the Shift key to maintain the correct proportions. The lizard photo did not have enough head-room for the new hairdo. The canvas was extended on the lizard photo, and the Rubber Stamp Tool was applied to the lizard layer to add more background. Parts of the folds of skin under the lizard's mouth were rubber stamped away to allow for a smoother transition into the emu beak.

To me the thing that art does for life is to clean it—to strip it to form.
—ROBERT FROST,
in *Fire and Ice: The Art and Thought of Robert Frost,* by Lawrence Thompson (1942)

Figure 6-8
Combination creature

Use a layer mask to transition one layer into another

The final, but the most important, step was to use a layer mask to transition the emu head into the scaly lizard body. I added a layer mask (Layer > Add Layer Mask) and painted the mask with a paint brush loaded with black. Anywhere on the mask that is painted with black will allow the image below to show through. If you make a mistake, you can simply paint with white to restore the top layer. Subtlety is important. Be sure to vary the size of the brush and its opacity to whatever the task at hand requires. Your work is done on the mask and not on the image itself, so no harm can come to your photos. They remain intact.

Figure 6-9
Barnyard possibilities

Figure 6-10
Does it croak or cock-a-doodle-do?

The rules of nature do not apply to your collages. You can make elements of your collage as big as an elephant or as small as a flea. They do not have to be the size that would seem natural. The following example plays with the idea of sizing. My morning cup of tea became the playground for an exercise in scale. My first impulse was to put a breeching whale into the cup.

Figure 6-11
A teacup and a whale to combine

Figure 6-12
Whale breeching a teacup, showing layers

Use Free Transform to scale down a component part
The whale was scaled down using Free Transform. A layer mask worked the seawater into the tea. To correct the color, I used a clipping mask on a Hue/Saturation adjustment layer, and I moved the hue slider to warmer tones.

The completed image is nonsensical and purely for fun; however, this approach is often used in advertising to grab our attention.

I love red so much that I almost want to paint everything red.
—ALEXANDER CALDER, in *The Artist's Voice,* by Katherine Kuh (1960)

Figure 6-13
Completed collage

Figure 6-14
Possible subjects to put in a teacup

Figure 6-15
Surfer in a teacup

Many photographers sit down with their contact sheets and think of various combinations and possibilities for combining images. I rely on my digital contact sheets and my file browser to explore those artistic possibilities. Using the teacup as the background, I found four more possible images for a simple collage that explores the ridiculous with the element of scale.

Figure 6-16
Furry critter says hello in a teacup

Figure 6-17
Potential collage elements of a fish and a boat

Figure 6-15 explores the idea of a Hawaiian surfer in the cup, Figure 6-16 uses an aquatic clown (actually I think it was an otter), and Figure 6-18 uses a small boat. The boat version was enhanced by the inclusion of a reflection from the boat. Figure 6-19 employs a fish on ice at a famous Seattle fish market. Notice that the body of the fish continues down into the tea. This transparency was achieved with the use of a layer mask. This is a fun exercise. Pick a photo, like my teacup, that can be the background, and look through your files for wacky or provocative combinations.

We become what we contemplate.
—PLATO,
  ION (350 B.C.)

Figure 6-18
Boat in a teacup

Figure 6-19
Fish and tea, anyone?

Figure 6-20
"Bonfire of the Vanities" collage

In Figure 6-20, the collage was very simple to execute. I had been photographing the fire in our fireplace on a snowy winter afternoon. The pattern that the fire made was really fascinating. I literally took over a hundred images that day for later use. I started thinking about the Bonfire of the Vanities in Florence, Italy. Many painters, like Botticelli, fell under the spell of the monk Savonarola. Their paintings, which were seen as vanities, were burned in the great Piazza della Signoria, in 1497. Later, Savonarola would be tortured and burned in that same plaza, on May 23, 1498. One can only speculate on the fabulous art that was lost to this political and religious movement.

One of the painters that burned his secular paintings was Lorenzo di Credi. I remembered that I had photographed a surviving nude of his in the Uffizi, when photography was still allowed in Florence. The painting of Venus depicts her in what is referred to as the "modest Venus" pose. Her hands are covering herself, with the help of a sheer piece of fabric. Yes, she was failing miserably at being modest. But, if she were wearing a coat, no one would identify her as Venus, Goddess of Love. Remember that most people were illiterate. Stories, myths, and biblical and historic events were told through a recognized symbolic iconography in paintings.

Voilà! A collage was born. My photo of the painting was dark (due to the inability to use a tripod in the museum) and purposely taken at an angle to the painting for a bit of distortion. I simply resized the painting image to fit with a photo of my winter afternoon fire, and combined the two using the Multiply blend mode and a little bit of a layer mask to soften the edges. That was an easily constructed collage. Nothing else was necessary. If you know the history of that period, it will make sense to you, and is again a piece of art telling a story. If not, it is still an engaging image.

Collage with Lighting Effect

Figure 6-21
Collage component parts

The next collage began with a wonderful tile floor photographed in Spain. The tiled corner was like a stage, calling out for actors to enter. Instead of a ceiling, a dramatic sky was selected and an antique songbook was selected for a foreground element. The component that would tie the images together was a bird (Figure 6-21).

Figure 6-22
Canvas enlarged at the top

> What lives in a painting
> is the personality of the
> painter.
> —EDWARD HOPPER,
> in *Edward Hopper,* by
> Lloyd Goodrich (1978)

Enlarge the canvas (Edit > Canvas Size)

The tiled corner was too short. The canvas needed to be enlarged. The background color was white. The canvas was extended visually by using the Crop Tool. The entire image was selected, and the top anchor point of the Crop Tool was pulled up, beyond the image. Pull it as far as you would like to enlarge your canvas. With this method, you can eyeball the amount of enlargement you want, instead of measuring it as you do with Edit > Canvas Size. Press Return to complete the crop. This is a quick way to extend your canvas. If you want white canvas, be sure that your background color is white.

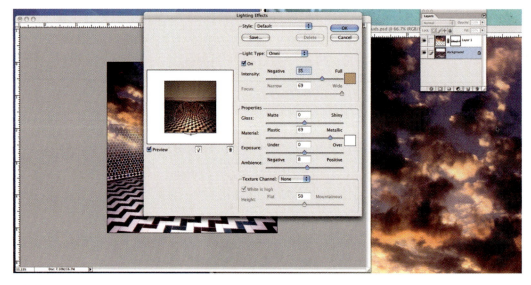

Figure 6-23
Lighting effect added

Add sky area on another layer and use a layer mask to integrate the sky into the floor area

Use Filter > Render > Lighting Effects > Omni to add omnidirectional light with a golden color

The sky area was placed in the collage as another layer, and a layer mask was used to blend the image into the tiled corner photo. The match was good, but the color was off and the sky presented a definite source of light that did not match the floor. This was corrected by using Filter > Render > Lighting Effects. An omnidirectional light was selected and shaped by pulling on the edges of the preview image. The color of the light was changed from white to a soft golden color, to match tones in the sky.

Figure 6-24
Layers of collage

Add antique songbook with Transform > Distort
Correct bird and color with Image > Adjustments > Color Balance
Paint a bird shadow onto a separate layer

Next, the book was placed into the foreground and shaped a bit to fit the perspective by using Transform > Distort. All that was needed now was the bird photo to connect the sky and the book visually. I corrected the coloring of the bird using Image > Adjustments > Color Balance before bringing it into the collage. Notice that the bird photo that was selected was lit from behind. If the bird were really flying into this space, as depicted, it would definitely be

I retain in the depth of my heart the memory of all my works.
—Eugene Delacroix, *The Journal of Eugene Delacroix,* translated by Walter Pach (1937)

Figure 6-25
"Grace Descends" completed
collage

casting a shadow. A bird shadow was needed. A new layer was created. Using a dark gray, at a low opacity setting, the shadow was painted onto the new layer. By confining the shadow to a separate layer, it can be altered and adjusted without harming the rest of the collage.

Suspend True Scale

Figure 6-26
Component parts for a collage

It is fun to push the edges of reality with collages. Suspend what is, and look for what could be. The egg has always been a symbol of birth and life potential. It is also a beautiful shape. Couple the egg with a door or portal, add in a little girl, and then set that combination in a beautiful rural landscape. This landscape was created as a panorama from ten photos taken in sequence (see Chapter 8).

A cast shadow was added for realistic effect
Finishing touches on this collage included an additional layer for the shadow cast by the egg. An elliptical shape with a feather of 15 was selected and filled with a 30% opacity of dark gray. Shadows were

Let the poses of the people and the parts of their bodies be so disposed that they display the intent of their minds.
—LEONARDO DA VINCI,
Treatise on Painting
(1651)

Figure 6-27
Completed panorama collage

added behind the little girl. Her dress was colored a pale blue and her skin was given some flesh tones. These colors were on a separate layer with the blend mode set to Color.

Themed Collages

Figure 6-28
*"Ruddick Family Collage"
uses a family quilt as the
unifying design element*

Family photos are a wonderful source for meaningful collages of family members. The collage in Figure 6-28 relied on the scan of a family quilt to be the textural element that pulled the separate pieces together. A double meaning existed regarding thoughts about the fabric of a family. Civil War muster roll records from the War Department at the National Archives were used to add meaningful text to the imagery. The migration of this family west was a direct result of their Quaker ancestor serving in the war and then moving his young family to Missouri. The collage tells the history of this family in a unique way.

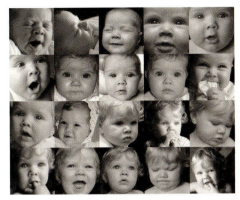

THE MANY FACES OF ANNE - YEAR ONE

Figure 6-29
*"Thank You Card" collage
celebrating a first birthday*

Collages can be used to celebrate special family moments. Twenty images were selected from the first year of life of baby Anne. The images ranged from her first hours of life and proceeded through that year to her first birthday. The image size for each photo was only an inch square. All the images were converted to a sepia tone to unite the small collage with a common color. Text was added to complete the card. This frameable thank you card was sent out to family and friends.

This technique could be employed on all types of family collages: a graduation, a marriage, or an anniversary. Pull those old photos out of the shoeboxes and the attic and see what you might create.

Suspend Reality

Figure 6-30
Venetian gondolier

I want to make of
impressionism something
solid and lasting like the
art in the museums.
—PAUL CÉZANNE,
    in *Paul Cézanne, Letters,*
    edited by John Rewald
    (1941)

The next collage began with a photo taken in Venice of a gondolier (Figure 6-30) and a photo taken in Seville, Spain, of a grand building (Figure 6-31). That gorgeous brick path was just calling for something to be progressing toward the building. The choice of the gondolier did obscure the brick path but opened up other imagery possibilities.

Figure 6-31
Spanish walk and building

Figure 6-32
Combining gondolier and background

Figure 6-32 shows the selection taken from the gondolier shot and imported as a new layer into the building background. It became apparent that more water needed to be created.

Figure 6-33
*Clone Stamp Tool used to
expand the water around
the hedge*

Use the Clone Stamp Tool to flood the walkway

With the use of the Clone Stamp Tool, water was cloned to expand out
and fill the area that needed to be flooded. Water flowed between the
hedges and up to the doorway, where an old man dressed in black,
holding a newspaper under his arm, was waiting.

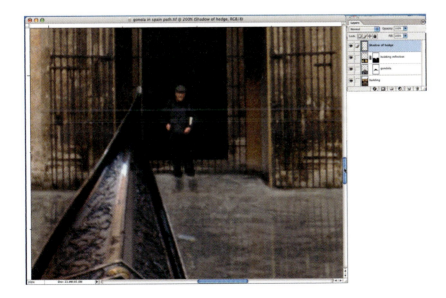

Figure 6-34
*The waiting man's lower legs
were submerged in the water,
using transparency*

For realism's sake, use the Dodge Tool on the man's sweater to lighten and separate it from the dark background
Use a layer mask to make the water transparent on the man's legs
Add a slight reflection of the building by copying and flipping it 180 degrees
Add hedge shadows for a realistic effect

What could be done to make this scenario more believable? Although the waiting man was a very small element in the building image, his presence created a sense of waiting for the gondola. Because the photo of the building was a grab shot taken as I toured Seville, I couldn't ask the gentleman to change his sweater, because it blended into my background, now could I? The Dodge Tool, which I seldom use, was great for lightening his sweater, separating him from his surroundings. I wanted him to be standing in the water, so a layer mask was used for transparency through the water. Another touch of realism was added with the reflection of the building into the water. The building was copied and flipped horizontally. Only a faint reflection was allowed to show by using a layer mask. The hedges along the path would also create a shadow and reflection. These were added on an additional layer and painted in. Tiny little details were added for realism, including painting with white, at a very low opacity, around the man's boots and doorway. This small touch made the surface of the water surrounding him more realistic.

Figure 6-35
Close-up of details added

The sky was very blank and overcast on the day that the building was photographed. More drama was needed. A new sky was found on another image. It was imported over into the collage. The sky would come with a bit of reflection in the water. The new sky was duplicated and flipped horizontally and merged into the collage lightly, using a layer mask. It just added a little of the blue from the sky above.

Figure 6-36
"Stray Gondola" completed collage in color

The completed collage was interesting in color (Figure 6-36), but what would it look like in black and white?

The whole collage was saved and then flattened. The flattened image was desaturated to achieve our monotone version.

I rarely start anything that isn't pretty clear to me before I start. I know what I'm going to do before I begin and if there's nothing in my head, I do nothing.
—GEORGIA O'KEEFFE,
in *Portrait of an Artist: A Biography,* by Laurie Lisle (1980)

Figure 6-37
Completed collage in black and white

Pile on the Layers

Figure 6-38
*"Holy City," a complex
collage created from a
previous collage*

A more complex collage (Figure 6-38) evolved out of another collage
(Figure 6-40).

Figure 6-39
*Component pieces for initial
collage*

-Gray added 85% Overlay
-Hydrangea 30% Normal
-Rose 50% Luminosity
-Rose 50% Luminosity
-Echinachea 42% Luminosity
-Echinachea 21% Luminosity
-Iris 52% Luminosity
-Oil on water 51% Difference
-Coffee Stained Paper

Figure 6-40
*Pearl Harbor failed collage,
later used for texture*

Sometimes you will make a collage that is simply unsatisfactory to your tastes. That is the case with Figure 6-40, which was created from the components shown in Figure 6-39. Those components included coffee-stained paper, flowers, and a blue-toned photo taken of an oil

The eye of imagination is dark and yet it fills with light, both from within and from without.
—ALEXANDER ELIOT,
Sight and Insight (1959)

Figure 6-41
*Spanish Cathedral dome, the
inspiration for our collage*

slick floating above the sunken ship at Pearl Harbor, Hawaii. The oil slick image was converted to pink tones using Hue Adjustment (found under Image > Adjustments > Hue/Saturation). Despite various attempts at different versions of this collage, it was an artistic failure. Despite that, it was not discarded. I suspected that the texture that it held might be useful later. And it was!

The dome of a Spanish cathedral was the starting point for the collage shown in Figure 6-41.

Figure 6-42

Failed Pearl Harbor collage combined with Spanish dome

Figure 6-43

Additional components to be added

The dome was combined with an earlier collage made with flowers and a piece of paper containing coffee stains (see Figure 6-40). The pieces were combined using the Difference blend mode set at 57% opacity, with the collage layer on top of the dome (Figure 6-42).

What lies behind us and what lies before us are small compared to what lies within us.
—Ralph Waldo Emerson,
Essays: First Series (1841)

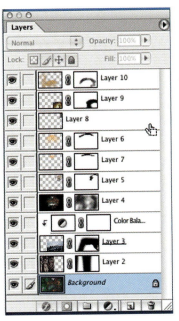

-Gold color 100% Color

-Fresco 38% Hard Light

-Grey color 61% Normal

-Gold color 55% Normal

-Gold color 97% Normal

-Lion 85% Difference

-Village segment 100% Normal

-Adjustment Layer - Color Balance

-Village 100% Overlay

-Statue 100% Hard Light

-Background Textural Collage

Figure 6-44
Layer structure of the combined, complex collage

The combined image seemed to call out for more imagery related to Europe and religion: additional photos (Figure 6-43) of Grenada in the fog, a lion from St. Mark's in Venice, a mosaic from St. Marks, and a statue on the face of the Cathedral in Toledo, Spain. It was a hodgepodge of origins, but I thought it might work.

The collage has been dissected for you in Figure 6-44, layer by layer. Each layer is further elaborated on with the opacity it was set to and the blending mode that was used on it. Almost all the layers used a layer mask for blending precisely into the entire collage. Notice that a golden glow was added coming from the top of the dome and on the village below. The golden color helps tie the entire collage together and helps emphasize the central focal point.

The forms of a model, be they a tree or a man, are only a dictionary to which the artist goes in order to reinforce his fugitive impressions, or rather to find a sort of confirmation of them. Before nature itself, it is our imagination which makes the picture.
—Charles Baudelaire,
Epigrams (1860)

Combining Diverse Objects with Blending Modes

Sometimes the creation of a collage has a lot to do with timing. As new imagery is fresh in my head, various pieces start to coalesce. Call it serendipity if you like, but some collages begin this way. I had just visited an antique shop that specializes in old paper ephemera. While there I bought some old books, antique photos, journals, and letters.

The next day I was scanning a pear before I ate it for lunch. Its shape was too beautiful to ignore, so of course I scanned it. In my mind, I started to put things together and before I knew it a collage was born.

Figure 6-45
Scanned pear

Blend modes, located in the Layers palette, are very important tools in creating a collage. I often encounter students who have never changed the blend mode from the default "Normal" setting. Blend modes determine how two layers will interact together. The two layers are the one that is currently active and the one directly beneath it. Each blend mode will change how that interaction occurs.

The following collage relies heavily on the use of blend modes.

Figure 6-46
Hand-sewn book added to pear

My first thought was to have the pear show stitching, as was the case in the old book I had bought. I used the Liquify filter to push and pull the book to fit the contours of the pear (Figure 6-46). The blend mode was set to Multiply on the book layer. Opacity remained at 100% on the book layer. A bit of masking was applied.

Figure 6-47
Carte de Visite gentleman was added

The next component I added was the gentleman from the Carte de Visite that I had purchased. I used the Soft Light blend mode on this layer and a small amount of masking. This new layer was set at 50% opacity.

Figure 6-48
Farmer's ledger from 1856 added

The next piece I added was a ledger from a farmer in 1856, accounting for the sale and purchase of various grains. It was blended with the Hard Light blend mode, and considerable masking on that layer allowed the pear to show through. It was set at 54% opacity. Notice the scratch effects around the outside corners of the piece, achieved by hatching marks on the masks.

Figure 6-49
Color tint added in areas

The overall color effect was too monotone. It needed a bit of spicing up. I applied some additional tinting using the Color blend mode at 100% opacity.

Figure 6-50
Cast Shadow applied

Although a man in a pear is certainly not believable, I continued the conventions of reality by adding a cast shadow. It was applied with an Overlay blend mode and that new layer was set at 73% opacity.

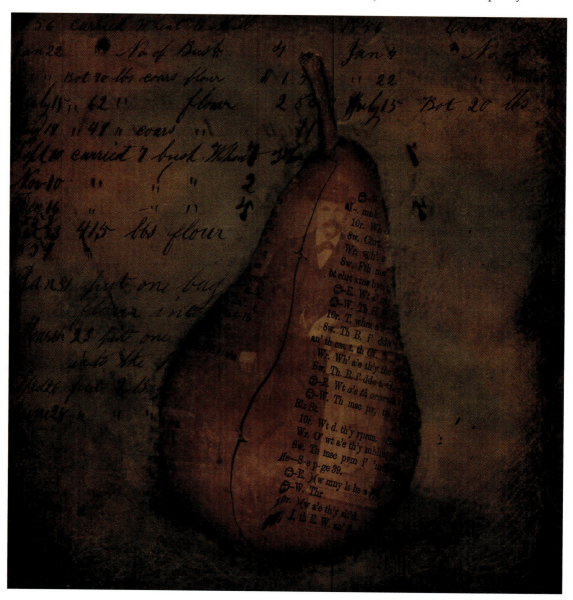

Figure 6-51

Completed pear collage

The collage entitled "Ruth's Life Pods" is in tribute to the great photographer Ruth Bernhard. I had the good fortune to study with Ruth and greatly admired her work. In a conversation one day she mentioned that she saw the human body as the seed pod of the next generation. That comparison always stuck with me. This multilayered collage has a female torso, flower blossoms, and lotus pods incorporated together to illustrate Ruth's statement about our own fragility and the cycle of life, death, and rebirth.

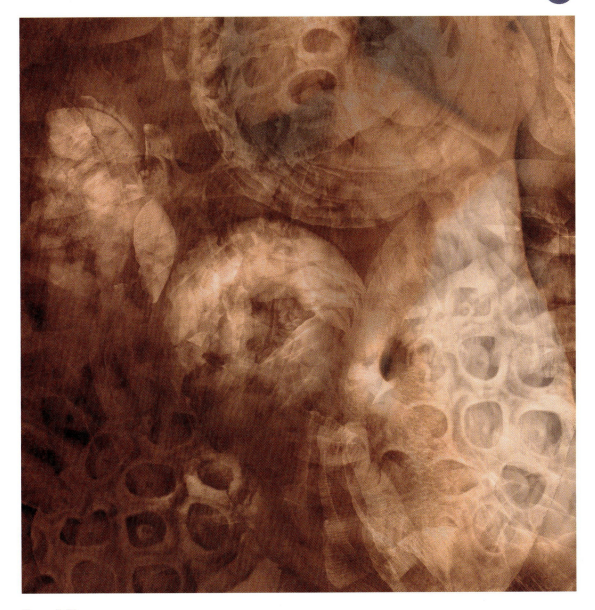

Figure 6-52
"Ruth's Life Pods"

. . . .

Shadow Power

Our next example began with a photo I had taken for a fashion shoot, many years ago. The model's eyes and expression had always made the photo a favorite of mine. In the original image the model was standing beside a Grecian column. I decided to turn the column into a tree and go with the feel of a wood nymph in this collage.

Figure 6-53
*Component pieces for wood
nymph collage*

Figure 6-54
Collage begins

We do not see things as they
are. We see things as we are.
—*THE TALMUD*

I first began by putting the model's eye into a leaf lying on a coral walk. The result was okay, but not really exciting. The next thought was to put the leaf and eye combination back into the face. That started to work better visually, and the concept became that of a wood nymph or the goddess Flora. Additional leaves were used to clothe the model. The column was replaced by a tree trunk. The other eye was festooned with flower petals and a background was imported into the composition. Notice the cast shadow from the leaf onto the face. It is a separate layer, with the color gray painted on. Shadows are the powerful component that unites this piece and creates the realistic effect.

Figure 6-55
Shadow layers turned off

This collage relies on separate layers of shadows that are painted into the piece with a low opacity of dark gray. Figure 6-55 illustrates the collage with the shadow layers turned off. It resembles pieces that were cut from magazines and glued in place.

He is nothing but an eye.
—Paul Cézanne,
    Writing of Claude
    Monet, in *Paul Cézanne,
    Letters,* edited by John
    Rewald (1941)

Figure 6-56
Layers of collage

Figure 6-56 shows the collage with the impact that shadows bring to the realistic rendering of this collage. Shadows create a modeling of light and form that was needed for a uniform, cohesive, and realistic rendering. There is a tremendous difference in the total effect.

The last step was to pull the saturation down, for a more subtle effect.

Figure 6-57
Final wood

Nymph Collage

Figure 6-58
"Nautilus Venus" collage

Figure 6-58 is part of a series of images that revolve around the concept of Venus. Component parts include a nautilus shell, patterned rocks, a statue, and a photo of a nude torso.

Figure 6-59
Butterfly/woman collage

Figure 6-59 is a very simple collage combining a model (photographed at dawn) with the wings of a butterfly. Cast your restrictions to the wind. Scale in real life is not important when you are putting a collage together. Stretch your imagination!

Gridded Collages

Gridded collages in Photoshop involve a structured grid and careful placement and sizing of design elements. Decide on the output size of the final printed piece of art. For our example, I will use the 13 × 19-inch (Super B) size of paper that can be printed on many midrange printers. The size of the final piece will dictate how large the file size needs to be for each element of the collage. This type of collage does not rely on a textural layer to give the design cohesion. Instead, the very structure of this type of collage fits together like a jigsaw puzzle.

At the very beginning of this project, establish the size of the borders. On this project I wanted a printed area of 12 × 16 inches. That size is a standard frame size. The choice of a standard frame size can be important when the piece is finally framed. Odd sizes will require custom-made frames. Standard frame sizes are easy to work with and will ultimately prove to be more economical. Nonprintable grid lines can be brought onto the canvas with the Move Tool. Simply pull a grid line from the ruler area onto the canvas. To dispose of a grid, just grab it with the Move Tool and pull it off the canvas onto the ruler area. Another way to lay down a grid is to use the automatic grid supplied by View > Show > Grid). It is accurate and easy.

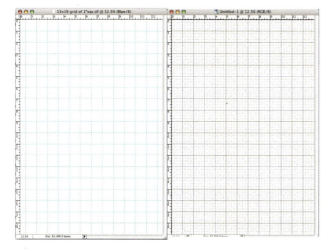

Figure 6-60
Grid to use as the bones on which to hang the images

In this next example of a wedding collage, a centrally located large photograph will be the focal point. It will be edged with other photos from the wedding day. Additional grids were laid down, being careful to line them up with the ruler marks. If you are placing the grid system yourself, be certain that the grid lines are accurately placed. I usually enlarge my viewing area, to be sure that the grid that I will use as my underlying armature is not placed slightly off center to a ruler mark. You can only be accurate with this underlying grid if you carefully go over the grid placement in a greatly enlarged view. The accuracy of this step will pay off in the future, as you place your images into the grid structure. Again, you may choose to use the built-in grid system in Photoshop (pictured on the right in Figure 6-60) using View > Show > Grid.

Place your focal point image first
Select more photos than you will really use. Be sure to have both vertical and horizontal images to select from. Place the large focal point image first and then work around it, adding images, as you progress.

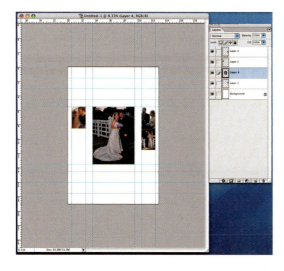

Figure 6-61
Beginning the layout

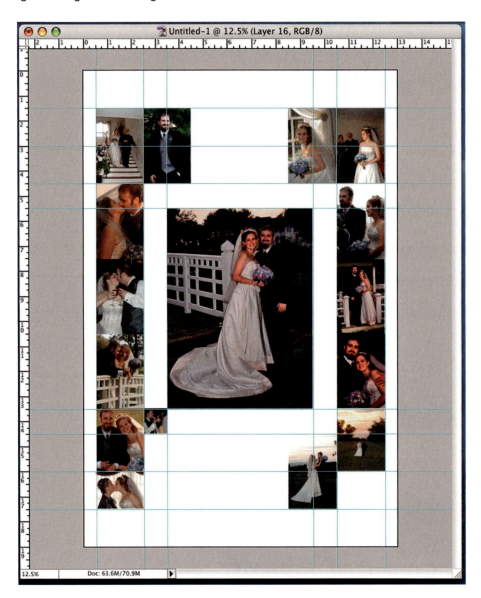

Figure 6-62
Add images into the collage

Beauty came to be my presiding ideal—whatever I did and whatever happened. I sought after beauty in everything, and the more my aesthetic satisfaction, the more thirsty I grew for it. Hence my idealism—which is nothing in effect but a perceptual craving of beauty.
—ANWAR EL-SADAT,
 In Search of Identity
 (1977)

Add photos, using Edit > Free Transform to resize (cropping may be necessary)
Add photos, resizing them as you go. Using Edit > Free Transform is an easy way to size your images on the fly. You can place them exactly using your grid. Once all the photos are in place, it is time for another evaluation. I thought the composition was too busy, and the color was distracting. I decided to desaturate the image, converting it to a black-and-white image.

Figure 6-63
Filled collage in color

More refinement was necessary. The small frame of photos that encircled the main photo did not stand out separately as a framing device, so I applied a glow effect to the edges of that "frame" of photos. The glow was also used on the outside edge of the entire collage. The image was flattened and converted to a sepia tone, and a small, thin, dark sepia border was added to the outside edge to complete the finished collage.

Figure 6-64
Collage in sepia tones with a glow effect to accentuate the small frame of photos

Figure 6-65
Another wedding collage

The grid technique is a good one for a variety of subjects.

There really are no limits to the subject matter for a grid collage. Likewise, there is no limit to the number or arrangement of grid lines to facilitate the placement of your photos. Remember that the grid lines do not print, so there is no need to clear the lines from your completed image before printing.

A gridded collage exercise has been provided for you in Chapter 11, and projects and files can be found on the accompanying website.

Figure 6-66
Sequence of photos of a little girl with apples

Figure 6-67
Collage of images from one person's life and family

Collage Possibilities for Wedding Photography

I am following Nature without being able to grasp her. ...I have gone back to things that can't possibly be done; water, with weeds waving at the bottom. It is a wonderful sight, but it drives one crazy trying to paint it. But that is the kind of thing I am always tackling.

—CLAUDE MONET,
letter to Gustave Feffroy, June 2, 1890, in *La Vie de Claude Monet,* by Marthe de Fels (1929)

Collage is a wonderful technique that you can really use if you photograph weddings. Although this example addresses weddings, you can certainly apply the same concepts to other purposes. I'll use the example of the wedding of Tess and Michael. Their formal collage is featured in Figure 6-65. They were a fun-loving couple who applied a sense of humor to their wedding day. After the wedding, we went out to the 50-yard line of the football field for an unusual shot with a fish-eye lens. Tess displayed her New York Giants garter belt and Mike threw his arms in the air in jubilation and machismo while holding her bouquet. It was wacky and fun. Their humor carried through to the top of their wedding cake with a statuette of a bride pulling an unwilling groom. Why not carry that humor one step further?

Figure 6-68
Transforming the cake topper with the actual bride and groom

I often photograph details at the wedding, such as the cake, flowers, champagne glasses, etc. The cake topper was too good to resist. I searched through the photographs that I had made of the couple and found two heads that I could use to substitute on the little statuette. I resized them using Transform and masked them into the original photo. It was easy and the couple was pleasantly surprised.

Figure 6-69
Album layout using collage techniques for a double-page spread

Figure 6-70
Collaged close-up

Figure 6-71
Original photos used in the collaged composite

Staying with the same wedding, collage was used to make a double-page spread for an album. The bouquet of roses was used as the background, at a low opacity. The photos were added on top, with the help of the grid system. The photos had a drop shadow and bevel and emboss added.

Figure 6-72
Fantasy collage

I really liked the intense look in the groom's eye in one of the shots, but part of his face was obscured with the bride's hair. I decided to use her profile with this shot and cast him in the shadows for a mysterious kind of look. Extra layers were added for shadows and sepia toning.

Taking it one step further into a fantasy kind of collage, I incorporated Tess's roses into her head. This may be over the top for some couples. You need to know your clients. It certainly will be different from their friends' conventional wedding photographs. Let your imagination loose. Follow your nose. Investigate options. Experiment. Have fun with it. Collaging can make your work unique among that of your peers.

Look to History

If you are going to be involved in the arts I think it is important to be looking at lots of art. Artists do not create art in a vacuum. They are inspired to create within the context of the times they live in. So much can be learned from viewing great art. If you have not become a regular patron of your local museums, please give it a try. Look at the colors used, the texture, the overall composition—in short, take the painting apart intellectually. What makes it tick? What is the artist trying to say? Take some time to ponder a work. Many great artists cite the impact on their work by artists of a previous era. We have much to learn from each other and from the artists who preceded us.

Figure 6-73
Birth of Venus

I like to try to incorporate fragments of art from other eras into my collage work. Sometimes it is subtle as in Figure 6-73, "Birth of Venus." This piece derives its content from the myth about the watery birth of Venus. It includes ancient mosaics that have a nautical theme, as well as infrared photographs of a fish and a female figure. It is a very large piece. The mosaic tiles provide part of the literal context and serve as the unifying texture for the piece.

Figure 6-74
Sacred and Profane

The collage entitled "Sacred and Profane" (Figure 6-74) incorporates many component parts from our collective art history background. In this collage, I've used both the sacred version of idealized beauty, the Virgin Mary, in combination with her secular counterpart, Venus or Aphrodite. Most of the ancient art component pieces were derived from a trip to Sicily, where I photographed the art in churches, museums, and excavation sites. The exception in this piece was the photograph of a Venus sculpture taken in Paris. On close examination you might spot several heavenly angel messengers. Look for the hands that might be making a blessing or offering caution to the viewer. The juxtaposition of elements is important in collaging. Be sure to watch the scale of each component and how it adds to or detracts from your overall composition.

I have a large library of images to pull from when creating collages. I photograph wherever I go, continuing to build my visual library collection. If you are involved in collaging you needs lots of visual material to draw from. I have DVDs devoted to skies, some to texture, some to foliage, etc. Become a pack rat of ideas and images.

Figure 6-75
"Love Poem" collage

Figure 6-76
Multiple exposure of pansies

Sometimes inspiration comes from experimenting in the process of actually making photographs. The collage in Figure 6-75 began with making in-camera multiple exposures of a bunch of pansy flowers (Figure 6-76). My camera allows me to dictate up to 10 separate exposures to be combined by the camera software in a multiple exposure. This capture of the pansies was about six exposures. It is interesting on its own but absolutely superb for texture and color in a collage.

Figure 6-77
Infrared water lily photograph

The next layer that was added was the infrared photograph of a water lily and the surrounding buds and lily pads. This photo was added on another layer with the blend mode set to Hard Light and 100% opacity.

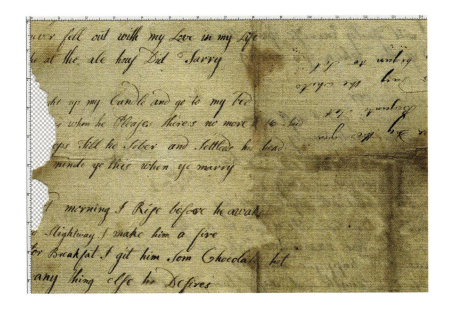

Figure 6-78
Tattered parchment with hand-written poem

The next layer was a love poem. It was a piece of parchment that was tattered and torn but still quite beautiful. I picked it up at an antique store and scanned it in. This layer was set to the Multiply blend mode at 69% opacity. I usually try all the blend modes out until I arrive at one that complements the progressing collage. The opacity for each layer is determined in process.

Figure 6-79
Layers assembled in
"Love Poem" collage

Simple Kaleidoscope Collage

Sometimes a collage can be as simple as making a kaleidoscope view of a single photo. In Figure 6-80, "Tapestry I," I simply expanded the canvas both horizontally and vertically and duplicated the original photo of seaweed taken with an infrared dedicated camera (Figure 6-81).

This mirrored Icelandic landscape (Figure 6-82) is even simpler. Iceland has many piles of rocks, or *cairns,* that memorialize areas that were destroyed by earlier volcanic action. Visitors often add a stone to an existing pile for good luck. Seldom do I previsualize which images will eventually become mirrored. As I review contact sheets, occasionally I will spot an image with potential for this simple technique. There is a fascination with what an image becomes when it is mirrored. It becomes more than a simple double of itself. Like those famous inkblots used in psychological testing, mirrored images open the imagination to a different reality.

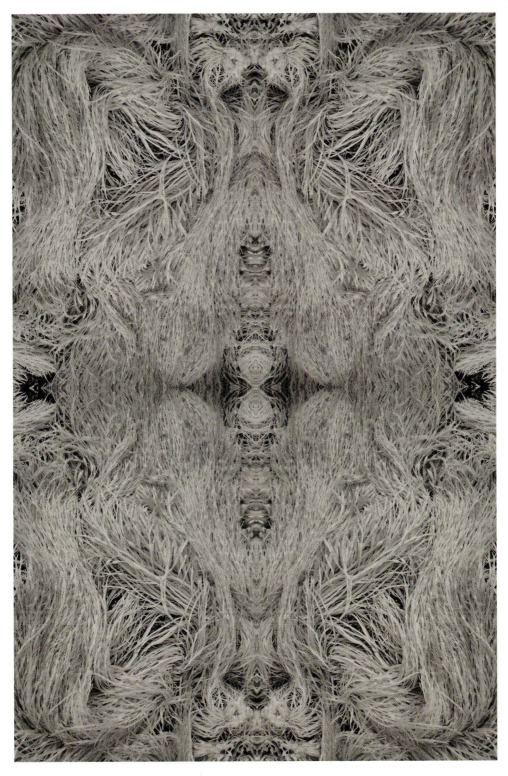

Figure 6-80
"Tapestry I" collage

Figure 6-81
Original seaweed photo taken with an infrared dedicated camera

Figure 6-82
Iceland landscape mirrored

Gradient Tool for Smooth Blending

Another wonderful tool for creating a collage is the gradient tool. It gives you a smooth transition from one image into another one.

Two Hawaiian photos were used on this simple combination created using the Gradient Tool. The water image was placed above the palm leaf image. A layer mask was added. To make a smooth, seamless transition, the Gradient Tool was used on the mask. In the modifiers for the tool, select the black to transparent option. Simply click and pull the tool, like pulling a window shade. It is so simple and yet effective.

Figure 6-83
Palm leaf

Figure 6-84
Vegetation reflected in water

Figure 6-85
Layer illustration of combining these two images with the gradient tool

Figure 6-86
Combination image

Figure 6-87
Swan introduced to pond

This technique can also be used and then customized for a more delicate mask rendition. Figure 6-87 shows a swan that I photographed in Germany. I placed the swan on a layer above a Maine pond filled with reeds and lily pads that was photographed in infrared.

Figure 6-88
Gradient Tool used on the mask

The Gradient Tool was pulled several times on the mask, creating a smooth transition. Using this tool gives you a head start on creating the perfect mask for this combination. Next, the standard brush tool was used to paint white on the mask, restoring the swan where it had become somewhat transparent. The size of the brush was varied as needed.

Figure 6-89
Fine-tuning the mask

Figure 6-90
Color photo is converted to sepia-toned black and white

Figure 6-91
Completed swan in pond

The next step was to use Image > Adjustments > Black and White. I checked the toning option at the bottom of the menu and used a slight sepia tone to match the background pond.

Sometimes, as artists, we have a variety of images that we would like to use in combination. There were no swans in the Maine pond, but with the help of masks we can combine images to create a new reality.

Figure 6-92
"Time Floats By"

Allow Yourself to be Flexible in the Creative Process

Sometimes you might start a collage with a preconceived idea that just doesn't work no matter how hard you try. Continue to work with that original impulse and try combining other imagery with your original background. Figure 6-93, "Time Floats By," was such a collage. I spent an afternoon unsuccessfully trying out combinations until I relaxed and opened my mind to other possibilities and imagery.

Figure 6-93

Weeds in the morning

Figure 6-94

Multiple-exposure flowers were added to start the collage

The collage began with a simple photo of weeds in the early morning light in a foggy meadow near my home (Figure 6-94). Those amber tones set the color palette for the following work. I then added two images of flowers that were multiple exposures. Each was added as a separate layer, and the blend mode was set to Luminosity, yielding the brownish collage seen to the right of Figure 6-95. At this point, the collage began to come together.

Figure 6-95
Floating leaf added

The next layer added was a floating leaf. I used the Overlay blend mode and a mask to integrate the leaf into the underlying collage (Figure 6-96).

Figure 6-96
Antique writing added

The final image to be added was some antique writing, which I scanned in and used a mask to blend into the collage. After applying the Multiply blend mode to the writing layer, the floating leaf was a bit too pale. I duplicated the leaf layer and used 40% opacity to give the leaf a bit more color saturation and presence to complete the collage.

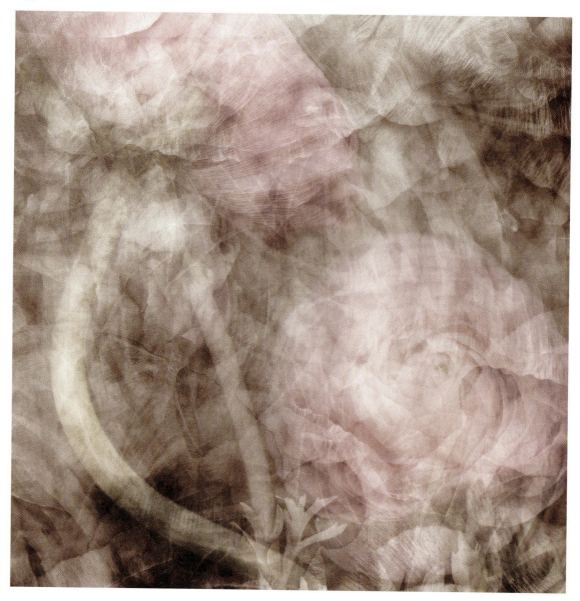

Figure 6-97
*Ranunculus collage using
dozens of layers, blending
modes, and masks*

In short, collage can be anything that you can imagine. Exaggerate scale, suspend reality, and let those creative juices flow. Keep in mind the need for unity to knit the piece together and you should be successful at collaging.

7

Assembling a Collage in Painter™

Each piece of software offers unique ways to work with pixels. Photoshop® is by far the first piece of software that comes to mind when contemplating putting a collage together. It has the tools that make resizing and placement of images easy; however, don't rule out Painter as a program for collaging. Painter offers some unique possibilities, especially for textural effects.

. . . .

Using Painter's Image Hose

Open all files in Painter
The completed nature-oriented collage shown in Figure 7-10 was created in Painter. The background layer was a scanned piece of art paper with a botanical feel (purchased from a bookmaking/paper

Art is nature as seen
through a temperament.
—JEAN-BAPTISTE-CAMILLE
  COROT,
in *Corot*, by Keith
Roberts (1965)

store). The other photo contributions were butterfly specimens that I photographed (Figure 7-1). Figures 7-2 to 7-9 demonstrate the collage processes. All the files were opened in Painter.

Figure 7-1
Original photographs used in Painter collage

Figure 7-2
Cloning butterfly

Clone the background paper (File > Clone)
Create a new layer
Change the File > Clone source to the open butterfly file
Clone the butterfly on the new layer
You will notice that the butterfly appears in the upper left-hand corner of the image. That is the location where the cloner begins. It shifts all image files to square-up to the upper left-hand corner. If that is not where you would like the image to appear, then take the Move Tool and place that layer where you would like it. Be sure to complete the cloning first.

Figure 7-3
Moving the butterfly

Use the Move Tool to reposition the butterfly

Some of the burlap cloth background on which the butterfly was mounted came along for the ride. That was deleted by erasing the cloth, using the Eraser brush. The blend mode was set to Shadow Map once the butterfly was in the desired location. Two more butterflies were added in a similar fashion. They were both set at the default blend mode, but the butterfly on the upper left was reduced to a 79% opacity.

Figure 7-4
Image Hose > Swallows and Look Selector > Passionflower Leaves

Image Hose was used to "spray" on swallows and leaves

There are some really wacky images that you can spill onto the page by selecting the Image Hose Brush. The size of these randomly thrown objects is determined by your brush size. Placement is not precise. The challenge here was to use these Image Hose components in a way that integrated them into the collage. Generally speaking, the Image Hose libraries are fun but not terribly useful when creating art. They are digital spin-art (discussed in Chapter 9). I chose the swallows from the Image Hose Library and the passionflower leaves from the Look Selector in Version 9 of Painter. Each version of Painter has new libraries of Image Hose images to choose from, or you can look back through previous versions for some oldies but goodies. Each of those components was sprayed from the Image Hose directly onto a new layer. Note that each upgrade of Painter has new Image Hose libraries. Some of the old libraries have some interesting items that are worth examining.

Art is the thing everyone has to use. There is art in the line of a jacket and in the shape of a collar as well as in the way one addresses a letter, combs one's hair, or places a window in a house.

—Georgia O'Keeffe,
in *Portrait of an Artist: A Biography,* by Laurie Lisle (1980)

Figure 7-5
Using the Image Hose

Spray the leaves on a separate layer with blend mode set to Overlay and opacity reduced to 56%

Spray the swallows on a separate layer with blend mode set to Gel

Add another new layer and use the Airbrush > Coarse Spray variant to spray a dark brown texture in segments of the piece, especially near edges, with a large brush, with the opacity set at 22%

The next challenge was to integrate these various components together to create a feeling of wholeness. That was achieved by varying the blend modes and spraying a coarse airbrush texture along the edges and in several locations to vary the tone.

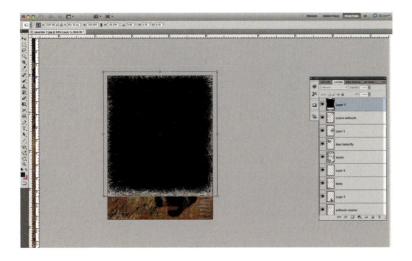

Figure 7-6
Adding scratchboard edges in Photoshop

Place the scratchboard file on a layer above the collage and resize with Free Transform in Photoshop

The collage could be complete now, but I decided to save it as a Photoshop file, thus preserving all the layers, and to open it in Photoshop. I also opened a file of a scanned piece of scratchboard. Scratchboard can be purchased from an art supply store or you can create your own. Scratchboard is a board coated with a chalky-like base (several coats of gesso will work) and covered with a layer of black ink. With a sharp stylus or pin, the artist scrapes through the ink, revealing the white layer beneath. The scratchboard used in Figure 7-6 was scratched around the edges with a few random marks throughout the board. It was scanned for my collection of edge effects (see Chapter 4). The scratchboard image was placed on a new layer above the collage, and Free Transform was used to resize the scratchboard to fit the edges of the collage.

Figure 7-7
*Close-up edge effect
(Difference blend mode)*

Set blend mode to Difference

I tried all of the blend modes to arrive at the best integration of the edge effect with the Painter collage. I settled on the Difference blend mode. That blend mode created a turquoise color for the edge effect that worked well with the color of the butterflies.

Figure 7-8
Layer effects completed

The layers remain separate for modification at a later time

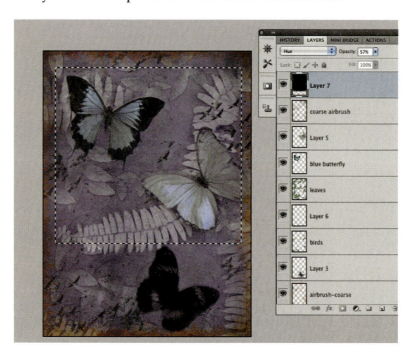

Figure 7-9
Blend mode set to Hue

Set blend mode to Hue

While trying out various blend modes, you may stumble on an unexpected rendition. The Hue blend mode created this interesting lavender version. I decided to crop out the edges, which appeared rather orange, and use only the top portion of the collage. This created an entirely different kind of look.

Figure 7-10
Completed collage

The completed Painter collage has a nature theme that was enhanced by the use of Painter's Image Hose.

The alternate image made from the collage would work nicely on a greeting card.

Beauty is not in the face; beauty is a light in the heart.
—Khalil Gibran

Figure 7-11
Alternate version of collage using Hue blend mode

Using Painter's Unique Brushes for Texture in a Collage

The next Painter collage relies on the wonderful surface texture effects that Painter offers. The collage consists of just two images (Figure 7-12). The one on the left is a scan of paper made from bark. The image on the right is sunrise in Venice. The goal was to push this image combination with a rough textural feel.

Figure 7-12
Original images

Figure 7-13
Selecting color of light

Place the Venetian image on another layer, above the bark paper
Set the blend mode to Multiply
Effects > Surface Control > Apply Surface Texture dialogue box appears
Select a golden shade of light color

The Surface Control > Apply Surface Texture offers a world of possibilities. It allows you to apply lighting effects that can be colored, like putting a colored gel over studio lighting. It can bring the texture out in the paper that you have selected. There are just tons of options and combinations. I chose Image Luminance as the type of surface texture that I wanted.

Figure 7-14 illustrates the settings that were applied to this image. The preview window allows a look at how the effect will appear.

Figure 7-14
*Apply Surface Texture >
Image Luminance*

Figure 7-15
Blend mode set to Multiply

One should not pursue
beauty so much as one
should be open to it.
—Mortimer J. Adler,
  Six Great Ideas (1981)

Set the blend mode to Multiply
Try all the blend modes to see which one will work best for the desired effect.

Figure 7-16
*Apply Surface Texture >
Paper*

Select Apply Surface Texture > Paper
Apply Surface Texture was used a second time, using the Paper Texture option.

Figure 7-17
Edges erased

Erase sharp edges

Using the Eraser brush, the straight and sharp edges were erased to create an irregular edge.

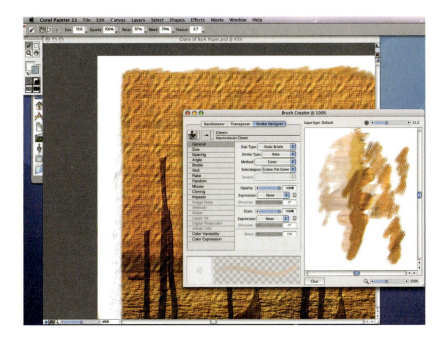

Figure 7-18
Brush creator creates custom brushes

Go to Window > Show Brush Creator

The Brush Creator allows you to make and test custom brushes. A custom-made Impressionist Cloner brush was created using a Static Bristle, Rake Stroke type, and a Grainy Flat Cover method of applying the strokes. Try the brush out in the area provided.

Figure 7-19
Rough edge applied with custom-made Impressionist Cloner brush

Apply rough strokes around the edges of the collage
Rough strokes, using the custom-made Impressionist Cloner brush, create a rough-hewn edge effect.

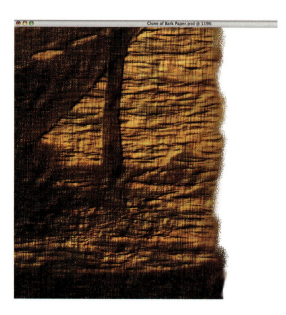

Figure 7-20
Straight Cloner "fills" within the painterly edge

Black is like a broken vessel, which is deprived of the capacity to contain anything.
—LEONARDO DA VINCI,
Treatise on Painting
(1651)

Use Straight Cloner to bring the textural effect up to the rough edge
The edge created a different textural look as it made the rough edges . To bring the textural image up to the rough edges, I used the Straight Cloner.

The completed Painter collage has a rough, bumpy, deep textural feel, thanks to the textural possibilities available in Apply Surface Control.

Using Colored Paper and the Lighting Effects

Size images in Photoshop
Preparing for a collage in Painter requires a bit of preparation. If you intend to clone from many different source files it is important that they all be the same size and resolution. Painter will place all of them in registration from the upper left-hand corner.

Knowing that little piece of information, I first prepared this example in Photoshop. The concept involved a stone archway and a swan. The swan photo had a nice reflection, so I decided to echo that with the archway. I prepared three files. I cropped the archway a bit and that became the file that established the base dimensions. Next I used free transform on the swan to size it to fit within the archway. The third file was the arch reflection, achieved by flipping it vertically.

Figure 7-21
Completed textural collage in Painter

Figure 7-22
Sizing the swan

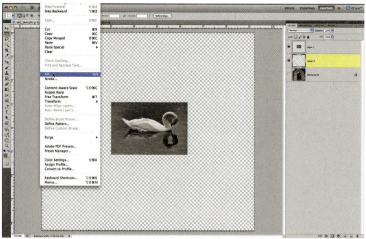

Figure 7-23
Adding canvas to the swan

I added a new transparent layer between the swan and the archway base. The water surrounding the swan was sampled with the Eyedropper Tool. The new layer was filled (Edit > Fill > Foreground) with this color.

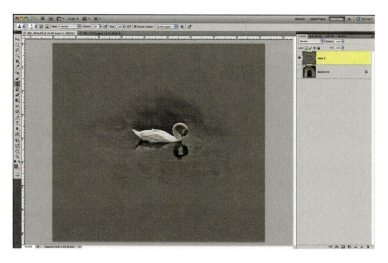

Figure 7-24
Enlarged swan layer

The swan layer was merged into the gray layer beneath it. Once joined, I used the Clone Stamp Tool with a light opacity setting of 20% to enlarge the water area around the swan, creating a soft edge that tapers outward.

Figure 7-25
Archway reflection created

The archway was duplicated and flipped vertically (Edit > Transform > Flip Vertical) and placed for accuracy.

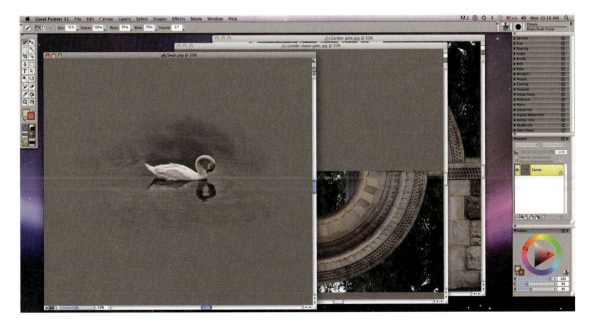

Figure 7-26
Three files opened in Painter

I then opened all three files in Painter.

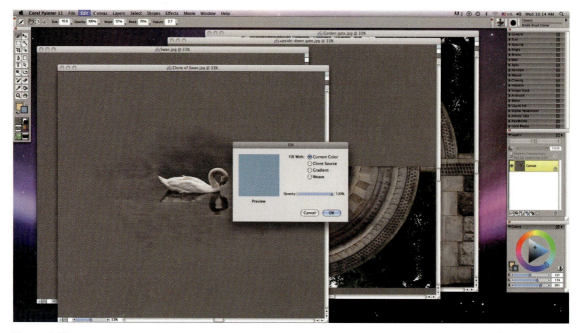

Figure 7-27
Cloned swan file

File > Clone was used on the swan file. Once it has been cloned, you can fill that clone with a color that simulates a colored sheet of paper. I chose a dusty blue color. Often this choice becomes a subtle undertone that peeks through the cloning and exaggerates any texture treatment.

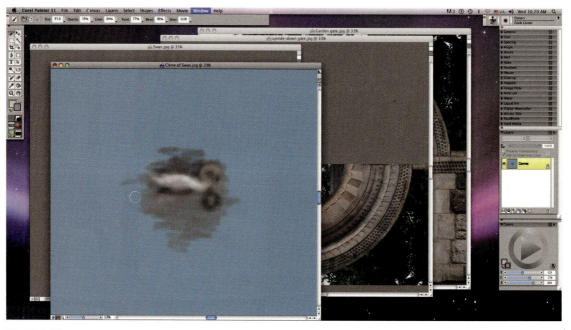

Figure 7-28
Chalk Cloner used on the blue paper

I selected the Chalk Cloner brush and used it to deposit a light application of chalk on the blue paper, thus beginning our collage piece.

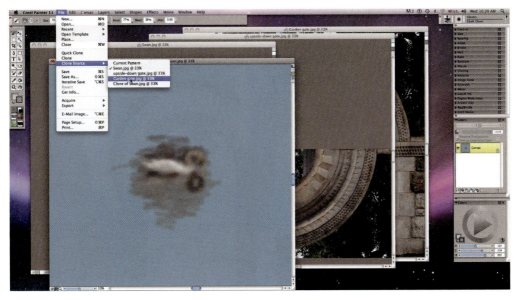

Figure 7-29
Switching the clone source

Cloning from multiple layers requires you, as the artist, to be aware of which file is the currently selected one for cloning. You can switch back and forth between source files by going to File > Clone Source and selecting the desired file to serve as the source of the clone.

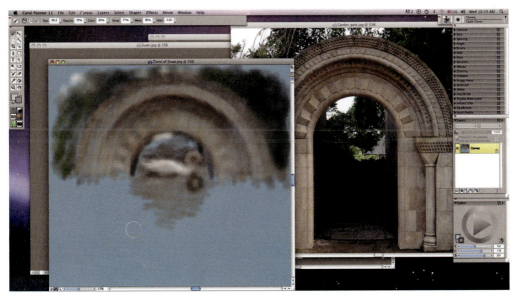

Figure 7-30
The archway roughed in

Using the archway as the source, the underpainting of chalk continues with the enlargement of the working area into the archway. Don't worry if you bring in unwanted areas, like the tree leaves, as they can easily be covered over by switching the source of the clone information.

Figure 7-31
Straight Cloner applied for detail

Next, I used the Straight Cloner at 2 to 4% opacity to lightly bring in elected areas of the swan and the archway.

Figure 7-32
Reflection of arch is added

Next, I added the reflection of the arch and cloned more of the gray color on the swan layer.

Figure 7-33
The Thick Bristle Cloner was used to add a bit of textured brushwork to the swan and the upright archway

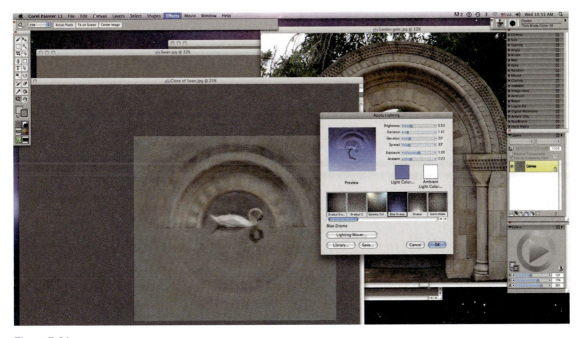

Figure 7-34
Apply Lighting gave the piece a night-time mood

Select Effects > Surface Control > Apply Lighting
Painter has a big assortment of unusual effects. The Apply Lighting command, found in the Effects > Surface Control, is a gem. I selected a blue that would produce a night-time feel.

Figure 7-35
Completed collage

Creativity can be described
as letting go of certainties.
—GAIL SHEEHY,
    Pathfinders (1981)

Combining the Power of Painter and Photoshop in a Collage

The next collage began as an out-of-focus Lensbaby® shot of some of my hibiscus flowers. The Lensbaby® attaches onto your SLR and has a tilt feature that can throw things out of focus. You could achieve a somewhat similar effect by using blur filters. It is a fun lens, especially

Figure 7-36
Lens Baby photograph

when you want to loosen up your imagery, concentrating more on color and shapes and less on detail.

I love to combine the potential of the two powerful programs, Painter and Photoshop. Each piece of software offers unique ways to make your creative mark. In this example, I will use Photoshop for the initial collage, followed by adding brushwork and textural effects in Painter.

Figure 7-37
Adding in portions of petal detail

Add detailed portions of hibiscus petals to the composition with a layer mask
Set the blend mode to Screen

Education for creativity is
nothing short of education
for living.
—ERICH FROMM,
   *Creativity and Its
   Cultivation* (1959)

In Photoshop, I selected additional petals from photos that were in focus. Portions of these images were added using a layer mask and setting the blend mode to Screen.

Figure 7-38
More petals added

I added more petals using a layer mask to blend them into the collage. Again, the blend mode was set to Screen on each additional petal layer.

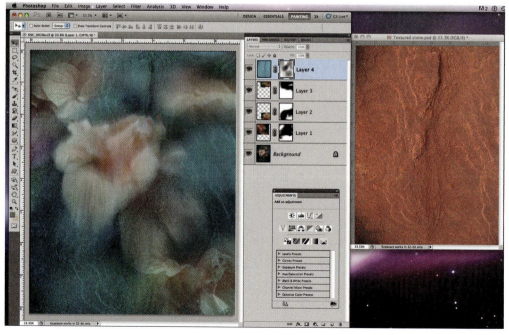

Figure 7-39
Eroded sandstone was added for texture

Add a new layer with a sandstone texture
Change the hue of the sandstone to an aqua shade using a Hue/Saturation adjustment layer
Set the blend mode to Hard Light

The image seemed a bit too soft, so I decided to add texture. I used a digital photo of a detail of an eroded sandstone tombstone in Scotland. I changed the color of the stone to an aqua shade by using Image > Adjustment > Hue/Saturation. I set the blend mode to Hard Light, which allows the texture to show with clarity.

I next opened the image in Painter and cloned it. Working on the clone, I applied some clone brushwork using brushes that gave me some depth (Wet Oils, Smeary Bristle Cloner, and Flat Impasto Cloner). These brush strokes were judiciously used in small sections. I didn't want to lose the texture of the sandstone throughout the piece. The brushwork was essentially used to accent areas.

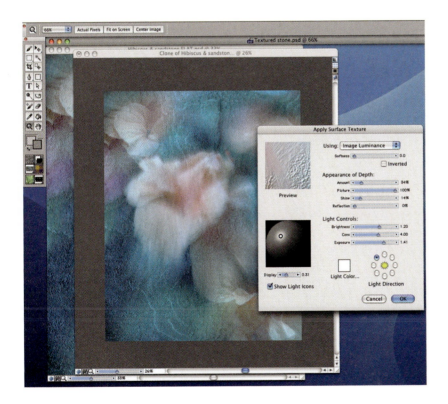

Figure 7-40
Surface texture applied

Looking at the landscape from an airplane, I began to understand Cubist painting.
—ERNEST HEMINGWAY,
The Toronto Daily Star
(1922)

Select Effects > Surface Control > Apply Surface Texture

Painter offers an interesting effect called Surface Texture. I chose the Image Luminance type. After adjusting the sliders to my satisfaction, checking the preview throughout, I applied this effect.

Figure 7-41
Effect was faded

Fade the effect (Edit > Fade)

If the effect seems a bit too strong, you can fade the effect, after it is applied. Fade is located under Edit, in the top menu.

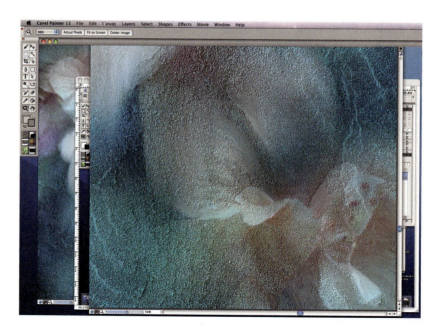

Figure 7-42
Close-up of surface control effect

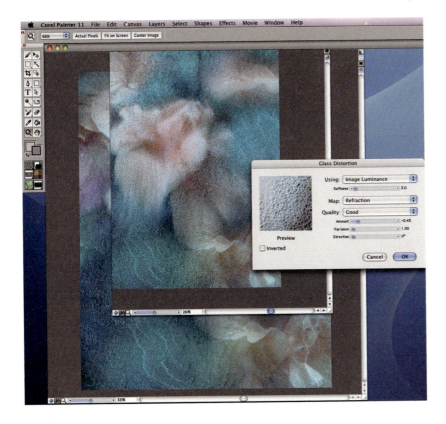

Figure 7-43
Glass Distortion applied

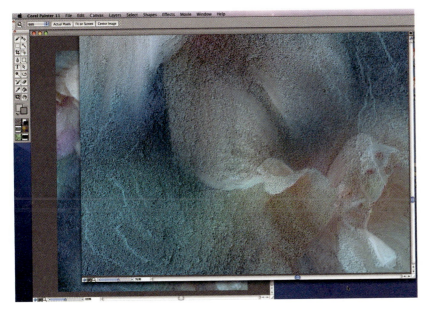

Figure 7-44
Close-up of detail in lower right-hand corner

Choose Effects > Focus > Glass Distortion

Another surface effect, Glass Distortion, was applied to enhance the textural quality.

When you are contemplating making a collage, remember that Painter can offer some unique effects and is especially good for a textural feel. I am constantly going back and forth between Painter and Photoshop for many pieces. Simply pick the tool that is best suited for the job at hand. Both programs offer a stunning array of options singly, but when you combine the power of both of them together you have a greatly extended range of artistic options.

Figure 7-45
Completed abstract collage made in Photoshop and Painter

8

The Paradox: The Absolute Truth and the Exquisite Lie—Creating a Panorama in Photoshop®

Concept and Preparation

A panoramic image may well be the ultimate collage. There are many ways to approach a panoramic project. There are prepackaged software programs designed to tackle this task. Photoshop even includes stitching software, called Photomerge, in their program. Photomerge is located under File > Automate. Or. you can elect to stitch your photos together yourself. Although the do-it-yourself approach may take you longer to construct your image, I really like it for two reasons: quality and control.

I feel like I need to wrap this chapter in yellow tape, saying *CAUTION*, like you see on the television crime shows. This process can become addictive. You will want to make panoramas everywhere you go, from your own backyard to exotic vacation locations. Travel spots are ideal material for this process. You know what it feels like

OPPOSITE PAGE FROM TOP TO BOTTOM: *"Fox Hunting, Pennsylvania;" "Boston Common;" "Cadillac Mountain, Acadia, Maine;" "St. Augustine, Florida;" "Cappadocia, Turkey;" "Capri, Italy;" "Garden Wedding, Maryland"* on vacation when you are standing in a beautiful location and you just want to soak it all up and carry this place home with you. You want to remember what it felt like to be at that spot in that place and at that time of day. You simply want to bottle it up. Snapshots seldom bring home the feeling you had on that spot. The panoramic process will certainly come closer to the real thing.

The concept is simple. You revolve around in a complete circle, taking photographs as you go. Those images are then pieced or stitched together. The result is one very long image that reveals not only what was in front of you at that spot but also what was at your sides and behind you. Now you can really have eyes in back of your head, just like you thought your Mom had when you were a child.

In some ways, this panoramic is the penultimate truth of that moment in space and time. You quite literally see it all. The flip side of that is that it is all an exquisite lie. Take the example shown in Figure 8-1, a panoramic taken in Florence, Italy. I had just come out of the Uffizi Art Museum in Florence, after spending many hours with some of the finest art on the planet. I walked through the colonnade (known as the Piazzale degli Uffizi) toward the Arno River. Through the colonnade I could still see, in the distance, the fake Michelangelo's *David* in the Palazzo Vecchio (remember, the real one is now in the Galleria Dell' Accademia). Behind me was the famed Arno River and to my side was the Ponte Vecchio, the bridge that dates from 1345 and is occupied by fine goldsmith shops. What a wonderful moment and place, I thought, and I proceeded to take about 60 photographs as I spun around.

In dealing with light, the photographer is dealing with one of the most fundamental, and mysterious, things in the universe. It is related, on the one hand, to the basic vital processes of all living things; on the other, to the inner nature of time. ...We are creatures of the light, and photography is one of the most creative ways by which we can re-affirm this relationship.
—CLARENCE JOHN LAUGHLIN, in "A Statement by the Photographer," March 1955, typescript for *Modern Photography* (never published)

Figure 8-1
Uffizi Museum in Florence, Italy

Look closely at the completed image. It is very much the truth of that moment, but it is such a lie, as well. The Uffizi Museum in the panoramic appears bowed, as it would through a fish-eye lens. How could that be? Consider the laws of perspective. What is closest to me will appear larger. Things further away become smaller as they recede into the distance. As I pivoted around, taking the images that I would later composite together, those same rules apply. As I joined those images in Photoshop they took on the bowed effect illustrated here. Anyone who has ever visited that museum or walked along the beautiful Arno River knows that there is no curve. It is a straight street in that vicinity. Therein is the lie, but the image is beautiful and fascinating nonetheless.

Another interesting concept, as you put together your panoramic image, is that you can juggle the pieces around to create your focal point, since it is really one long continuum that interconnects together. Picture yourself with this long print literally wrapped in a

circle around your head. You choose what will be the center of interest. Consider the panoramic in Figure 8-2, which illustrates that point.

Figure 8-2
Wedding ceremony

This panoramic was taken inside a country church during a wedding ceremony. I'm standing to the rear of the main aisle. The stained
glass windows are behind me. The windows, with their bright colors
and shear largeness of scale, easily dwarf the bridal couple. The completed image should be about the wedding, not the windows. I split the
windows in half. By delegating the stained glass windows to the edges
of the finished print, I've downplayed their importance. The drapery
of white tulle fabric that lined the aisle leads the viewer's eye toward
the front of the sanctuary and the ensuing ceremony. Notice how the
church pews appear to bow, like our previous example of the museum.

Figure 8-3
*Carroll County Courthouse
in Maryland*

In Figure 8-3, a panoramic of the Carroll County Courthouse, the
emphasis needed to be on the courthouse. As I stood in the middle of
the street, the area behind me was really boring and contained some
parked cars. In the finished piece that area was delegated to the sides
as unimportant. Another way to cope with an unattractive area is simply to not show it. Instead of a 360-degree image, you could reduce it
to 280 degrees, or whatever works for the image. You get to call the
artistic shots. Include or delete what you deem appropriate.

In Figure 8-4, I'm sitting on a hillside, watching a preseason football scrimmage. This image is not quite 180 degrees. I didn't want to
include close-ups of the people to my sides or behind me. Due to the
bowl-like nature of the terrain, I would have been looking up into the
nostrils of the people behind me. I really didn't want to include that!
I did, however, want the flag to the left and decided to balance that
with the knee and the hand holding a pair of binoculars to my right.
Remember that you are in charge. There aren't any digital police that
will slap you with a fine for not making the image a complete 360
degrees. Include what seems right for the completed image. In some
places, a complete 360 degrees does not make artistic sense. Use your
own judgment.

Figure 8-4
Football scrimmage

Speaking of judgment, let's play with the idea of a complete circle. Anything in the complete circle can be the center of interest. You can deconstruct your panoramic, after it is completed and rearrange the parts if you are looking for a different effect or area of interest. In Figure 8-5, I liked making the lighthouse and buildings the central design element, and the rock strata provided a good directional line into the composition, leading you to the lighthouse. You can always change your mind later. You can rearrange the pieces of this puzzle. The huge, boulder-like, light-colored rocks could be more prominent if the panoramic was rearranged (Figure 8-6).

Figure 8-5
Pemaquid Lighthouse in Maine

Figure 8-6
Pemaquid Lighthouse reformulated

Another peculiar thing that happens with panoramas, which can be really interesting, is the ability to see in front and behind at the same time. In Figure 8-7, I was standing on the suspended walkway that leads from the shore to the lighthouse. As I pivoted around, the walkway became dissected. In a circumstance like this, you will have two large directional elements that can be used to your advantage in the composition and placement of the images. This will happen whenever you are on a road or path. You will have the path in front of you and also the path behind you.

Figure 8-7
Marshall's Lighthouse in Maine

My work is my sensuous life. ...To make the subject become more beautiful took my full attention, the attention of a lover for his beloved.
—RUTH BERNHARD,
in *Ruth Bernhard: Between Art and Life,* by Margaretta K. Mitchell (2000)

Exposure Controls, Proper Overlap, Tripod or Not?

What do you need to know before you take those photographs for your intended panoramic? Important issues to keep in mind are exposure, overlap, and tripod usage. Let's start with exposure. Normally, we photographers abhor taking a photograph when the sun is directly above us. There are no long shadows to carve out our subject matter, but for a panoramic that can be the ideal time of day to capture your imagery. Think about it. If the sun is not directly above you, somewhere during your time pivoting around, you will be looking into the sun. Likewise you will also be looking away from the sun, during some portion of your exposure. Sometimes the sun can be hidden behind a tree, building, or cloud. Sometimes it is simply unavoidable. You can imagine how this might wreak havoc with your exposure settings.

My rule of thumb is this: Stand with your shoulder to the sun. You are at a 90-degree angle from the sun. Take a meter reading. Make a mental or written note of the settings. If you are using the automatic exposure setting on your camera, change it to the manual mode and dial-in that suggested exposure setting. That exposure setting will be used on *all* of the images that will be used for the finished panoramic. All of your photographs will be taken with the same *f*-stop and shutter speed setting. Why, you ask? In automatic mode, the exposures would be the best ones for each and every shot, but they would vary too greatly from one another to be blended together cohesively. You would be surprised at the difference, especially in the sky areas, from one exposure to the next. Saturation will also vary. For this task, I want a uniformity of tone for easier blending as I join the pieces together.

Figure 8-9 illustrates a series of four exposures taken with the same exposure settings on all, using the manual setting. Figure 8-8 illustrates that same series taken with an automatic exposure setting.

There are exceptions to this rule. A good example of this is a panoramic that I made as I entered the Scottish Highlands. The weather and sky were dramatic that day. Remember, your digital camera has a finite tonal range, just as film does. Knowing that piece of information, and sensing a huge range of tones in front of me, I actually pivoted around three times to obtain the shots for Figure 8-10, taking in excess of 150 photographs. I used three different meter settings. On one sweep, I metered for highlights; on another sweep, I metered for midtones; and on the final sweep, I metered for shadowed or dark areas. I knew that was the only way I would come close to the tonal range I saw that day. I wouldn't recommend this technique for the first dozen or so panoramas that you construct, as it can be quite a challenge,

1/320s at f/9   1/250s at f/9   1/320s at f/10   1/320s at f/9

Figure 8-8
Automatic camera exposure

1/400s at f/10

Figure 8-9
*Manual exposure setting of
1/400s at f/10*

Figure 8-10
Scottish Highlands

but once you are a seasoned panoramic photographer you may want to try it for those difficult scenes that exhibit an enormous amount of tonal variation.

Another issue may be a bit of vignetting from your camera lens. We can fix that later as we blend the images together.

Let's look at the issue of overlap. I always overlap at least a third, sometimes more. I need a large area of overlap to blend one image into the next one. Some subjects are trickier than others. If there is a vertical element in my series of photographs, such as a pole or tree, I make sure that the vertical element is in the middle of at least one exposure. Curvature of the lens will bow the vertical element as it progresses to the edge of your photographs (see Figure 8-11). You need at least one exposure where that flagpole or tree is standing straight upright.

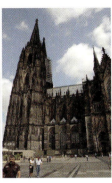

Figure 8-11
Cologne Cathedral—curvature of the lens will bow vertical objects on the edges of the frame

To use a tripod or not is the question. The answer should be "Yes, always!" But, alas, the real world intervenes and I don't always walk around with one. I especially don't carry them in cities when I travel. There is only so much I can carry anymore. Short of hiring an assistant or Sherpa, I'm on my own, and I would rather carry an assortment of lenses. Are the images sharp, you ask? They probably could be a little bit better if I used the tripod, especially in low light situations. But, I've made literally hundreds of panoramas without a tripod that I consider to be rather nice, indeed. So, don't dismay if you find yourself somewhere without your trusty tripod. You are only using a sliver of each image in the total compilation. When those slivers are amassed together, you will discover that you will have a huge image file. Those slivers add up quickly and the result is an image that can easily be 400 to 500 MB, or more.

There are wonderful panoramic heads for this process. Many photographers are fanatical about discerning the nodal point, the use of special tripod heads, spirit levels, and more. I applaud them and the tenacious attention to detail that they use to achieve a beautiful panoramic image. My simple instructions are just that—a way to create lovely panoramics without much expense, elaborate camera equipment, and instructions that require an engineering degree.

Another tip is to always hold your camera vertically. This gives you more image area to work with. You can include more sky and ground. It also covers a multitude of sins, so to speak. Because you may be taking these images without a tripod, the extra headroom afforded by a vertical orientation can be helpful. You will need to eventually crop

There is no best way or only way. We learn from the past, in order to understand the present. The past is our foundation, the springboard into the future. Tradition and past ideas are important bases to begin with, but can be traps if misunderstood.
—ARNOLD NEWMAN,
in *Arnold Newman*, by
Philip Brookman (2000)

the final image, due to the slight variations caused by holding the camera. That is especially true if you are standing on an incline, as you make a circular sweep of the area. Some people go really nuts with this tripod thing and use levels and precise incremental overlaps, etc. That is fine, if that is how your mind works. I don't work that way. I can work fast and move on to another interesting area before my photo friends have set up their tripods, leveled them out, and gotten their meter readings. I've done so many, that I have it down to a science now. You may need that extra piece of time and patience later when you're waiting for that distracting person who stepped into your picture frame to move on.

Beware of moving people. If you are panning in the direction that someone is walking, you will have that person in multiple shots. Sometimes you can put them in one spot and delete them from others. It depends on the surroundings. This is always an issue when shooting in a crowded area, where people are moving about. Take extra shots to be sure that you are covered when you make the panoramic.

Making panoramas has also made me more aware of the sky. I am now constantly amazed at how different the sky is in front of me, compared to behind me, at any given moment. There doesn't have to be an approaching storm to see a vast difference in sky from front to rear. The colors of the sky and the cloud formations are much more variable than I would have suspected. Take a look around.

Relying on Layer Transparency and Layer Masking: Step-By-Step Panorama Instructions Using Collaging Techniques

I usually take about 60 photographs to make a single panoramic image. That is a lot of photographs to merge into one image. But, remember that I will only be using a sliver of each frame that was shot. To begin, I open about five to six images in succession. I miniaturize the images on my desktop and place them off to the edges of my monitor.

As you can see I have 60 images shot in a garden in Bamburg, Germany. There are 10 horizontal images taken after I shot the 360-degree ones. These are my insurance policy to cover any possible difficulties with areas, especially buildings with lots of windows and doors. Because I shot this without benefit of a tripod or a pano head that ensured the use of my lens' nodal point, these architectural features may be problematic.

Open five or six sequential shots, with a generous overlap, in Photoshop
Starting with the first image in this photographic sweep, I immediately add canvas (Image > Canvas Size). Be sure to have white as your background color. The canvas will be the color of your background. A neat trick I frequently use is to employ the Crop Tool and drag it beyond the photo base, as seen in Figures 8-13 and 8-14.

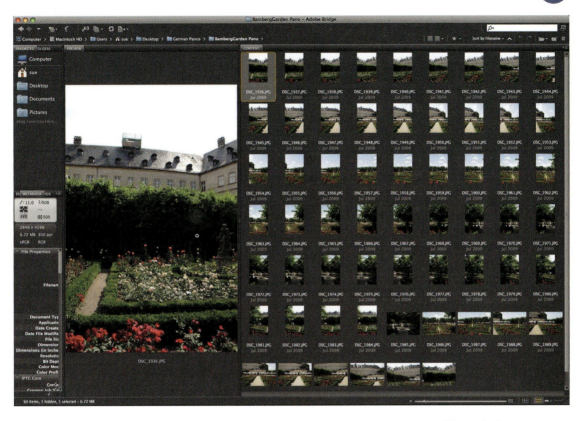

Figure 8-12
Bridge view of the sequence of panoramic shots

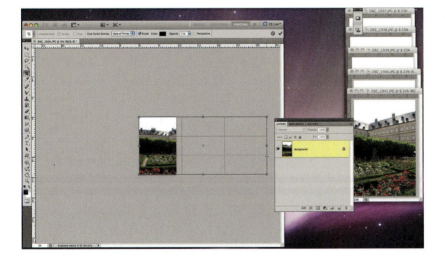

Figure 8-13
How my monitor looks as I begin and using the Crop Tool to expand the canvas

Add canvas width to the first image in the direction that you will be adding images

I add canvas in the direction that I moved while taking the photos. If I pivoted to the right as I was photographing, I add the canvas to the right side of the current picture. I usually add a little room on the top and bottom also. It will be cropped later.

Figure 8-14
Additional canvas is added

Figure 8-14 illustrates the expanded canvas. The extra canvas will allow room for the inclusion of successive photos to the right.

Add the next layer
You can copy it and paste it onto the panorama, or simply use your Move Tool and drag the image onto the panorama. Once the second image is on its own layer, there are a couple ways to position the new layer. You can lower the opacity on the new layer and use that transparency effect to exactly position the new layer. I prefer to switch the blend mode to Difference. This blend mode will look for the differences between the layers. You want a solid laydown of black. That means that where the black occurs the new layer is in perfect synchronization with the previous one. This technique allows for precise positioning. Remember that there is a built-in curvature of your lens that will not allow all portions of the new layer to be in exact sync with the previous layer.

On an image like this I'm particularly interested in lining up the roof line and architectural elements. Foliage is easier to manipulate to work in the image. Once you have shifted the image to fit as well as possible, return to the normal blend mode and add a layer mask. Using black on the mask, paint black until you have successfully blended this image into the one beneath. Do this with each successive image.

Look for the whole thing, the ensemble.
—WILLIAM MERRITT
    CHASE,
    in *William Merritt Chase
    in the Company of Friends,*
    by Ronald G. Pisano
    (1979)

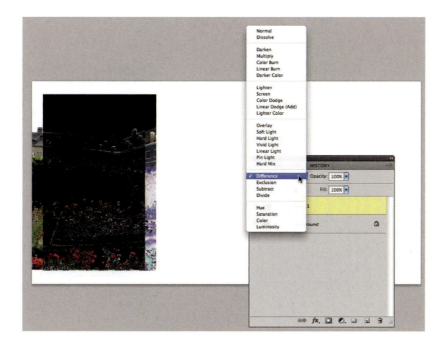

Figure 8-15
Difference blend mode used to line up the images

Set the blend mode to Difference to precisely line up the photographs
After aligning the images, return the blend mode to Normal
Add a layer mask to blend the two images together
Continue to add layers and layer masks for each layer
By using the layer mask, everything you do is reversible. If you were to use the Eraser instead, areas could possibly be lost. Remember, using white restores any areas that you have deleted by using the color black.

Continue this process by adding the next layer. Use the Difference blend mode again for accurate placement of the new layer.

Merge these layers after close examination for any flaws
Continue opening additional photos, in sequence, and repeating the steps listed above
Collapse those layers together and open five or six more photographs that will be added into the composite.

Whatever you can do or dream you can, begin it. Boldness has genius, power and magic in it.
—Johann Wolfgang von Goethe, *Proverbs in Prose* (1819)

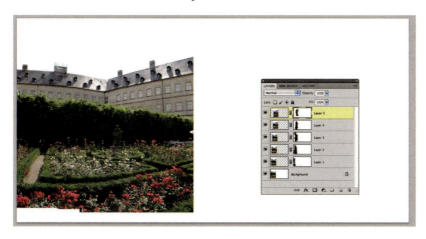

Figure 8-16
Six images stacked together

Figure 8-17
Six more images added

This stair-step effect is due to a slight difference in the position of the camera, as the images were taken without a tripod. Using a tripod would have been helpful. Ground and sky areas can usually be cloned easily, for the sake of size and unity.

> If I have been able to see farther than others, it is because I have stood on the shoulders of giants.
> —Sɪʀ Isaac Newton,
> *Isaac Newton's Papers and Letters* (1958)

Add more canvas, as needed
You can add more canvas by going to Image > Canvas Size again.

A neat trick to add more canvas is to use the Crop Tool. Pull the handle beyond the image in the direction you are going
You can also add more canvas by using the Crop Tool. Select the whole panoramic. Notice the handles on the bounding box. Pull the handle on the right to extend it beyond the image edge. Hit the Return key, and you automatically have additional canvas. It is quick and easy.

I continued to add more layers, each time using a layer mask for blending.

If there are voids in the panorama, such as gaps in the grass or sky area, you can rubber stamp the area to clone more grass or sky or use Content Fill Aware.

The layers were merged and new grass areas were cloned to fill in the empty spots. Cloning in additional sky, grass, and bushes is pretty easy. Some things are not easy at all, like a tangle of tree branches. You will gradually discover what is possible as a convincing clone and what is not.

Crop as needed
Because of our perspective and chosen lens, the buildings do bow quite a bit. You might like that effect, reminiscent of a fish-eye lens. If you want to reduce that exaggeration you can employ the devilishly wicked Liquify filter.

Figure 8-18
Completed panoramic image of Bamburg garden

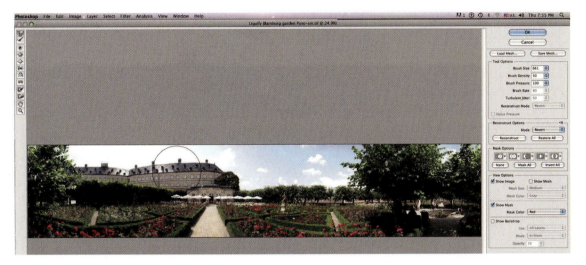

Figure 8-19
Liquify filter modifies the exaggerated bow of the building

Figure 8-20
Modified panoramic

Creating panoramas is like sitting at a movie with a box of popcorn. You can't eat just one piece. One piece leads to another, time and again. Here, you can't wait to see how it will turn out.

Some panoramas will work better if they are not a complete 360 degrees. Usually that determination is made on the spot. That was true of the panoramas shown in Figures 8-33 to 8-37. A distracting background, clutter, and moving people can be some of the many reasons. It is up to you, as the artist, to determine how much you will choose to include in your final panoramic.

These files can become quite large; the garden panoramic was 340 MB in size. Panoramics are generally printed on roll paper, and you may want to reduce the size of the image for printing. Some printers limit their printing length to 40 inches. Consult your printer manual.

Man's environment becomes his mirror. A person comes to know himself by expressing himself.
—JOSEPH CAMPBELL,
The Hero with a Thousand Faces (1949)

Figure 8-21
Venice at dawn (see insert)

Figure 8-22
Pemaquid, Maine (see insert)

Figure 8-23
The Gates, Central Park bridge (see insert)

Figure 8-24
Bryce Canyon, Utah (see insert)

Figure 8-25
Grand Canyon, Arizona (see insert)

Figure 8-26 *Pantheon, Rome, Italy*

Figure 8-27 *Inside the Colosseum, Rome, Italy*

Figure 8-28 *Keukenhof Gardens, the Netherlands*

Figure 8-29 *Small cove in Maine at dusk*

Figure 8-30 *Sepia tone: Cimitiere du Pere Lachaise, Paris, France*

Figure 8-31 *Olympia, Greece*

Figure 8-32 *National Cathedral Wedding, Washington, D.C.*

Figure 8-33
Capri, Italy

Figure 8-34
Outside Colosseum, Rome,
Italy

Figure 8-35
Spanish Steps, Rome, Italy

Figure 8-36
Baltimore Ravens football
game

Figure 8-37
McDaniel College, Maryland

Figure 8-38
Venice at dawn (see pages 430 and 431)

Figure 8-39
Pemaquid, Maine (see pages 430 and 431)

Figure 8-40
The Gates, Central Park NYC bridge (see pages 430 and 431)

Figure 8-41
Bryce Canyon, Utah (see pages 432 and 433)

Figure 8-42
Grand Canyon, Arizona (see pages 432 and 433)

"Grab Shot" Panoramas

Figure 8-43
Individual photos made from a moving car

Occasionally, you may find yourself at a disadvantage in your ability to achieve proximity to your subject. In the case of Figure 8-43, I was in a moving car, traveling through the Scottish Highlands with friends. We had stopped frequently to allow for making photographs, but where would it end? Around each bend we found new and beautiful vistas! Instead of asking the driver for yet another pullover, I simply made these quick grab shots through the window as we were traveling. I never intended to make anything of them. Later, when I was looking through my contact sheets, it occurred to me that a combination of these two images might just work.

In Figure 8-44, those two photos, with different exposure settings, were combined using a layer mask and adjustment layers to correct the color and contrast.

The secret of "Fusion" is the fact that the artist's eye sees in nature … an inexhaustible wealth of tension, rhythms, continuities, and contrasts which can be rendered in line and color; and those are the "internal forms" which the "external forms"—paintings, musical or poetic compositions or any other works of art— express for it.
—SUSANNE K. LANGER, *Mind: An Essay on Human Feeling* (1967–1982)

Figure 8-44
Grab Shot panorama

Figure 8-45
Small Irish panorama

Figure 8-45 is a small panorama made from just six photographs. This small-size panorama could easily be done with Photoshop's Photomerge ability. The photos were taken at the ruins of an Irish castle.

Figure 8-46
Individual photos used in
Figure 8-48

Faux Panoramas

If you are feeling ambitious and want to really stretch your ability to integrate one photo into another, you might try making a faux panorama. Figure 8-47 was created from just eight separate images (Figure 8-48). These were taken from a moving tourist bus on a Scottish island. Although the exposures were not the same, the overcast and sometimes rainy day lent a similar lighting feel to all the pictures. This faux panorama was created from separate photos taken in different places throughout the bus trip. This scene does not exist in reality. It is utterly and completely false.

Figure 8-47
Faux panorama on a Scottish
island

Figure 8-48
Separate photos that were combined

If an image exists in your mind, perhaps you can bring about its creation. I began with the side of the cottage and the clothes hanging out to dry. I blended those together in Figure 8-49. The opacity was lowered on the top layer to accurately place the clothes. The bus I was on had been moving, so my perspective changed. I had fired off several shots in passing. I needed to transform the clothes to make them the right scale. Adjustment layers were used to correct color and contrast.

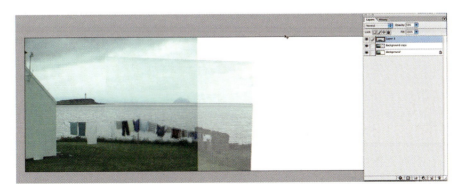

Figure 8-49
Combining clothes on the line

I began to work on the right-hand side of the panorama, adding in a cove and some boats. The image began to take shape as additional layers were added.

Figure 8-50
Adding in a little cove and small boats

There is a right physical size for every idea.
—HENRY MOORE,
The Sculptor's Aims (1966)

The tone in the sky was a big problem above the boats, and a foreground with grass detail was needed for the middle of the panorama.

Figure 8-51
Vegetation added in foreground

Vegetation was brought in using additional photos, shown in Figures 8-52 and 8-53.

Figure 8-52
Hedge row

Figure 8-24
Bryce Canyon, Utah (see page 432)

Figure 8-25
Grand Canyon, Arizona (see page 432)

Figure 8-53
More local vegetation was added from additional photographs

I used the Clone Stamp Tool to clone the sky to even out the tone and color of the sky. I also added one last group of vegetation to complete the composite.

Figure 8-54
Last bit of vegetation is scaled using the Transform command

The completed piece relied heavily on changing the scale of various components and altering the tonal qualities and color balance for an even-looking integration. Although all of these images were made on

Everything is impossible.
And yet ... I have all the
more desire to work.
—Alberto Giacometti,
Alberto Giacometti, by
Peter Selz (1965)

the same day on the same island, it certainly could be possible to construct a faux panorama from various pieces taken around the world. There is no limit to what you can imagine. You could transport an igloo to a desert vista. You could put lions in Central Park. It is simply the horizontal length of this collage that puts it into our discussions on making panoramas. In reality, panoramas are simply another technique for collaging images together.

Themed Panorama-Style Linear Collages

Figure 8-55
A different type of collaging that simply relies on the panoramic format

With the idea of collaging in mind, why not make a long, linear, panoramic-like piece that uses images that are not meant to form a continuum of one particular image? Figure 8-55 illustrates three such pieces. You can throw scale out the window. Close-up details of a sculpture can be used with rural vistas. Here, one image was blended into the next with layer masks. These are fun to put together, especially using favorite photos from a trip, as seen here.

TIP: This type of collage could be used as a ribbon of images that frame a newsletter or magazine article.

The same idea can be used for a collection of family images or bridal photographs, as shown in Figure 8-56.

Figure 8-56
Bridal panoramic collage

Mirror Images in Panoramic Format

Figure 8-57
Icelandic rocks

Figure 8-58
Icelandic vista

There is something fascinating about creating mirror images. Maybe it is the symmetry. They become so much more than just a doubled image. Just double your canvas (Image > Canvas Size). Copy your original image, transform it horizontally, and paste. It is way too easy. Iceland is a place of primal energy and austere beauty, a great place to photograph, indeed.

Hurry-Up Panoramas—Using Photoshop's Photomerge

Photoshop's marvelous Photomerge process can be used to stitch panoramas together. It is especially good for smaller, less complex panoramas. You access Photomerge via File > Automate > Photomerge. Photomerge can also be accessed through Bridge. Simply select the images in Bridge that you want to merge together and use Tools > Photoshop > Photomerge from the menu. Photomerge will open up a new window dedicated to the Photomerge operation.

Auto-Align and Auto-Blend

Another way to approach aligning your images is by using Bridge to go to Tools > Photoshop > Load Files in Photoshop Layers. This puts all the selected photos into one document in Photoshop.

Figure 8-59
Bridge view of panoramic capture shots (Load Files into Photoshop)

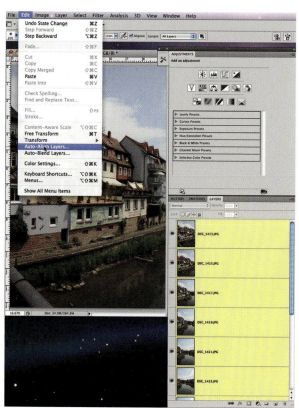

Figure 8-60
Auto-Align Layers

Figure 8-61
Auto-Align Layers choices

From there you can go to Edit > Auto-Align Layers. This will set a process in motion that checks the pixels of one image against the next one, aligning them as precisely as it is able to do. This can save a lot of time when trying to align images together.

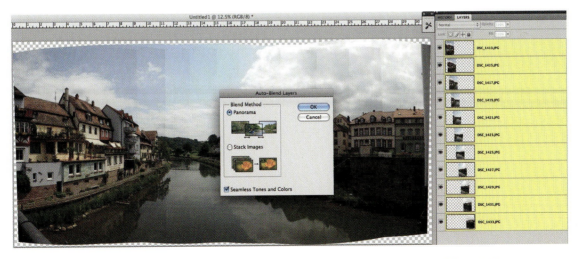

Figure 8-62
Auto-Blend menu

The great use of life is to spend it for something that outlasts it.
—William James, to W. Lutoslawski, November 13, 1900

Once all the images are properly aligned, each on its own layer, you can then use Edit > Auto-Blend. Check Panoramic, not Stack Images (which is used for multiple exposures of different depths of field). Often, this technique will be sufficient to make a very fine panorama.

Figure 8-63
Finished, cropped, and enhanced panoramic image of Wertheim, Germany

This 11-image panoramic was assembled quickly using the Photomerge possibilities in Photoshop. After the blending was completed and I checked for any errors, I cropped the image, and the saturation and contrast were increased.

If you find that streaking happens to your panoramas in Photomerge, try clicking on the box labeled Save as Layers. This will give you more options to correct any flaws that you notice in the resulting panorama.

The resulting panorama will come with all the layers intact and separate. In this technique, you will notice a stair-step feel to the finished image. The Photomerge operation has placed the photo layers for you but has left the blending to you.

It is not always necessary to proceed to the next step, but in this case it would be wise to apply layer masks to each layer. It is a relatively quick process to add a layer mask and quickly paint with black on the mask to blend one layer into the next. The layers have already been placed correctly in the Photomerge operation.

I have far more images than I shall ever be able to do.
—Francis Bacon, in Francis Bacon, by Lorenza Trucchi, translated by John Shepley (1975)

If you have a very large panorama that requires extensive stitching or blending, you could choose to create the panorama in small sections. Try combining the photos in groups of four layers each using Photomerge. These small panoramas can then be combined for a larger image. For large panoramic images with 50 or more photos, doing the panoramic in these smaller subsets allows for quicker production time.

Printing Panoramas

Printing panoramas requires roll paper. There are so many different surfaces available now. You can print on luster, matte, watercolor, gloss, canvas, and more. I often find that I can purchase the odd ends of paper rolls on clearance sale. Short rolls work quite well with this type of image. The images are long, but not very tall. Search for a bargain on your favorite paper surface.

Fractured Panoramas

Figure 8-64
Fractured panorama of Rockport, Maine, harbor

Normally when I'm photographing component parts for a panorama, I want the images to go together seamlessly, as if they were taken in one shot. That is not true in our next example, which I call a fractured panorama. These resemble the photographic collages made by the painter David Hockney. The images vary in tone, color, and scale. There is no attempt to make a seamless sky. Variations in tone can be quite appealing in this type of work. You can almost haphazardly photograph these images, twisting and turning your camera. You can vary the white balance, ISO, shutter speed, and more. You can let the camera make the decisions by setting it on the automatic or program setting. It is a virtual free for all. Have fun with this one. It is stress free.

The master of this type of panoramic work, in my mind, is Pep Ventosa. Check out his work at www.pepventosa.com.

Precision-Oriented Panoramics

The world of panoramic photography is incredibly varied, from precise instrumentation tools for the truly devoted practitioner to a more freewheeling approach. I'll try to touch on the variety of techniques, but to truly understand this field one could write several books, not a chapter. I include panoramic images because I love to make them and in their truest sense they are a collage of many images.

Autopano

Autopano is a wonderful piece of software by the French company Kolor. It allows for planar, cylindrical, or spherical panorama building. It does a fabulous job, precisely creating the panorama accurately and very quickly. It relies on the premise that the photographer has created the photos with a tripod and knowledge of the nodal point in your lens.

You can determine where your particular nodal point is located from your lens manufacturer. The nodal point is also sometimes called the *entrance pupil.* The concept is that the camera should rotate from that nodal point, keeping all photo elements in precise alignment for future stitching.

To achieve this kind of precision you really need to purchase a panoramic head for your tripod. Unfortunately, this kind of precision does not come cheaply. There are some pano heads available that allow you to rotate your camera for a single row of images. There are even pano heads that allow you to tip your lens up or down for several rows of panoramic photographs or simply one that is done from an angle, like looking up in a cityscape, to include the tops of the buildings.

You will also need to carry a small level to keep your tripod and the head level. I would suggest purchasing a simple small cube type with the bubble inside. Some tripods have the level contained on the tripod itself, as do most of the pano heads.

GigaPan

Another interesting approach involves a robotic device mounted on your tripod that holds your camera. GigaPan manufactures three sizes: one for compact digital cameras (Epic), one for a normal DSLR (Epic Pro), and one for a larger point-and-shoot or small DSLR (Epic 100).

This robotic camera mount allows the photographer to take rows and columns of photos that will eventually be stitched with their software. Literally many hundreds of photographs can be used. You can also zoom in for more detailed imagery. If you zoom, you will need to use many, many photographs for the ultimate piece, as you will be gathering many small details. It is actually very simple. You set up your gear and determine what will be your upper left corner and the lower right corner for your panoramic. The robotic gear then takes over, while you enjoy a cup of coffee.

If you have people walking through your image area you may have only their heads, upper torsos, or legs in your stitched panoramic. You may need to return to your original captures to cut and paste or use the Clone Stamp Tool in Photoshop to remedy this issue. The new Content-Aware Fill option in CS5 may be a real help in this task.

Many devotees of this type of panoramic photography are posting their gigantic images online in various forums, sharing their accomplishments. These panoramics are often so huge that they are measured in gigabytes. Many will not fit on a DVD. To print these images, they must be significantly reduced in size.

I would recommend looking at these websites. A fabulous example taken in Paris measures 26 gigapixels. The image contains 2346 single photographs, and you can zoom in on the famous monuments of Paris. When you think that 1 gigapixel is 1 billion pixels, this ambitious project is truly awe-inspiring. It took hours to photograph and was stitched together with Autopano Giga.

Pano Sweep Technology

Figure 8-65
Times Square, New York City

At the other end of the panoramic spectrum is a very exciting technology from Sony. Sony has introduced a Sweep Panorama™ technology in some of its inexpensive point-and-shoot cameras. These cameras can sweep up to 224 degrees horizontally and 154 degrees vertically. The images are processed in camera. The maximum resolution is 7152×1080 for an ultrawide horizontal. That is a 22-MG file, large enough to print at a decent size but not huge. It is fun and easy. You simply stand still and sweep the area with the camera moving. It allows folks with a simple point-and-shoot camera to make panoramics without the aid of a computer, tripod, or special software.

These advances do make you wonder what will become standard issue in upcoming camera designs.

Figure 8-66
Tourist moves through the panoramic, causing repeat fragments

Figure 8-66 illustrates what happens when a moving object—in this case, a tourist—walks through the panoramic area as you scan it. You can only sweep from left to right. Actually, I found this interesting and calculated that there must have been approximately 30 photos in this panoramic. I think photographing motion, dance, etc., could be lots of fun with these panoramic sweep cameras.

Panoramas are quite simply addicting. They present another way of documenting our world. They can be incredibly time consuming and inordinately expensive for precision accuracy, or they can be as quick as a couple-second sweep with a point-and-shoot camera. The choice is yours. Match yourself up with what your patience and budget will permit. They hold an inexplicable fascination. I hope you jump in with both feet and explore your hometown and beyond.

III

Artistic Considerations

9

Filters

Using All the Great Filters Available in Photoshop

Do you remember as a child going to the local carnival or fair? Remember the booth that offered "spin art"? It consisted of a turntable from an old record player, some mustard and catsup squeeze bottles filled with paint, and a piece of tagboard. The concept was a simple one. Anyone could be an artist. You stepped up to the turntable, placed the tagboard on the spindle, and with the board whirling quickly around you proceeded to squirt paint onto the board. You were finished in seconds. *Voilà!* An interesting, random spin pattern emerged, and your art was destined to hang on Mom's refrigerator. It was mindless and fun.

Today we have digital spin art in the name of filters. Don't get me wrong ... filters are fun and many are very useful. Some are really wacky, some are artsy, and some are ridiculous. You need to play with all of them. Explore what they do. Move those dialogue box sliders. Try one on top of another. Change the blend modes. Spend time just playing with filters.

My word of caution is this: Filters do not make photos "art." Putting a photo through a watercolor filter does not make it a watercolor painting. You may just end up with digital spin art. Just because a filter is available doesn't mean that it is right for your image or concept.

When the Macintosh® computer was first introduced, several of my friends and I loosely formed an informal Macintosh Users Group. We pictured ourselves as the brave pioneers. In those early days, everyone got excited about the variety of fonts available. Because most people had never studied typography, they made horrendous mistakes in their written documents. They used so many fonts (in various sizes, bold, italic, underlined, etc.) that the written page looked like a ransom note cut from magazine pages. The sheer joy of using all those fonts and their variations overrode what their eyes were seeing. Filters can be as seductive as those early fonts. Just because they exist doesn't mean that you should use them.

Picture yourself with a large tool belt around your waist. That tool belt contains all those filters, art tools, etc. As a carpenter would pick the right tool for the job, you need to think about the selection of your digital tools. Don't fall in love with a filter and render all your images through it, like meat being pushed through a meat grinder for hamburger. Just because that filter gave you a great effect on one image doesn't mean that it is appropriate for all your images.

With that word of caution declared, let's have fun!

Photoshop ships with a huge variety of plug-in filters. Despite that enormous range of options, there is a market for more filter plug-ins. Various software companies offer more plug-ins that can be added into your Photoshop plug-in folder. On top of that, there are also plug-ins for different edge effects for your images. I've shown you how to make your own edges in Chapters 4 and 5. There are also free shareware filters available online that can be downloaded. The range of options is overwhelming, and more filters are coming on the market every day.

In Chapter 4, we looked at the use of various artistic filters available in Photoshop that could be used alone or in combination for a painterly effect. Some of my favorite filters are the Watercolor, Underpainting, Colored Pencil, and Rough Pastels filters. They tend to have the ability to render brush-like applications of color. And, of course, the art materials available in Painter are virtually endless.

It almost always happens that true, but exaggerated, coloring is more agreeable than absolute coloring.
—MICHEL-EUGÉNE CHEVREUL, *The Principles of Harmony and Contrast of Colors* (1839)

Figure 9-1
Original water lily photo and close-up

Let's start with the original photograph of a water lily on a local pond (Figure 9-1). We will experiment with filter-like effects from both Photoshop and Painter.

Figure 9-2
Painter Watercolor Runny Cloner

In Painter, I cloned the water lily using the Watercolor Runny Cloner, saved it as a Photoshop file, and reopened it in Photoshop. In Photoshop, this runny watercolor version can be used with other filter effects on its own separate layer. (See Chapter 5 for painterly cloning in Painter.)

Figure 9-3
Painter Impressionist Cloner

Figure 9-3 illustrates the use of the Impressionist Cloner in Painter. This was also saved in a Photoshop format and reopened in Photoshop.

Figure 9-4
Photoshop Underpainting filter

Figure 9-4 shows the use of Photoshop's Underpainting filter. Notice in the close-up how this filter affects the edges of objects.

Figure 9-5
Photoshop Find Edges filter

The most impressive edge tool in Photoshop is the Filter > Stylize > Find Edges filter. This tool looks for contrast differences on edges and can give the effect of a pen contour drawing. I used this filter twice for a stronger look.

One becomes in time so sensitive to color harmony that the instant one puts on a false spot of color it *hurts,* like the wrong note in music.
—WILLIAM MERRITT CHASE, in *William Merritt Chase in the Company of Friends,* by Ronald G. Pisano (1979)

Figure 9-6
Finished water lily, made from bits and pieces of all the previous filters and clone effects

The final compilation of all these filters working together is shown in Figure 9-6. It uses a little sampling from each of the filter effects that were applied to the water lily. You can vary the types of filters used in your artwork, and they can come from a variety of software options.

You can combine the filters in Photoshop with cloners in Painter or third-party filters. You are the artist; you decide what is appropriate. Remember, we are selecting how we will make marks. The quality of those marks and how the effect will work with the final image are the important considerations.

Most software will allow you to save and open your image in Photoshop. If you have been consistent in the size of the original image, in every effect or filter that you have used, you can put each version on a separate Photoshop layer and use layer masks on each layer to determine how much of that layer will be used or hidden. If you couple that range of options with the ability to vary the blend modes on each layer, the possibilities become mind boggling.

Favorite Photoshop Filters

Find Edges

Figure 9-7
Using the Filter > Stylize > Find Edges

In the most "commonplace" objects marvelous new realities lie hidden, ordinarily unperceived relationships of forms, new combinations or psychological connotations, new aggregates of symbolic meaning.
—CLARENCE JOHN LAUGHLIN, typescript for a lecture, *Some Observations on the Functions of Photography* (1939)

Select Filter > Stylize > Find Edges
As mentioned earlier, Find Edges is a wonderful filter located under Filter > Stylize in Photoshop (you may recall seeing it in Chapter 4, Figure 4-58). This filter is wonderful to use in connection with another layer or two. It creates a line drawing around the contours of anything that exhibits contrast.

Using the Find Edges filter creates a line drawing everywhere that contrast exists. It is as if you had outlined the edges with a fine-point pen. Some color remains and can even appear somewhat bizarre in tone.

Select Image > Adjustment > Desaturate
I eliminated all color by using Image > Adjustment > Desaturate. This allowed only the line drawing effect to remain.

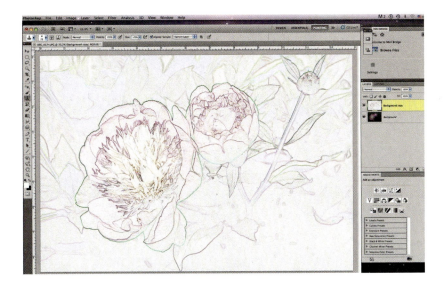

Figure 9-8
Resulting edge effect, maintaining color

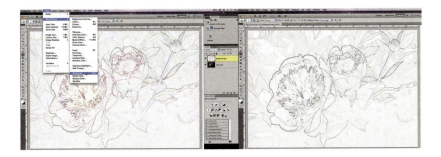

Figure 9-9
Using Desaturate to create a black line drawing effect

Figure 9-10
Increasing the contrast in Curves

The Stylize > Find Edges filter does not have sliders to adjust the line drawing effect. It is sometimes helpful to apply a curve or level adjustment to increase the contrast, allowing mid-tones to drop out.

Figure 9-11
Close-up of the Find Edges layer applied over the original photo

I applied the Multiply blend mode to the Filter > Stylize > Find Edges layer. The Multiply blend mode makes the color white disappear, letting only toned areas show, thus giving a line drawing effect on the photo.

Experiment with blend modes when using filters

Figure 9-12
Original photo taken in Venice

Continuing to experiment with the Find Edges filter takes us to an example that kicks this concept up a notch or two. The original photo was duplicated and the Find Edges command was used to create an outline sketch effect.

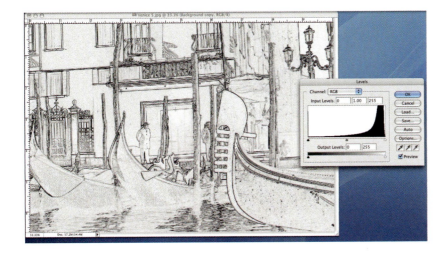

Figure 9-13
Photoshop Filter > Stylize > Find Edges effect taken into Levels adjustment

Select Filter > Stylize > Find Edges
Select Image > Adjustments > Levels
After using the Find Edges filter you may find many small areas that are gray-like whorls of tone. They make the effect appear dirty. The next step is to eliminate those pesky areas.

A clean-looking black-and-white outline sketch was achieved by using a Levels layer adjustment on the Find Edges layer.

Figure 9-14
Find Edges layer applied over the original photo using the Exclusion blend mode

Change the blend mode from Normal to Exclusion
Make a habit of trying out different blend modes. Remember that the blend mode determines how the selected layer will interact with the layer beneath it. I tried several before I arrived at the right one for this image.

Figure 9-15
Find Edges layer applied over the original photo using the Difference blend mode

Set blend mode to Difference
Set blend mode to Linear Burn

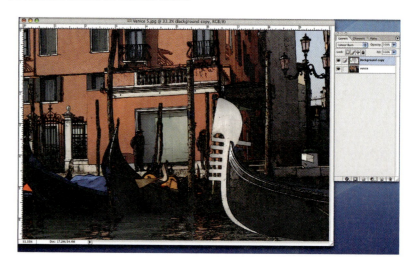

Figure 9-16
Find Edges layer applied over the original photo using Linear Burn blend mode

The great artists …
never really stopped
experimenting. …Titian
continued to use different
techniques until the end of
his long life. Renoir grew
even more experimental as
he grew older.
—KIMON NICOLAÏDES,
    The Natural Way to Draw
    (1941)

Figure 9-17
Find Edges layer applied over the original photo using Overlay blend mode

Set the blend mode to Overlay
The Overlay blend mode appeared to have the most potential for this image.

Add a layer mask for selective effects

Figure 9-18
Layer mask added to fine-tune the edge effect on the photo

Figure 9-19
"Waiting in Venice" completed photo illustration

Isolate and Blur

Figure 9-20
Original color photograph

If you have ever tried to capture children at a wedding, you know the perils and joys that can ensue. Josie, the little flower girl in Figure 9-20, was posing with her parents and young baby brother. As often happens, as the parents struggled to position the baby, little Josie was quietly trying to independently do her part. She was the only redeemable portion of this photo. But why not use her alone? Josie was cropped out onto her own photo page.

Figure 9-21
Completed sepia-toned image of Josie

Crop photo
Select Image > Adjustments > Desaturate
Select Image > Adjustments > Color Balance (to add yellow and red)
Duplicate layer
Create new layer using Filter > Blur > Gaussian Blur
Add a layer mask to allow the crisp photo to appear through the blurred image in selected areas
Paint the background a soft, dark-brown tone

After I cropped the photo and copied it onto a new canvas, the color was converted. First, the photograph was desaturated into a black-and-white image. Next, I applied color back in by adding red and yellow in all three of the tonal areas (highlights, mid-tones, and shadows). I then duplicated that layer and blurred the duplicate layer using the Gaussian Blur filter. This step gave me that soft, ethereal effect on the edges. Josie was a fairy princess that day, in her flower girl role—why not enhance that sense of a magical, romantic moment in time? The original photo was allowed to peep through by using a layer mask on the blurred layer. Finally, the background was painted a soft, dark brown.

The independence or detachment of the creative individual is at the heart of his capacity to take risks and to expose himself to the probability of criticism from his fellows.
—JOHN W. GARDNER,
Self-Renewal: The Individual and the Innovative Society (1963)

Photoshop Photo Filters

Photoshop comes loaded with several photo filters, like the ones you would attach onto your lens. Of course, these are digital ones that you apply after the photograph has been taken. These photo filters resemble the ones you used to attach to the front of your camera lens for colorful effects. Now you do not need to carry all of that gear in your camera bag. We can achieve the effects in our digital darkroom.

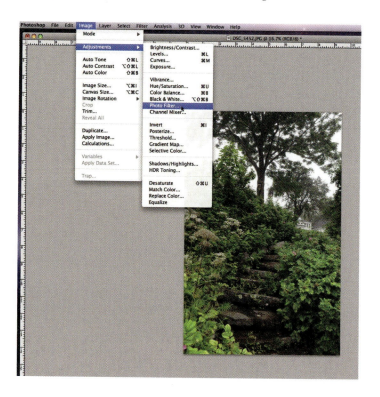

Figure 9-22
Locating Photo Filters

Select Image > Adjustments > Photo Filters

The most commonly used filters here are the warm-tone sepia filters. Just to give you another possibility I chose to use the Underwater filter for this foggy landscape.

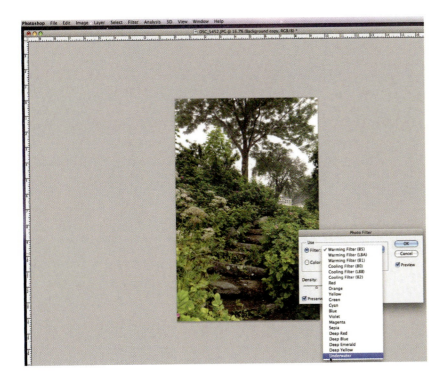

Figure 9-23
Selecting from many filters

Figure 9-24
Underwater Filter selected

I applied the Underwater filter to a copy layer. That layer was sitting on top of the original photo.

Figure 9-25
*Filtered layer masked to
reveal warmer tone steps in
the original capture*

I liked the very cool green and aqua tones but thought a bit of warmth might be nice as an opposite color for a bit of tension. The steps were masked to reveal the warm tones of the stone steps. Personally, I like the mood that this color filter gave to the image. If you use one of these filters on a duplicate layer, remember that you can lower the opacity of that layer to diminish the effect, if you so desire.

Creating a Black-and-White Pencil Sketch Effect Using Filters

If you are artistically challenged and want a pencil sketch feel from a favorite photograph, this is the trick for you. It can be used as a line drawing or in combination with other images. Give it a whirl. It is different than the previous effect of Find Edges.

Figure 9-26
Original photo

Duplicate the background layer twice
Desaturate both layers
On the top layer, apply Image > Adjustments > Invert (it will appear as a negative)
Set the blend mode to Color Dodge. Surprise! The image should now be entirely white!
This is like a magician's hat trick. You will soon be pulling the bunny out of the hat. If you are the kind of person that has to know why this magic happens, think about it. The images have cancelled each other out.

Apply the Gaussian Blur filter to the inverted image
Voilà! The rabbit has come out of the magician's hat! The trick in this step is to disregard the preview window on the Gaussian Blur. Look only at the image itself. Adjust the slider to achieve the look you are after for the sketch.

The supreme misfortune is when theory outstrips performance.
—LEONARDO DA VINCI,
Treatise on Painting
(1651)

Figure 9-27
Gaussian Blur applied

Figure 9-28
Soft pencil sketch effect with Curves used to increase contrast

Add Curves adjustment to create contrast

This young woman was a cheese company employee on a river cruise through Holland. Unfortunately, other passengers were in the rear of the photo.

Figure 9-29
Completed pencil sketch

Background painted with white

To finish this sketch, I painted the background white, eliminating the background distractions. This simple technique is great for turning a photo into a lovely soft pencil sketch that is ideal for portraits.

Nothing great was ever achieved without enthusiasm.
—RALPH WALDO EMERSON,
  Essays: First Series (1841)

There are no days in life so memorable as those which vibrate to some stroke of the imagination.
—RALPH WALDO EMERSON,
  Conduct of Life (1860)

Similar Effects in Photoshop and Painter

Original Photo

PhotoShop Cutout Filter

Painter Woodcut Effect

Figure 9-30
Similar, yet different, effects: original photo, Photoshop Cutout filter, and Painter Woodcut effect

Occasionally you will notice that an effect in Photoshop is similar to one in Painter. Good examples are the similar effects shown in Figure 9-30. I applied the Photoshop Cutout filter to the carousel horse for an effect that resembles silkscreening. A similar effect, Woodcut, is found in Painter. Both effects are great for photo illustration work.

Third-Party Filter Plug-Ins

Many companies offer third-party plug-ins or stand-alone programs with a myriad of filters and edges. You can find most of them on the Internet. Some sites offer free filters. It would be impossible to address all of them in this chapter. I will just provide a brief glimpse at a few of the more popular ones that are on the market. Keep in mind that a snazzy filter does not make up for a poor photograph. Use these filters to create a mood or graphic effect that is appropriate to the photograph that you want to enhance. Be careful not to overdose on filters. They can be seductive and fun, but I've seen some photographers go overboard on these effects, like a child in a candy store with all of their allowance to spend. Try them out. Find the effects that work with your own personal imagery. There are so many options. Have fun with it but maintain your photographic and artistic equilibrium.

Inspiration is to work every day.
—CHARLES BAUDELAIRE, *Epigram* (1860)

Nik® Color Efex Pro™ 3 Filters

Figure 9-31
Original photo of lawn chairs and butterfly nets

One of the most popular third-party plug-in filter offerings is the Nik Color Efex Pro 3. It offers a huge range of filters that simulate the filters that are normally applied directly onto your camera, as well as many unusual special effects filters. The same company also makes a wonderful piece of software that sharpens your images, another that is devoted to black-and-white conversions, and more. The Nik Sharpener Pro™ plug-in modifies the amount of sharpening needed on your image according to your printer and paper types. It can also be brushed on in selective areas.

The idyllic look of the photo shown in Figure 9-31, taken near dusk as children had deserted their bug-catching efforts, suggested nostalgia to me. I wanted a softer, moodier feel for the image. The completed image yielded the look I was aiming for.

Figure 9-32
Nik software interface

Select Filter > Plug-in > Nik Color Efex Pro 3 > Monday Morning Sepia

I love the Monday Morning filter that yields a soft, ethereal, glowy look. You can modify the image effects using sliders. One of the viewing options in the dialogue box of Nik Color Efex Pro allows you to view the image and its corrected version at the same time. This side-by-side comparison is very helpful. Once you press OK on the filter, the effect is rendered on a separate layer with a built-in mask. You can then paint the filter effect in segments of your photo or over the entire image.

Figure 9-33
Filtered layer with mask in place

In Figure 9-33, the mask was painted with black, revealing a bit of the original photo in selected areas of the photograph. A touch of color remained, especially in the butterfly nets, which I liked; however, I wanted a warmer feel, with a stronger sepia effect.

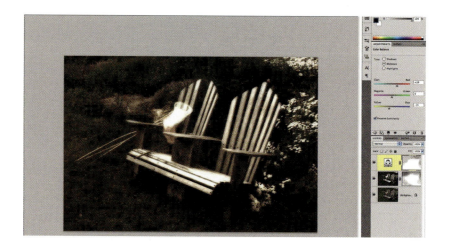

Figure 9-34
Color Balance adjustment layer used for more warmth

Use Adjustment Layer > Color Balance to increase red and yellow
A stronger sepia effect was created by pulling in more reds and yellows.

Figure 9-35
Flattened photo has vignette feel

Flatten all of the layers
Clone out the dirt mound using the Clone Stamp Tool
I added a new layer and with a wide, soft brush set to a low opacity (18%) painted a vignette effect along the edges.

Now for the finishing touches. The image was flattened. The bare mound of dirt beyond the chairs began to bother me so I cloned in more grass, using the Clone Stamp Tool. A new layer was added. A dark brown color was softly painted at a low opacity with a big brush. The blend mode was set to Multiply.

Instinct preceded wisdom.
—GEORGE LILLO,
    Fatal Curiosity (1736)

Figure 9-36
Completed photo

Black-and-White Conversion

Figure 9-37
Original color image of Amish buggy

There are so many ways to convert to black and white that an entire book could be devoted to the topic. There is the standard black-and-white conversion within Photoshop, as well as time-honored, step-by-step procedures in channels or luminance that some photographers prefer. Nik offers a separate piece of software called Silver Efex Pro™. There are also black-and-white options within Color Efex Pro and additional toning filters to push it a step further. The image of the Amish buggy in Figure 9-37 was rather flat in contrast and the color was dull, except for the neon red caution sign that all buggies are required to have on the rear of the carriage.

Figure 9-38
Nik Black and White Tonal Enhancer filter was applied

Apply the Nik Color Efex Pro Black and White Tonal Enhancer filter
The answer to enhancing this image was to convert it to black and white and increase the contrast. There are many options for black-and-white conversion filters among the Nik filters. Again, choose the

one that is right for your image. The Black and White Tonal Enhancer offers different contrast possibilities with sliders for refinement. This filter solves the problem of contrast that usually comes with desaturating a color image.

Figure 9-39
Paper Toner filter applied

Those of you who come from a traditional, wet darkroom background will remember the days when you stocked a variety of paper types, from cool to warm toned. We often added an additional toning bath to achieve our desired tone. This effect is now easily achieved with the Paper Toner filter in Nik Color Efex Pro. Accompanying sliders allow adjustment of the effect and tonal variations.

Figure 9-40
Close-up of caution triangle sign that is a problem and was darkened

My eyes kept being drawn to the triangular traffic caution sign required on the back of all buggies. It was super white because of its reflective nature, and distracting. My first thought was to darken it. I selected the triangular area with the Magic Wand Tool, expanded the selection outward by 1 pixel (Select > Modify > Expand), and shifted the tonal range with a levels adjustment, as seen in Figure 9-40.

Figure 9-41
Sign eliminated

It wasn't enough! So, although it is illegal to do what I picture here, I cloned out the sign for a better overall composition. I'm happier and I doubt we will have any digital photo accidents. It is clear that I'm neither a purist nor a documentary or bust photographer .

Applying Filters Selectively

Figure 9-42
Original photo taken at the doorway of a mosque in Istanbul

Funny thing about painting, you don't know what makes it right but you know when it's wrong.
—CHARLES HAWTHORNE, in *Hawthorne on Painting* (1938)

Sometimes you only want a filter to be applied to a portion of the image, not the entire photograph. The original photograph in Figure 9-42 was inviting, but the color of the rolled-up doorway did not complement the blue rug.

Figure 9-43
*Nik Color Efex Paper Toner
#2 filter applied selectively*

Select the Nik Color Efex Pro Paper Toner #2

My favorite color of toner (Paper Toner #2) was applied to the image, but not everywhere. Using a layer mask and a low opacity on the brush, areas of color were allowed to appear slightly.

Figure 9-44
*Nik Color Efex Pro Indian
Summer filter added
selectively*

Select the Nik Color Efex Pro Indian Summer filter

To warm up the overall look, a second filter (Indian Summer) was applied selectively in some areas, especially the wooden door. Again, a layer mask was used to apply the effect in specific areas only.

Lucis® Pro 6

One of the most exciting pieces of software I've seen in a while is Lucis Pro 6. It was originally designed for scientists to discern more detail from microscopes manufactured by Image Content Technology LLC. It has the uncanny ability to bring out detail in shadows and restore content to areas that are blown out. It is fabulous for emphasizing edge detail. The look of this filter's effects can often resemble a high dynamic range (HDR) image, giving a more illustrative look to a photograph.

The creator of this software has always had a passion for the arts, and she saw how it could be beneficial to photographers. The software is pricey, but the effects are fabulous. Like many pieces of software today, it looks at the edges of things. This software can magically produce shadow detail that you didn't know was there. Conversely, it can restore detail to highlights that I thought were virtually blown out. It loves busy photos with lots of detail.

Figure 9-46
Lucis Pro interface

I usually slide the Enhance Detail slider to the left in a generous manner. You can add the original color back in, which is especially important in any portrait work. It loves wrinkles, stubby beards, etc. It would, unfortunately, make a blemish more pronounced, so it is not for every image.

Figure 9-47
Enhanced Lucis Pro 6 cat

As you can see, it has an illustrative look with a huge jump in detail clarity.

Other Sicilian Photos Enhanced with Lucis Pro 6

Figure 9-48
Sicilian food market in the street

Figure 9-49
Hillside town

It is easy to go overboard with this filter, as it is often so exciting to see how the image will be rendered. I sometimes use it for just a little punch to an image, almost like a little over-sharpening. I'll run the filter and then quickly go to Edit > Fade, to dial in as much of the effect as I want.

In the current version you can even control each channel, giving you loads of control over your image. This filter has become a must-have in my digital toolbox.

The program requires that you plug the supplied dongle into one of your USB ports. The dongle resembles a USB flash drive and is supplied with the software to prevent software piracy. If you are forgetful, order two dongles when you place your order. The program will not run without it.

This filter is particularly good for a grungy kind of look, like men with scruffy beards and wrinkled faces. It is *not* flattering to a bride's

Figure 9-50
Flower stand

complexion, as it reveals every blemish, although it could work very well on the lace of her dress. For this kind of subject, I recommend using a mask to get the best of both worlds, as you can see in Figure 9-55.

Craig's Actions

Craig's Actions were created by Craig Minielly and are included here, as the effects of Actions are similar to running a filter effect. I find that as I travel, teaching workshops, many veteran Photoshop users have never opened or used the Actions menu. That is unfortunate, as Actions can be a speedy and effective way to modify your imagery. Access the Actions menu from the Window menu. As for all third-party software, the manufacturer will give you instructions for installing your new actions on your computer.

Figure 9-51
Before and after using Craig's Actions

There are a ton of actions available. Our example in Figure 9-51 shows the original photo on the left and the Craig's Actions BW Hurrell action version on the right.

Figure 9-52
Craig's Actions menu

In Figure 9-52 you can see the menu interface for Craig's Art Vintage Spot Color action and Craig's Art Illustration action. These actions are well designed and frequently give you instructions and helpful hints as you run the actions. You can also look at all the steps involved in creating the action. Often, adjustment layers and masks are created as the action runs, allowing you to go back into these adjustment layers to modify the action effect. To use an action, simply press on the arrow at the bottom of the menu to "play" the action.

Totally Rad Action Mix

Figure 9-53
Original photo on left and Prettyizer action on the right by Totally Rad Actions
Photo Credit: Rod Lamkey, Jr., for Amy Deputy Photography

Another wonderful collection of actions is the Totally Rad Action Mix. Like Craig's Actions, you can pick the action effect that you desire and run the action on that image, eliminating lots of steps and time. These actions are especially good for studios doing production work.

Our example is the aptly named Prettyizer. It gives a boost in saturation and introduces a smoothness in skin tones. As you can see, when completed, the action sits above the image in a group. This, again, allows you to modify the effect to suit your image.

Figure 9-54
Totally Rad Prettyizer action creates a layer group

Combining Filters and Actions

Figure 9-55
Original shot, Lucis Pro added, and finally Craig's Actions Portrait Warm Extra Soft N on the right

In Figure 9-55, the far left image shows the original bridal shot. The photo background layer was duplicated and Lucis Pro 6 was used on the duplicate layer. Using a mask, I allowed the face area and skin from the background layer to show through. This kept the face and skin clear of detail blemishes and reduced exaggerated noise. The embroidery on the dress was amplified with the use of Lucis Pro. The final image, on the right, was treated with the Craig's Actions Portrait Warm Extra Soft N action. This warmed the shot, in keeping with the setting sun behind the bride. Overall, the photo has more snap and presence, and more detail was revealed on the dress and flowers.

Once you have learned the variety of possibilities available and how they look, through trial and error, you can make good choices for combining various effects. Feel free to combine existing Photoshop filters, third-party filters, and actions. They are all great tools for enhancing your imagery.

Topaz Lab Filters: Adjust 3, Simplify, Clean 2

Figure 9-56
Various versions of Topaz filters, from the top down: Original Photo, Topaz Adjust 3 Spicify, Topaz Simplify Painting Watercolor, Topaz Simplify Cartoon, and Topaz Clean 2 Flat Style

Another very good value is the Topaz Adjust filters. Again, there are many choices here and a variety of software packages. This manufacturer gives you a large preview window and loads of sliders to modify the filters. It is very user friendly. The Spicify filter, like our old friend Lucis Pro, does very interesting things with details, rendering a hyperreal kind of look. The Simplify Painting Watercolor filter provides a good start for digital paintings as it eliminates details and looks at large areas of color, like an underpainting. The Cartoon filter found in the Simplify package is just plain fun. Another good one for an underpainting is Topaz Clean 2's Flat Style filter.

Figure 9-57
Topaz software interface for Topaz Adjust 3 and the Spicify filter

I really appreciate the large preview window and the ability to zoom in on a portion of the image to see what the effect will look like.

Totally Rad Dirty Pictures

Figure 9-58
Bridal portrait original and using Dirty Pictures' Starla Fontaine option
Photo Credit: Amy Deputy, Amy Deputy Photography

Although technically not a filter, the Totally Rad company, mentioned earlier, also makes a plug-in called Dirty Pictures. Don't be looking for any X-rated images here. These are textured images that overlay your image with a blend mode.

Figure 9-59
Dirty Pictures options: Cinnamon Windsor, Johnny Thunderpants, and Starla Fontaine

The user interface allows you to control the strength of the overlaying layer and the blend mode used. When the choice is complete, the effect appears as a group above your image. Feel free to use a mask, as I did, to restore some of the original image. In this photo, the skin and wedding gown were masked to restore them a bit, getting rid of the overlaying marks that were distracting. The control is in your hands. If the overlaying image is depositing debris, weird marks, etc., on a part of the image that is adverse to the overall image, simply use a mask to restore those areas. The funky names of these photo overlays are hilarious in themselves.

Note, if you are so inclined, you can photograph your own textures and apply them over your photographs, varying the blend mode to achieve the desired effect. Personally, I take photos of texture everywhere I go for this option as well as collage possibilities.

Alien Skin Snap Art

Figure 9-60
Original photograph of a Scottish castle entrance

This photo lends itself to a thick application of paint due to those massive stones.

Figure 9-61
The Snap Art option appears in your Filters menu bar and opens the program

I selected Oil Painting as the type of art medium. I duplicated the background layer twice. On the first background copy I used Brush with the small and short strokes option. On the other background copy layer, I applied Landscape with the more color variations option, under Oil Painting. I like to use the split-screen option to view the changes live.

Figure 9-62
Two different renditions of oil painting were used: (left) Landscape, more color variations, and (right) Brush, small and short strokes

I liked the loose and free application of paint on the left side using Landscape, more color variations, but more detail was required in other areas of the painting. The second background copy layer gave us much more detail using Brush with small and short strokes. A combination of the two renditions was what I needed. Nearly all oil paintings have areas that are loose in approach and other sections that are a bit more detailed. That was what I wanted.

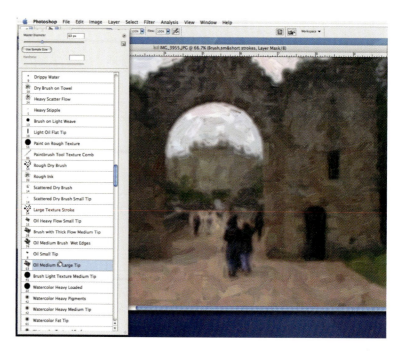

Figure 9-63
Brush selection narrowed down to the Oil Medium to Large Tip brush

To combine these two renditions I needed layer masks. The brush to be used on the layer mask should match the feel of the renditions, so I chose the Oil Medium to Large Tip brush from the Wet Media Brush Library.

Figure 9-64
Stacking order of the layers

The top layer was the rendition using small, short, more detailed strokes. That layer had a Hide All Layer Mask attached. The mask was painted with white, using the oil brush mentioned above. That allowed the more detailed rendition to show through in selected areas. The original background layer remained intact, in case it was needed later.

Figure 9-65
Completed Alien Skin's Snap Art Oil Painting

We could use this image as a completed work or use it as a base for the further digital painting.

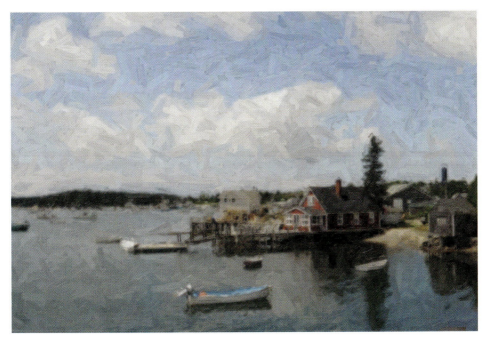

Figure 9-66
Alien Skin's Snap Art oil painting of the harbor at Vinalhaven, Maine

Bokeh

Figure 9-67
Original photo of bullrider and bull

Bokeh is made by Alien Skin and does a wonderful job of selective focus. I most often see it used in connection with portrait work, where the background is thrown out of focus by using this filter in Photoshop. It is wonderfully designed, with lots of sliders and control points for you to manage its usage. In my example of a bullrider being thrown off a bull, the crowd can make the background too busy. I want the viewer to concentrate on the action of the moment, not the entire venue.

Figure 9-68
Bokeh effect

One method might be to use the factory-default oval shape that can yield some selective focus and vignette effects, especially if you are in a hurry.

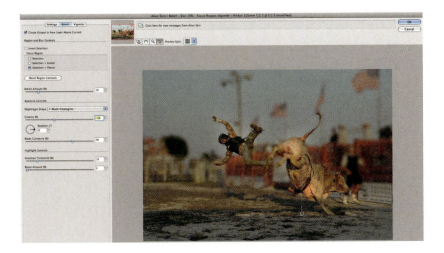

Figure 9-69
Another Bokeh approach

If you have the time to create a selection of your subject—in this case, the bull and the rider, you can give yourself more control over the image. I loaded in my selection and then set the Selection + Planar control points. This allowed the gravel to gradually fade out, and the distracting background. There was one problem apparent to me—the rodeo cowboy, whose job it is to distract the bull and allow the rider a safe exit. He was close enough to have more focus but was not important enough to the general emphasis of the image to be sharper. The answer was to add a layer mask and lightly pull him back in just a little.

Figure 9-70
Completed mask and Bokeh rendition

The completed image used that mask and a small Curves adjustment layer to bring in more contrast and snap.

Exposure 3

Do you hanker for the old days of film? Do you remember how we purchased specific film for its color palette or grain structure? Do you miss those days? If so, you are in luck. Alien Skin has created Exposure 3 for you. You can choose from over 500 options, including cross-processing, Polaroid® films, infrared, and even vintage daguerreotypes.

Figure 9-71
Original photograph, Polaroid Creamy Brown highlights, Color > Golden Hour > Orange More

This software is easy to use, and there are many, many choices of both color and black-and-white film, as well as options for vignetting and a range of exposures and grain.

Figure 9-72
Fuji® Velvia 50 and Kodak® Tri-X 400

I used lots of Velvia 50 for those luscious greens when I was shooting slides. Likewise, good ol' Tri-X was a workhorse of a film and was always in my camera bag. Isn't it nice to revisit these old friends digitally?

It is both impossible and impractical to show you all of the third-party filters and actions currently available. More are being added all the time. My purpose is to highlight a few that I use and to give you a bit of a feel for what is possible. All of these products, and many more, can add to your artistic arsenal. The tools are only valuable if you use them in an intelligent and judicious manner.

In conclusion, filters are fabulous tools that can bring great creativity to your work. But they are tools, like any other. As an artist, you must be the arbitrator of what is appropriate for your imagery. It is important to know your tools well. Know their limitations as well as their positive attributes. Filters can easily be overdone. Try not to fall in love with a filter and use it on your work indiscriminately. Filters work when they truly enhance the image, and only then.

Figure 9-73
"Sara," is a bridal portrait enhanced with the Nik Midnight Sepia filter and Nik Vignette Blur

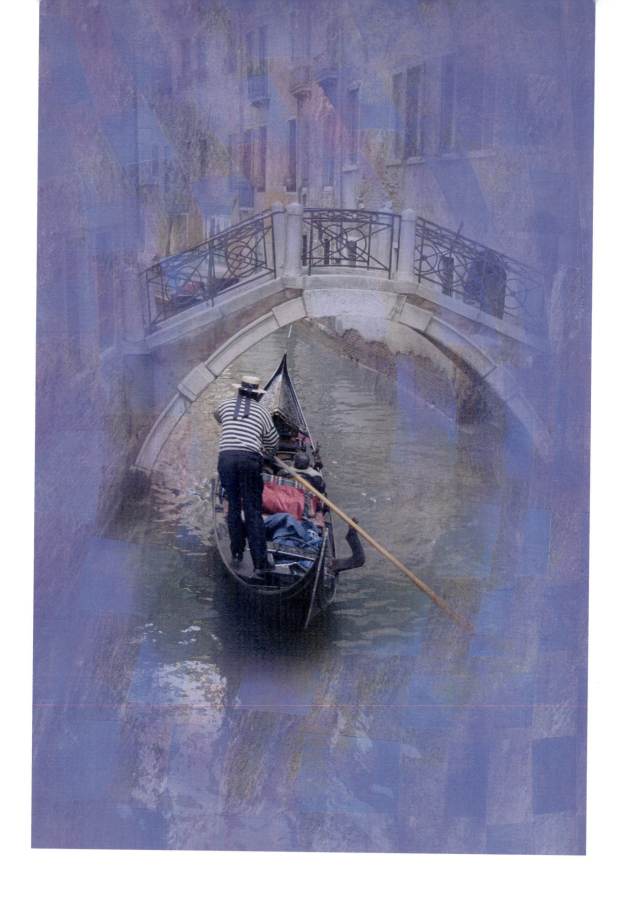

10
Experimentation

Chapter 10 takes the restrictions off where you might go with your digitally produced artwork. There is every opportunity available to combine various media. Some of the artists featured in Chapter 3 employ a variety of traditional art mediums in their digital work.

I would encourage you to keep a scrap bin of discarded prints that can be used for experimentation. Feel free to tear them up and collage them with other elements or draw and paint on them—in short, have fun with the imagery and see where it might lead you. We'll begin by recapping traditional printmaking processes.

Combining Traditional Media with Digital

Printmaking: Woodcuts, Intaglio and Lithography, and Silkscreening

Artists throughout time have been fascinated with the idea of making more than one copy of a piece of art. In the example of an oil painting, only one patron or client can own the work. This exclusivity comes with a high price tag to compensate the artist for his time and talents. Over the centuries, many processes have been developed to allow artists to make multiple copies of their work.

In the woodcut printmaking technique, a design is chiseled or gouged out of a piece of flat wood. The areas to be inked and printed are the remaining sections of the wood that have not been removed. Gauguin used this technique often. A more modern version of this technique uses a piece of linoleum to substitute for the wood. Painter™ offers a technique that resembles a woodcut.

Figure 10-1
Woodcut in Painter

Engravings, or intaglio, are made with a metal plate that is coated with a tar-like substance (to protect the plate). That covering is then scratched with a stylus of some type, revealing a line of bare metal. When the drawing is completed, an acid is applied to etch the drawing into the plate. In turn, the plate is inked, and run through a press that pushes the soft printmaking paper into the inked areas, resulting in a print. Many editions can be made from the plate, as evidenced by the fine engravings by Albrecht Dürer.

The lithography process is similar to the intaglio process, but instead of a plate of metal a thick, flat stone is used. In this technique, the drawing is made directly onto the stone with a greasy pencil. The stone is etched and inked, and an edition is made. A good example is the beautiful art nouveau work of Alphonse Mucha.

Both intaglio and lithography can be made with more than one plate or stone, multiplying the effect. It was also very common in the past to employ artists to handcolor the black-and-white prints. The coloring was sometimes done with stencils for each color added, or with handpainted watercolors.

Other printmaking techniques that have been popular over time include silkscreening, as seen in the work of Toulouse-Lautrec. Modern uses of silkscreen are more confined to T-shirts and mass commercial productions, but the process is still used in artwork today. An example would be the work of Andy Warhol. A separate screen of silk is made into a stencil for each color used in the completed work.

What does all that have to do with digital printing? We are, of course, making prints. We can make multiple copies of our work, creating an edition. We determine how large or small that edition will be. The fewer the copies produced, technically the more rare the print. The more rare print can command a higher price.

Historically, in lithography, after the images had been pulled for an edition, the stone was ground down, removing the drawing and preparing the surface for the next drawing to be made on that stone. In intaglio, the plate was destroyed by slashing through the image area, marring the drawing, or actually melting the metal down. The ethics of the digital artist are perhaps not so clear cut. The master digital file could be destroyed to assure collectors that no more than the stated edition number will be made of that print. The waters get a little muddy when artists make another edition of that image at a different size or on a different type of paper. I will leave it to you and your own personal ethics and business practices to work out a system that works for you and your clients and that is fair to all concerned.

As we are making prints, there is no reason that we cannot make monoprints. *Monoprint* is a term used to describe an image that is only made once.

No person is real until he has been transmitted into a work of art.
—GEORGE BERNARD SHAW,
The Sanity of Art (1908)

Overprinting and Collaging

For our uses in the digital print arena, we can make a drawing on a piece of paper and then feed that drawing through our printer, applying a digital overprint. We could reverse that concept and draw or paint on our digital prints, creating one-of-a-kind artwork. We could apply translucent layers of rice paper or fabric onto our prints. There is no end to the possibilities of digital printmaking, especially if we open our minds to include other art materials.

Encaustics

When you hear the term *encaustics*, think wax. Pigment is joined with wax and damar varnish. Wax, as you know, is affected by heat. Encaustic paints are applied with the use of heat, which can be supplied in a number of ways, from a hot plate to a hand-held heat gun to a tjanting tool (used in the art of batik). And, of course, wax also varies, from white paraffin used to cover jellies in canning to soft, buttery, smooth beeswax. You can even achieve an encaustic effect by using crayons and heat. Heat and wax can be quite dangerous, so always use precautions and have a fire extinguisher handy.

Lazertran onto Marble, Glass, Tile, Fabric, and Silk

Figure 10-2
Lazertran for silk

There are times that you do not want your image to be on paper. You may want the image to be on glass, tile, metal, or marble. What do you do? You can be sure that your warranty would be void if you tried to put a piece of marble or glass through your printer. The answer can be found by putting your image on a material that transfers that piece of art over onto the substrate that you desire. You will in essence be creating a decal. This can be a lot of fun to explore.

A company called Lazertran, based in the United Kingdom, has developed a product that will allow you to put your digital image on all sorts of surfaces. One of their transfer papers goes directly into your inkjet printer; another type relies on the use of a color laser copier. The company also carries separate types of materials for transferring your images onto cloth, including silk, even dark fabric and metal.

Don't try to learn a formula, but to become sensitive, to feel deeply.
—Kimon Nicolaïdes, *The Natural Way to Draw* (1941)

Figure 10-3
Digital images transferred to marble and ceramic tiles

inkAID™—Making Your Own Inkjet Paper

Figure 10-4
Inkjet coated print, using inkAID on charcoal paper

inkAID is a product that allows you to paint an inkjet coating onto your favorite charcoal, watercolor, or drawing papers. Like most artists, I have favorite types of papers that I like to use. Sometimes I want a soft paper with a high rag content; sometimes I prefer a paper with embedded flecks. And, of course, I always look for a paper that is archival, that will resist decay by acid.

In Figure 10-4 shows charcoal paper coated with two coats of inkAID. Use good ventilation and observe the safety precautions listed on the product. I found using inkAID to be quite simple. I allowed time for the applications to dry and then treated the sheet of paper like any other paper going through my printer. Remember, there is no white-colored ink in your inkjet printer, so the lightest areas of your image will be the color of the paper. Choose your image wisely for printing on toned paper. Darker images stand a better chance of making good use of this process.

Golden Artist Colors, Inc., also manufactures an inkjet coating for nonporous surfaces, such as glass and metal, and a gloss and matte digital ground for porous surfaces like papers. These products are also very good.

These inkjet coatings that you apply open up the world to all kinds of printing surfaces. There are tons of artist papers on the market, as well as metal surfaces, fabrics, and more—let your imagination run wild.

Japanese Inkjet Coated Papers

Figure 10-5

Sampler test sheets printed on a variety of Japanese papers

If you like the look of your work on paper that is not the standard inkjet paper offerings, you might like to try some of the exotic Japanese papers offered by Digital Art Supplies that are unique in texture, composition, and transparency. You can purchase a sample pack that has two sheets of each type of paper available. When I get a sample pack of new papers I run a test image on one sheet of each. Your test image should be representative of the type and color of images that you typically make. You might want to include flesh tones, bright colors, and subtle colors or a black-and-white image on your test page. Print that same test page on all of the different types of papers. Does the ink bleed out more on some papers (excessive dot gain)? Do the dark areas block up? Does the texture overwhelm the image? Consider all these factors and more. This will help you decide what paper is best for your needs and imagery. Be sure to label your experiments for future reference.

Moab Paper also has a beautiful line of inkjet coated paper called Moenkopi Washi, which is available in three surfaces (Kozo, Unryu, and Bizan) in both sheets and rolls. Using the rolls, you can create a long, scroll-like image.

. . . .

Thinking Creatively: Paint It, Draw On It, Tear It, Glue It, and More

Add pastels, watercolors, colored pencils, gouache, and more

Figure 10-6
Two photos the same size

For those of you who like to draw and paint with traditional materials, you should feel free to use those materials on your digital prints. Depending on what printer and inks you are using, you may need to spray a protective coating onto the digital print to keep the inks from becoming soluble. An example of a digital print on which drawing and painting have been applied is shown in Figure 5-85.

Figure 10-7
Woven photos

Weave two images together
It is always liberating to experiment. We often consider our art in a way that is too precious. What would happen if we tore it up or cut it into strips? In an experiment, I selected two photos that were the same dimensions. The photo on the left in Figure 10-6 was taken from a boat circling a heather-covered Scottish island. The photo on the right, taken at Pearl Harbor, Hawaii, was of the water above the memorial (the sunken vessel still leaks oil that creates these marvelous rainbow patterns on the water surface). I cut the first image into horizontal strips and the second image into vertical strips and then wove them together.

The most important education you get is your own—the one you learn in solitude.
—ERICA JONG,
  "The Artist as Housewife: The Housewife as Artist," *Ms. Magazine* (October, 1972)

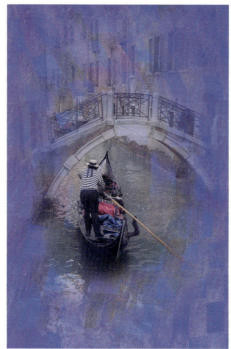

Figure 10-8
Sponge-applied paint in Painter

Figure 10-9
The final image combined the woven image with a straight photo

Art seems to me to be a state of soul, more than anything else. The soul of all is sacred.
—Marc Chagall,
My Life (1922)

Some forms of success are indistinguishable from panic.
—Edgar Degas,
The Notebooks of Edgar Degas, translated by Theodore Reff (1976)

After the photos were woven together, I scanned them on my flatbed scanner. I liked the idea of weaving but wanted to soften the effect a little.

In Painter, apply paint with the Sponge brush
The woven photo scan was opened in Painter and colors of paint were selected and applied with the Sponge brush to soften the look and provide a bit more color continuity.

The completed image was layered together in Photoshop using layer masks. The bottom layer was the straight photo of a gondolier in Venice. The next layer was the woven piece. That layer supplied color and texture. The top layer was a blue tone reduced to 49% opacity and selectively used with the use of a layer mask.

Combining Drawing and Photography

Figure 10-10
Combining drawing of leaves with the actual leaves

I'm fond of experimenting with using several art media together. I'm always looking for new avenues of expression. Figure 10-14 began in such a manner. I found a cluster of leaves on the sidewalk. I decided to draw them and then to photograph the drawing with the actual leaves. On a piece of drawing paper I made a sketch of the leaves with a simple, soft, 4B drawing pencil. I made the drawing in such a way as to allow space for the actual leaves later. I then positioned the leaves on the drawing so that they and their shadows interacted with the drawing. I liked the interplay of the two different ways to capture the leaves. I especially liked how light worked with me compositionally, as the shadows became a design element in both the drawing and the photo.

Talent is habitual facility of execution.
—Ralph Waldo Emerson, *Natural History of Intellect and Other Papers* (1893)

Photo Tex

Photo Tex is a removable adhesive substrate fabric material that can be printed in your inkjet printer. You can attach it to any non-porous flat surface (wood, glass, metal, and more). It can even be used outdoors. The importer says that you can take it down, without damaging the walls. It is reusable and can withstand all weather conditions. How about that for versatility? It is virtually impossible to rip or wrinkle it, and it is waterproof. Retailers are using it for large displays, but what about us artists? I began to think how I might use this material.

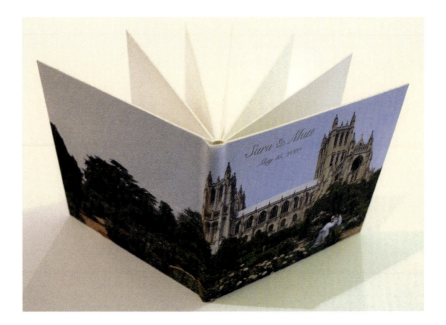

Figure 10-11

Photo Tex used as cover of a blank book

Figure 10-12

Photo Tex used on cradled artist panels
Photo Credit: Amy Deputy Photography

Frankly I was amazed at the fidelity of the colors and the density of the blacks. And, yes, you could easily reposition the photograph. I applied a wedding panoramic image to the cover of a blank board book from the local crafts store (Figure 10-11). Next, I applied photos onto cradled artist panels (Figure 10-12). This approach allows you to create wall groupings.

The cost of framing is often a problem for artists. I've found a home décor outlet store near my home that I browse occasionally looking for frames. The art in the frame is disposable in my mind. I'm looking for framing and matting that I can use. Figure 10-13 is

Figure 10-13
*Photo Tex photograph of
sheep in Iceland in a floating
premade frame*

an example of that. This frame and matte had a free-floating small painting inside. I simply applied my Photo Tex image on top and, *voilà*, instant framed art! If I get tired of that image, I can peel it off and add in another one from my Icelandic adventure.

Creative Use of Papers for Albums

Something is happening now with albums, handmade books, and journals. Paper arts, calligraphy, and handmade books are rising swiftly in popularity. Scrapbooking is a huge hobby and, for some, an art form. I believe that scrapbooking has added to the interest in personalized books that can present visual and verbal information in a unique manner. The publishing industry caught a whiff of this self-publishing trend and now has small book-on-demand printing operations, even at the large publishing houses such as Random House.

A very nice array of companies now offers beautiful album components. The wedding photography business is also changing how companies look at albums. In the past, wedding albums were primarily constructed of pages that had inserted mattes that were die-cut in particular shapes (rectangles, squares, ovals, etc.). Now, brides want photojournalistic photography in addition to the standard portraits. They want those images in a book that is personal to them. Some of the high-end books look like slick coffee-table books. Companies such as Asuka Books (see Chapter 12) create lovely bound books in a variety of sizes on magazine glossy stock. These can be used for weddings or slick-looking portfolios.

The handmade book is being reborn and it is very exciting. The following discussions present a few examples of bookmaking tools that are currently available.

iPhoto® Books

Figure 10-14
Medium-sized, soft-cover iPhoto books

The object isn't to make art, it's to be in that wonderful state which makes art inevitable.
—ROBERT HENRI,
The Art Spirit (1923).

Apple® came out with a book-on-demand service with their iPhoto program, which allows you to download and organize your images, order prints, create slide shows (you can even add music), and publish small books. These books can be soft cover or hard cover. There are four sizes: a little book that is 3.5 × 2.6 inches, a medium-sized book (6 ×8 inches), a large book (8.5 × 11 inches), and an extra-large book (13 × 10 inches). The prices are economical. There are easy templates to follow: You just drag and drop your images into the page format. There is also quite a bit of flexibility to customize a book to your needs.

Epson StoryTeller™ Photo Book Creator Kits

Epson has entered the fray with a kit that comes in two sizes (5 × 7 and 8 × 10 inches). It can be purchased at the super office supply stores. The kit includes Epson high-end premium glossy paper, a

Figure 10-15
Epson StoryTeller book

bound book, software (only for PC, not Mac), and a glossy cover. The books can hold 10 or 20 pages. You print the book, you assemble it. It is easy and very attractive.

Kolo® Albums

Figure 10-16
The Kolo album has a distinctive window in the cover

Everyone wants to understand painting. Why don't they try to understand the song of the birds? Why do they love a night, a flower, everything which surrounds man, without attempting to understand them? Whereas where painting is concerned, they want to understand.
—Pablo Picasso, "Conversation avec Picasso," *Cahiers d'Art* (Vol. 10, No. 10, 1935)

You may have noticed Kolo albums at art supply stores, bookstores, and fine stationers. This company makes a huge array of albums, from itty-bitty, really tiny paperback ones to luxurious leather-bound albums with a post construction. These albums can have inkjet-printed pages (they sell their own brand of double-sided inkjet paper that corresponds to the size of the album selected), scrapbook pages (even the old-fashioned black pages with photo corners), and journal pages. They are versatile for many different needs. They even sell protective sleeves to cover the pages (see Chapter 12).

Blurb Books

Figure 10-17
Blurb book samples

Blurb books have caused quite a sensation in the photo world. Photographers are crafting their own soft- and hard-covered books using the Blurb book templates. Again, they are available in a variety of sizes, and you can upgrade to a premium paper stock. You can even sell your book on their site and apply your own studio logo. These books can be ordered as image wraps, where the photo is the cover, or you can have a separate paper cover that has a French flap around the edges of the book.

Art Leather Books

Art Leather offers a black board book with a black leather cover. The pages have a peel-back adhesive attached. Simply print your pages on whatever photo paper you like and then adhere them in this classy album. You must be a professional photographer to use Art Leather.

Figure 10-18
Classy black leather album

HP® Photo Book

Figure 10-19
Do-it-yourself vacation albums made with the HP Photo Book kit

Hewlett-Packard has a different kind of photo book. This hardcover book, with a window on the cover, pinches shut. A kit contains glossy HP paper, Photo Book software (for Windows only), and the cover. The pinchable cover allows you to add and delete pages easily. The cloth cover is classy and comes in several colors.

Other Album and Book Possibilities

I'm always on the prowl for a neat album cover that I can use with my own "insides." I found lovely wooden-inlay covers at an import shop. They had flimsy plastic pages for inserting 4 × 6-inch photos. I took those out and printed my own pages, customized to the size of the cover. Printing your own albums or books can be a rewarding experience. There are a few tools that you probably will want to have (bone folder, good scissors or knives, archival glue or spray adhesive, etc.). If you print your own, you can choose the paper type, texture, and weight that you prefer. You can even print on double-sided paper for that real book feel.

Figure 10-20

Hinges added to printed page, converting it for album use

Depending on the album or cover that you have chosen, the binding procedure can be a little tricky. Post-bound albums usually work well, but you will notice that the high-end, manufactured pages have a scored bend in the paper to allow the page to lay flat. You can try to mimic that effect by scoring and bending with a bone folder. Another possibility is to try flexible hinge binding strips that are prescored, hole-punched, and archival. These strips come in several popular album sizes. Your paper attaches with the removal of a covering over an adhesive portion of the hinge. These provide a sturdy, archival way to use your favorite papers without physically creasing the paper (see Lineco in Chapter 12).

Handmade books, portfolios, and albums are definitely a practical approach to displaying your digital artwork and a wonderful way to package a body of work. Perhaps you have a collection of photographs taken in parks and gardens or a series of images made abroad. With these options you can create a book for each series of art that you produce. There are just so many materials and options available now—your own coffee-table book is just waiting around the corner.

DASS Film and the Hand-Sanitizer Transfer Method

Artist Bonny Lhotka was waiting in an airport and was bored. She looked at what was in her pocketbook and discovered her hand sanitizer and began to read its label. That was an "ah-ha" moment. She then began to experiment with the idea of using this material to transfer a photo image onto another substrate.

Bonny sells instructional DVDs and supplies through her Digital Art Studio Seminars (DASS™). The website can be found in Chapter 12. One of the many products she sells is DASS Transfer Film. This transparent film is coated for use in an inkjet printer. It comes in sheets or a roll.

Print your photo image on the DASS film. The finished transfer will be a mirror image, so you may need to rotate your image 180 degrees, especially if there is any writing in your image area.

Figure 10-21
Tools for the DASS transfer

Coat your substrate with hand sanitizer, rolling it on evenly with a soft brayer. I especially like to use soft, deckle-edged handmade papers for this technique, but most papers will work fine. I like the paper to be slightly saturated, but not soggy with the sanitizer. Carefully place your DASS film image (ink side down) onto your paper and burnish it. You can use your hand, a bone folder, or even the back of a spoon. Apply some pressure and carefully peel up the DASS film, leaving your image on the paper. The film should be transparent again, having transferred the ink to the new substrate. You will get different effects with different papers, especially textured papers. Disposable gloves are recommended. Always follow the manufacturer's instructions.

Figure 10-22
Composited Sheep rendered in Painter's Woodcut option

Give this technique a try, especially on papers that are virtually impossible to run through your printer. It reminds me a bit of the old days of Polaroid® transfers. Transferring images can be loads of fun.

Printing Tip

Another tip for paper that is too delicate or too small to run through your printer is to use a carrier sheet. The disposable cutting mats sold in grocery stores to use when cutting meats or vegetables are great. They are rigid enough but thin enough to go through most printers. I've used double-stick tape to secure small sheets to the cutting matt and it works like a charm.

Figure 10-22 was constructed from two separate sheep photographs and was primarily rendered with the Painter Woodcut filter.

11

Essential Photoshop® and Painter™ Techniques to Master

Although this book is not meant for absolute beginners in Photoshop and Painter, I realize that you may still need to improve some of your basic skills. What are the essential skills that are necessary to be proficient in these programs? This chapter addresses the most basic techniques that will form the foundation of your digital knowledge base.

If you pare Photoshop down to its barest essentials, it does two things: it allows the selection of an area of pixels to change and then the action that changes those selected pixels. That's it!

Novices are frequently overwhelmed by all the tools and options. What tool should I use and when? The answer is to use the tool most suited to the task at hand. In order to make that determination, you need to be thoroughly acquainted with your options. Be methodical in trying out the tools and making notes to yourself. Keep a notebook

A picture is something which requires as much knavery, trickery, and deceit as the perpetration of a crime. Paint falsely, then add the accent of nature.

—EDGAR DEGAS, in *The Notebooks of Edgar Degas*, translated by Theodore Reff (1976)

next to your computer, and keep notes. Also, buy a few books by the leaders in the field, or go to a workshop for hands-on instruction. Some folks learn best by actually seeing someone do it. You know best how you learn effectively.

My Soapbox Lecture: Another strong recommendation is to set aside a certain number of hours each week to devote to learning this new digital artistic medium. Perhaps a Tuesday evening would work each week. Whatever fits in your schedule is right, whether you can devote three hours or twenty hours a week. Be focused and hold yourself to it. Discipline yourself to hold that time for your digital learning. Too often folks will do some productive work and then let weeks or months slip by, and they forget what they knew. Learning any new discipline requires practice. Compare it to a sport, such as biking. Lance Armstrong didn't pick up a bike and immediately win international races. Practice was required. A concert pianist has spent countless hours learning to play. You, too, need to be serious about learning these new skills and need to be focused in your approach. Success awaits the well-prepared person.

While I'm on my soapbox, I would really recommend taking a drawing class. Learning to draw will teach you so many things. It trains the eye to slow down and be attentive to line, light, shapes, contours, shadows, and more. It is all about seeing and recording what you see, whether it is with a camera or a pencil. Increase your sensitivity to your environment by drawing it and photographing it.

Additionally, while I'm still on this soapbox, I urge you to go to museums regularly. Learn at the feet of the masters. Degas, da Vinci, and van Gogh are no longer here to sit beside you and teach you their techniques, but they left a body of work to speak for them. If you make it a ritual to go to museums regularly, you will be surprised by the inspiration and technical tips you can pick up. Stand in front of a painting in two different ways: close-up, to look at brushwork, and from afar, to see the overall composition and design. From a distance, you can see how the artist decided to use the four edges of the canvas. What was the "crop" used in this piece? How did that aid in the composition? What is the overall color impression? Although we often love a painting for its emotional impact on us, we will stick to basic techniques for the practical lessons. A close-up view can reveal traces of underpainting, layering, glazing, the size of the brushes used, the amount of paint used, the directionality of the strokes, and, most importantly, the colors used. In short, there is a gold mine of tips awaiting you in your local museums.

One more plea for developing your knowledge base is to take art history classes. So much can be learned. A class on the era of Impressionism will teach you so much about color usage. A class devoted to Japanese painting will be sure to affect your sense of design and composition. It is all related. Life is short; learn as much as you can as fast as you can.

I'll step down from the soapbox now to address some of the basic skills you should have tucked into your digital art tool belt.

Photoshop Selection Tools

There are many ways to select an area. The tool you choose to use depends on the nature of the selection at hand. Honestly, it is just common sense. Is the selection a large global one or a tight, precise one? Pick the tool that will do the job.

Figure 11-1
Rectangular and Feathered Rectangular Marquee Tool

Large global selections are most frequently made with the Marquee Tool. The Rectangular Marquee Tool will make a precise rectangular selection. If you feather the selection, you will get a soft edge (the higher the number of pixels that are feathered, the softer and more gradual the edge). If you want a perfectly square selection, hold down the Shift key to constrain the selection to a square.

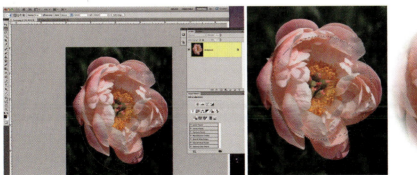

Figure 11-2
Elliptical, Circle, and Feathered Circle Marquee Tool

Nested with the Rectangular Marquee Tool is the Elliptical Marquee Tool. You can make an oval-shaped selection, a circular one (by holding down the Shift key), and a feathered selection. The feathered oval shape is great for the traditional vignette used in portraiture.

Figure 11-3
Lassoed selection

If you need to make an irregularly shaped selection, you can use the Lasso Tool or Magnetic Lasso Tool. It is nearly impossible to make a careful selection in one move. Instead, make a preliminary, rough selection. Then, modify the selection by adding to it (using the Shift key) or deleting from the selection (with the Option key held down). The Magnetic Lasso Tool is really good for this task, also. Simply drag the end of the lasso around the edges of your object. This technique is especially good if your object is different in color or contrast from the surrounding background. It does not work as well if the tones are too similar.

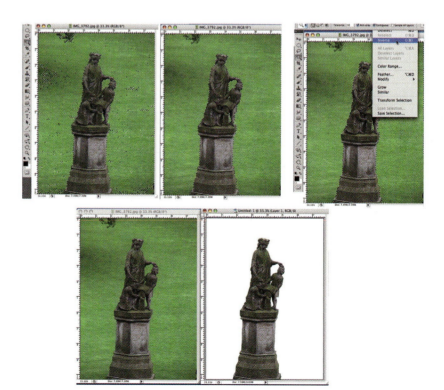

Figure 11-4
Magic Wand Tool with a tolerance of 30, completed selection, and inversed selection

If the background is sufficiently different from the object to be selected, you might decide to use the Magic Wand Tool to make your selection. In our example in Figure 11-4, the background grassy area is sufficiently different from the statue. The tolerance of the Magic Wand Tool was set at 30. That did not quite get all of the area. The missing sections were added to the selection with the help of the Lasso Tool. What was now selected was the grass, not the statue, so the selection was inverted. With the statue selected, it could be easily copied and pasted onto a transparent or white background.

Painting is with me but another word for feeling.
—John Constable,
    letter to John Fisher
    (October 23, 1821)

Figure 11-5
The Quick Mask mode button is located under the foreground/background icons

If it is easier to paint with the Brush Tool, you might choose to use the Quick Mask option to make a selection.

Select the Quick Mask mode (shown in Figure 11-5), and paint with your brush, using black. It will appear red on the screen, simulating the Rubylith™ material used for masking in the printing industry. If you make a mistake, use white to correct it. A soft-edge brush will yield a feathered selection. A hard-edge brush will give you a selection with precise edges. You are actually selecting the area you did not paint. Click back onto the button to return to a normal selection mode.

Photoshop: Transforming for Scale

You will often need to resize an object, especially when you are making a collage. Most likely, the easiest way will be to use the Transform command located under Edit. *NOTE:* Transform will not work on a background layer. You can bypass that dead end by simply giving the background layer any other name. The shortcut is Command (key with apple icon on a Mac) + T. Memorize this shortcut, as you will use it a lot.

A small note of caution here for the perfectionists among you: Transform is a destructive technique and will harm pixels. As a rule, we try to take nondestructive steps so we can easily restore something. Transform will alter the original pixels, but it is a perfect tool for this particular job and we love it nonetheless.

Figures 11-6 through 11-11 demonstrate a simple exercise for working with layers and Transform.

Figure 11-6

Component parts for our scale exercise

This project began with a shred of old foreign currency bought at an antique market and two scans of seashells. I had the idea to incorporate the long shell as a framing device and use the cross-cut shell as a kind of headdress for the woman on the currency. As the project evolved, more fine-tuning was done.

Figure 11-7

Long shell added

Place long shell on a new layer

The long shell was moved over onto the currency fragment. It occupies another layer. You can use the Move Tool to drag the shell onto the currency image (easiest) or copy and paste it.

Figure 11-8
Long shell rotated and resized

Go to Edit > Transform
Using the Edit > Transform command, I rotated the shell and scaled it smaller. If you want to keep the proportions the same, hold down on the Shift key as you transform.

Figure 11-9
Second long shell added on third layer

Duplicate the shell layer by dragging that layer icon to the new layer icon at the bottom of the Layers palette
Flip horizontally

I duplicated the shell layer by dragging that layer icon to the new layer icon at the bottom of the Layers palette. The new shell was then transformed by being flipped horizontally.

Figure 11-10
More shells added

Create two more layers and rotate the shells to create a frame

I added two more shell layers, rotating and flipping them vertically to complete the framing effect.

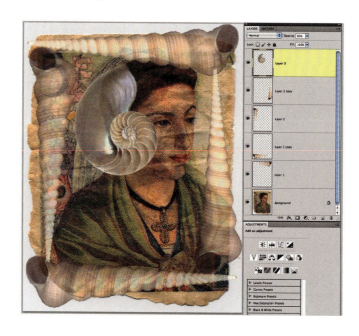

You know a painting is finished when it no longer says, "Do something." Do something different, change that color. If it sits there mute, leave it alone.
—BERNARD ARNEST, in *Colorado Springs Gazette Telegraph* (April 28, 1984)

Figure 11-11
Cross-cut nautilus shell added

Add, rotate, and scale a new shell

Use Transform to slant the new shell in its Distort version

The round cross-cut shell was added on yet another layer. I used Transform to rotate, scale, and distort it.

Adjust opacity on each layer

The long shells were each set at 68% opacity. The cross-cut shell was set at 83%.

Learning to routinely use Transform is an essential collaging skill. Remember that each layer has its own ability to be opaque or some value of transparent. Also, every layer can use a blend mode, altering how it will interact with the layer beneath it. These are all powerful tools.

Photoshop: Layer Adjustments

Figure 11-12
Adjustment Layer icons

There are three locations where you might select a layer adjustment. One is located under Image > Adjustments (in the top menu bar). If you use this method, the adjustment cannot be changed much later in the process. If, however, you choose the symbol that looks like a yin–yang, at the bottom of the Layers palette, you can always go back and change the adjustment later. Another access area is the icon palette for Layer Adjustments.

The Levels adjustment layer is helpful in describing the file. A histogram tells you where the pixels are located. On the left you have

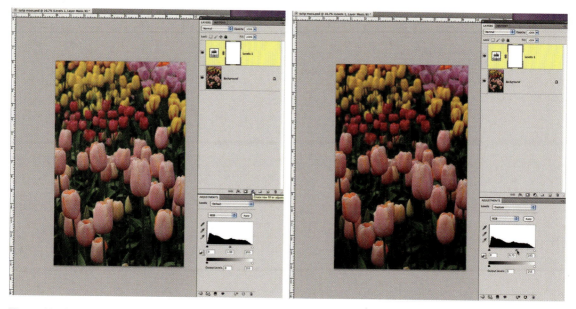

Figure 11-13
Levels adjustment layer

solid black, and on the right is solid white. The middle slider indicates middle tones. The pixels in the photo are represented by the black mounds in the histogram. This allows you to see how the pixels are distributed tonally in your photo. You can see that by moving the middle slider to the right, I created more dark pixels. You can easily shift the overall tonality of the image.

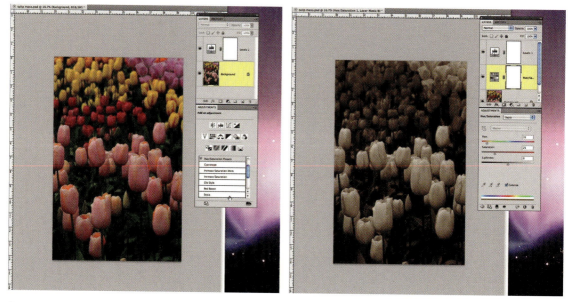

Figure 11-14
Hue/Saturation preset: Sepia

Using the list located under the adjustment icons, you will discover lists that expand. Illustrated here is the Sepia option listed under the Hue/Saturation presets. This is a quick way to apply a preset. The Channels palette, with sliders, lets you customize the conversion.

Nothing in life just happens … you have to have the stamina to meet the obstacles and overcome them, to struggle.
—GOLDA MEIR,
My Life (1975)

Figure 11-15
Maximum White in the Black and White preset assortment

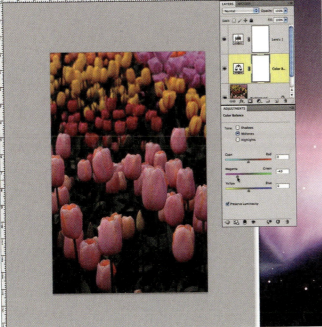

Figure 11-16
Color Balance adjustment layer

The Color Balance adjustment layer allows you to change the color tone in the highlights, mid-tones, and shadow areas of a photo. In our example, the image was pushed toward magenta in the mid-tones, drastically changing the image.

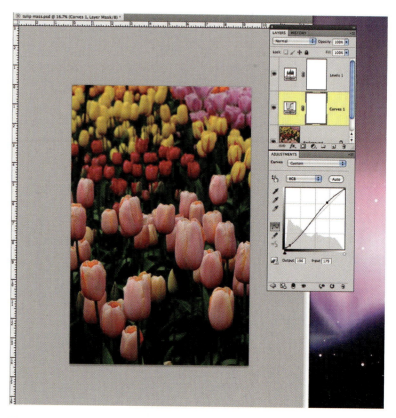

Figure 11-17
Curves adjustment layer

Curves is one of my favorite adjustment layers. Like Levels, it displays a histogram, illustrating the distribution pattern of pixels in your photograph. Again, you can move the black-and-white sliders at the bottom. However, greater modification occurs when you select a point on the diagonal line and nudge it up or down, changing the tonal range. If you introduce an S curve, like our example Figure 11-17, you automatically increase contrast. You are deepening the blacks and increasing the highlights, creating contrast. If you make a mistake, don't despair. You can pull outward on the dot, like snapping a rubberband, and it will restore the default setting.

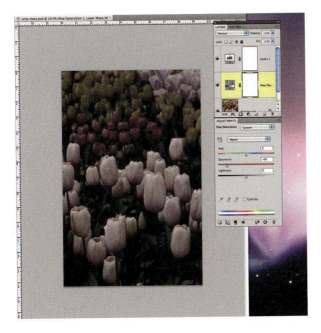

Figure 11-18
*Hue and Saturation
adjustment*

In Figure 11-18, the Saturation slider has been moved into negative numbers, creating a more subdued look, similar to a hand-colored image.

Figure 11-19
*Hue slider severely changes
the color*

Still using the Hue/Saturation adjustment layer, the Hue slider completely changes the look of the photo by changing the Hue. You may notice that we are working on the "Master." You can also modify each channel individually.

Photoshop: Layer Masks

I often say to my students, "Layer masks are your friend." I use a layer mask on almost every project that I work on. For some unknown reason, this technique seems to be the least understood of all the basic skills. Make the effort to understand layer masks and you will be amazed at how wonderful they are.

Figure 11-20
Base image of Civil War re-enactors

When love and skill work together, expect a masterpiece.
—John Ruskin (1819–1900)

Think of a layer mask as a way of blending one image into another, with spot precision. With a layer mask, you can choose to reveal or conceal any portion of the layer beneath. For this exercise, we will use a photo shot at a Civil War re-enactment event as our background image. The intent is to give a vintage, distressed look to the image.

Figure 11-21
Scan of coffee-stained paper

Scan a textured paper

The watercolor paper shown in Figure 11-21 was stained with coffee, and I supplemented the color with pastels. Use your imagination to create a library of textural images that you can use in your collage work. Experiment!

Figure 11-22
Coffee-stained paper added to base image

Add the coffee-stained image on top of the base Civil War image

Because we have no sense of appropriate scale for a stain, it was easy to Free Transform the stain to fill up the whole page, stretching the stain layer. The blend mode was set to Overlay.

Figure 11-23
Curves adjustment layer added

Use Curves adjustment layer to increase contrast

Figure 11-24
Clipping Mask applied

To confine the Curves adjustment layer to *only* the coffee stain layer, apply a clipping mask
That little downward-pointing arrow on the adjustment layer indicates that it is only affecting the layer directly beneath it, not the entire layer stack.

Figure 11-25
New layer added at the bottom of the stack and a layer mask applied to the coffee stain layer

Place a new layer under the Civil War re-enactors and fill it in with brown
Lower the re-enactor layer opacity to 68%

I added a layer mask to the coffee-stain layer. Masks can be obtained from the bottom of the Layers palette. It is the symbol that looks like a circle inside a rectangle. I lightly painted that mask with black, using a soft brush at a low opacity. This helped reveal the women a bit more, but still left a distressed look.

Keep in mind that masking is a nondestructive process. It does not harm or eliminate any pixels. Anywhere that you paint with black on a white layer mask reveals what is underneath. If you paint at 100% opacity you will have visually restored whatever lies beneath your black marks. If you use a black brush with a light opacity, you only partially restore the image, allowing both areas to be seen.

Figure 11-26
Vignetting added

Place another layer on top of the layer stack

I painted this layer lightly with a dark brown color at a low opacity. Because I used a large, soft brush, the paint also fell on the women. To restore them, I used another mask. The darkened edges help direct the viewer's eye to the women and subdue the vegetation.

The final touch was to add another layer on top, set to the Multiply blend mode. The final layer was a handwritten poem from that era that I scanned in.

Figure 11-27
Completed vintage look collage

Good painting is like good cooking; it can be tasted, but not explained.
—MAURICE DE VLAMINCK
On Painting (c. 1901)

Photoshop: Art History Brush Tool

The Art History Brush Tool allows you to lay down the pixels from your photo in a unique manner, depending on the brush you have selected.

Figure 11-28
Original photo

Open your photo

Figure 11-29
Dab brush style used with a 21 pixel brush (left) and 90 pixel brush (right)

Select a new layer
Fill the new layer with white (Edit > Fill)
Select the Art History Brush Tool (icon with a curly-cue top, bundled with the History Brush Tool)
Under Style (in the top modifier menu bar), select Dab

Figure 11-29 shows the use of brush sizes 21 and 90. There are lots of different brush styles to choose from; some effects resemble strands of lint from your clothes dryer—try them out. They are quite simply wild!

Figure 11-30
Painting created using Art History Brush Tool with Dab method and the Fuzzy Cluster Loose brush from size 20 to size 200 pixels

It seems to work best if you pick a large brush first, laying in an underpainting, then progress to smaller sizes for more detail. Whether you choose the Dab method or the Tight short, you can choose from the huge range of brushes that Photoshop offers.

Build Your Own Brush

Although there are loads of great brushes available to you, you can make more and it is easy.

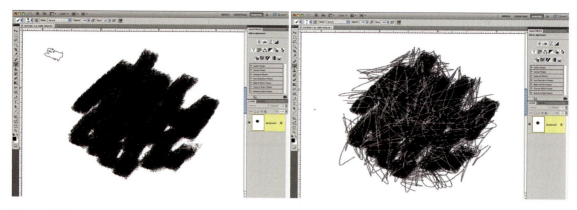

Figure 11-31
Making marks to construct a new brush preset

Make marks on a white layer to simulate the effect you want your brush to have

I wanted a rough-edged, scratchy brush. I started with the Pastel on Charcoal Paper brush, loaded with black. This brush creates a look of skipping over raised, bumpy-textured paper. I used large brush strokes at first, followed by helter-skelter small marks with black and white.

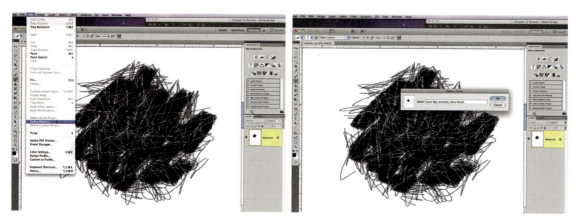

Figure 11-32
Creating a Brush Preset

My voyages have been in my work and in my so-called reality. I have the world, right here, "in my own backyard." And truly I don't need anything else. There is so much work to be done that I can move an inch and circle the world.
—LOUISE NEVELSON,
   Dawns and Dusks:
   Conversations with Diana
   MacKown (1976)

Simply go to Edit > Define Brush Preset

Name your brush; mine is Sue's Big, Scratchy, Hairy Brush 1. It is 828 pixels large—super big. You can always reduce it down in size.

Your very own personalized brush will appear at the bottom of the brush menu. Doesn't that make you want to make more brushes?

Let's use that scratchy brush on an Art History Brush Tool painting.

Use the large brush to establish the scratchy edges that you desire for your artwork. It is way too big to create any detail, though, so simply lower the brush size. The smaller the brush that you use, the more detail that will appear.

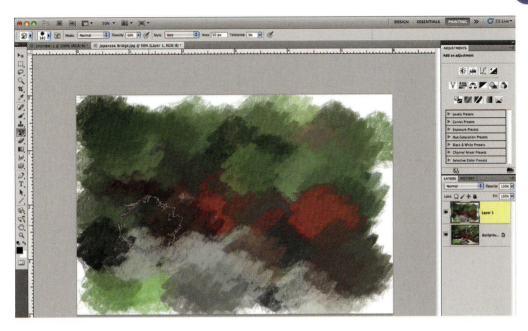

Figure 11-33
Large scratchy brush used to lay down colors

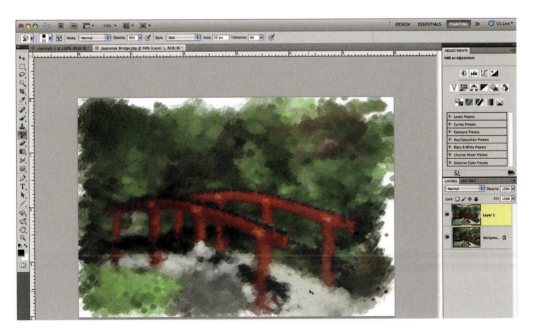

Figure 11-34
Lower the size of the brush to bring in details

Use a smaller brush to bring out more detail. It will still be somewhat clumpy, because it is a Dab stroke. The colors will be more true to the original photo, because the brush is smaller and isn't sampling a larger area. You are laying deposits of colored pixels.

The study of what is excellent is food for the mind and body.

—LEONARDO DA VINCI,
Treatise on Painting (1651)

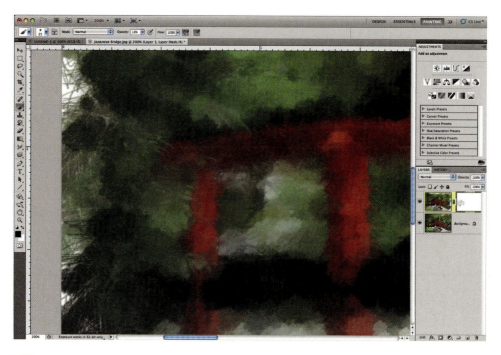

Figure 11-35
Detail of the painting, bringing in some leaves using a layer mask

Add a layer mask if you want more detail

If the image does not have enough detail for you, use a layer mask on your painted layer, and with a light opacity black brush stroke back some details from the original into your painting.

Figure 11-36
Art History Brush Tool painting

Figure 11-37
Accent Colors added on a new layer

If you want to add some additional color accents, as we did, add another layer, setting its blend mode to Color
With a light opacity brush, paint in your color accents. It is like glazing additional color on an oil painting.

    NOTE: The regular History Brush Tool was described in Chapter 4.

Sculpture is the art of the hole and the lump.
—Auguste Rodin,
  in *Art by Auguste Rodin*,
  translated by Paul Gsell
  (1912)

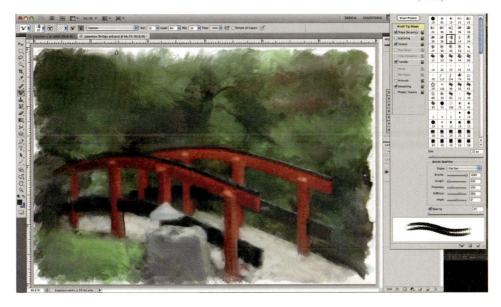

Figure 11-38
New Mixer Brush Tool blends and pushes paint around

If you want to continue you can move onto the new Mixer Brush Tool, described in Chapter 4. We used the Cloner mode here.

Figure 11-39
Completed painting

We painted out the rock and path lighting cone with the Mixer Brush Tool, loading it with a variety of colors depending on where we were painting.

Photoshop: Blend Modes

I know folks who have worked with Photoshop for years and have never taken the blend mode off the default, normal setting. Strange, but true. Blend modes are powerful ways to determine how two layers will interact. There are loads of blend modes. You need to have a minimum of two layers to use blend modes. I'll discuss the ones that I use most frequently.

Screen

Screen is absolutely invaluable! A quick fix for an underexposed photo is to duplicate the image and set the blend mode on Screen. It feels like you used a fill flash.

Multiply

Multiply is a very versatile blend mode. In this mode, white disappears. The line art of the fish in Figure 11-41 was placed on top of the aerial photo. It is a bit of a pun on flying fish. The white background of the line art magically disappeared.

Figure 11-40
*Underexposed image lightened
with the Screen blend mode*

Figure 11-41
*Multiply blend mode makes
white disappear*

If you have a photo that is overexposed (too light), simply duplicate the image and set the blend mode to Multiply. *Voilà!* If the effect is
too strong, just lower the opacity of the duplicate layer. This trick may

increase your saturation a little and it may have to be reduced separately. Multiply and Screen are opposites in the world of blend modes.

Color

Figure 11-42
Color blend mode used to hand color

Color is the ideal blend mode to use for handcoloring. It will work on every area that is not pure white. Handcoloring is performed on a separate transparent layer, where corrections can be made without altering the actual photograph. Color will appear on any area that is not pure white.

Overlay

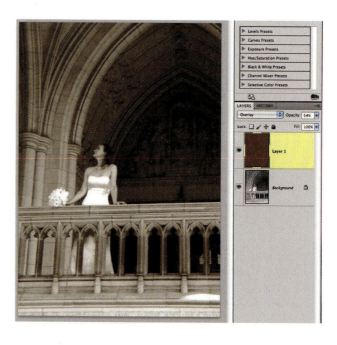

Figure 11-43
Sepia effect using Overlay blend mode

The Overlay blend mode is a great way to make consistent sepia-toned prints, and it is so easy. Select a black-and-white photo that is an RGB or CMYK image, not a grayscale image. It must have color channels to work with the color we will add.

Select a shade of brown that you like, and use it to fill a new layer
Often the tone is too much. To tone it down, just lower the opacity. The color will not affect pure white at all.

Reduce opacity to 40% on the Overlay layer
If you write down the numbers for the fill color (in this case, Red 241, Green 155, and Blue 71) and use it exclusively, you will have consistent sepia-toned prints. *HINT*: You could write an action for this task if you repeat it frequently.

Photoshop: Using Adjustment Layers, Layer Masks, and Blend Modes Together

Since we have just learned some uses for blend modes and a little layer masking, let's take these techniques out for a spin.

Figure 11-44
Original tombstone image

I was touched when walking through a New England cemetery to spot the simple tombstone of a young mother who had been preceded in death by two young daughters. The gesture of the hand holding a rose in full bloom was symbolic and tender. Upon looking at the image later, I thought I should bring the flower to life, using a real rose.

Things are not difficult to make; what is difficult is to put oneself in a state to make them.
—Constantin Brancusi, in *Brancusi: A Study of the Sculpture,* by Sidney Geist (1968)

Figure 11-45
Curves and Hue/Saturation adjustment layer used to increase contrast and change color cast

We need no instincts but
our own.
—Jean La Fontaine,
Fables de La Fontaine
(1664)

Add a Curves adjustment layer for contrast

The photograph was flat tonally, as it had been taken in heavy shade. A slight S-curve was added with a Curves adjustment layer to increase the contrast.

Add a Hue/Saturation adjustment layer to warm up the image

Figure 11-46
Rose added

Add a photo of a real red rose

Figure 11-47
*Hue and Saturation
adjustment layer lowers the
saturation*

The rose was a bit too bright for the entire image.

**Add a Hue/Saturation adjustment layer confined to the rose layer by
introducing a clipping mask**
The saturation on the rose was lowered to a softer tone, but the color
was still not correct for the overall image, so I shifted the hue.

Art happens—no hovel is
safe from it, no prince may
depend upon it, the vastest
intelligence cannot bring
it about.
—James Abbott McNeill
    Whistler, *The Gentle Art
    of Making Enemies* (1890)

Figure 11-48
*Soft green tones handcolored
on a new layer*

Add a new transparent layer with the blend mode set to Color
Select various shades of green and paint onto the new layer with a
low-opacity brush
In an effort to tie the sculptural relief on the stone to the rose layer, the
leaves and vines were handcolored.

Figure 11-49
Shadow added under the rose

Beauty is the sense of life
and the awe one has in its
presence.
—Willa Cather,
   Song of the Lark (1915)

Add a new layer for a slight shadow under the rose layer; paint a
brownish-gray color onto the new layer to create a shadow

Editing Your Images: Retouching—Cover-Girl Skin, Brightening Teeth
and Eyes
Retouching can be a great way to put your Photoshop skills to good
use. Our example (Figure 11-50) features a bridesmaid, my daughter,
Emily, at age 25, photographed in natural light under the edge of a
pavilion.

Although Emily was still quite young, several summers of working
as a lifeguard had taken a toll on her skin. She has, in this photo, light
lines on her forehead and wrinkling near her eyes. Retouching will
even out the skin tone.

Select the area you would like to correct with the Spot Healing
brush
This is such a fabulous tool! It is so much easier than matching up skin
tones using the Rubber Stamp Tool.

Figure 11-50
Before and after retouching

Figure 11-51
Spot Healing brush used on the forehead wrinkles

Use the Patch Tool on darker areas under the eyes
There was too much of a difference, so I used Edit > Fade to restore some of the original.

Remember, you don't want to eliminate the natural lines of the face, just lessen their impact. You still want the image to look like the person, just a bit more refreshed.

The sense of the beautiful is God's best gift to the human soul.
—WILLIAM HENRY HUDSON,
Green Mansions (1937)

Figure 11-52
Patch tool used

Figure 11-53
Working on the teeth and eyes

Lasso the teeth with a feather of 2
Use a Curves adjustment layer to brighten the teeth—apply a Clipping mask.
Teeth whitening is all the rage. In this case, it didn't cost a penny. I simply lightened Emily's teeth using a Curves adjustment layer.

Lighten the whites of the eyes, just a little, using that same process
Use a mask to blend in the eyelids, which were captured in the eye layer
No matter how rested you are, the whites of your eyes can appear bloodshot and too dark. We can help them out by adding a little sparkle to the image.

The image is perfectly good now, but if you want to go for the flawless cover-girl look, proceed to the next step.

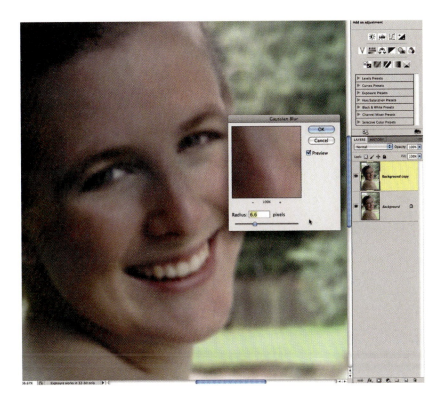

Figure 11-54
Gaussian Blur used for perfect, blemishless skin tones

Flatten the image
Duplicate the image
Apply a Gaussian Blur filter to the copy layer

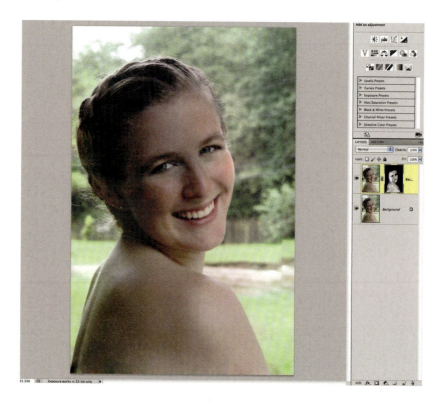

Figure 11-55
Gaussian Blur layer added to base image

Move the slider until all if the blemishes, freckles, etc., are gone
Choose Add Layer Mask > Hide All (an all black one) to bring paint into the soft, blurred complexion where needed
Keep the detail in the eyes, lips, hair, edge of nose, edge of face, etc. This leaves the face blemish free and flawless. If it is too flawless, just lower the opacity on that layer. The foliage in the background was already out of focus and didn't need to be altered.

A side-by-side comparison of the close-ups (Figure 11-50) reveals the difference that retouching techniques can make.

Painter Basic Papers

A wonderful tool in Painter gives you the ability to simulate various paper textures. These textures can enrich your artwork. Try them out and see what works for your imagery. Figure 11-56 shows a few.

Paper textures vary in different versions of Painter. You can import old textures and create new ones. The paper texture can really affect the look of your artwork, depending on which art medium was used.

Figure 11-56
Paper choices in Painter

Figure 11-57
How each paper affects the look of the artwork (left to right): Artists Rough Paper, Sandy Pastel Paper, Retro Fabric, Wood Grain, Coarse Cotton Canvas, Pebble Board, and French Watercolor Paper

Painter Cloner Brushes

Some of the most important tools for a photographer in Painter are the Cloner brushes. Each one handles color, saturation, and dispersal of the pigment in a different way. Some Cloner brushes increase the color saturation; some let the pigment actually run. Try them out, vary them—they can be used successfully in combination.

Figure 11-58 shows the effects of the following Painter Cloner brushes.

Cloning without a Cloner Brush

Although most users of Painter will only use the existing Cloner brushes to clone a photo, don't stop there. The painting in Figure 11-62 was achieved with a brush that was not a Cloner. You can make other brushes become Cloner brushes by selecting the cloning option (looks like a Rubber Stamp Tool) in the Color Picker. Follow along on the steps that were used to create this painting of geraniums in a windowsill.

Choose File > Clone
Choose Select All > Delete

Figure 11-58
Various Cloner brushes

A	Coarse Spray Cloner
B	Camel Oil Cloner
C	Impressionist Cloner
D	Watercolor Wash
E	Thick Bristle Cloner
F	Furry Cloner
G	Graffiti Cloner
H	Fiber Cloner
I	Flat Impasto Cloner
J	Straight Cloner
K	Van Gogh Cloner
L	Melt Cloner
H	Soft Cloner
N	Oil Brush Cloner
O	Watercolor Run Cloner
P	Cloner Spray

Figure 11-59
Clone the photo

Figure 11-60
Oils > Thick Wet Oils 30 fat brush

When working from an existing photo, open the photo in Painter and choose File > Clone. From there, choose Select All and delete the image. This appears to leave a blank page. It seems counterintuitive. Simply click on the box at the upper right-hand top edge of the image and you will see your original image through a faux layer of tissue paper. Another (faster) way to achieve this is to go to File > Quick Clone.

Choose Oils > Thick Wet Oils 30
Select the Cloning option in the Color Picker palette
Paint the entire canvas with a large, thick brush
A good way to see your composition more clearly is to paint initially with a large, thick brush. This allows you to better visualize the large blocks of color, contrast, and organizational design.

A little smaller brush (#16) was used to bring a bit more detail into the piece. Next, I added a new layer and lightly applied blue to the upper windowpanes with the Oils > Glazing Round brush set at a very low opacity. This increased the blue color saturation in the upper portions of the window.

This painting was deliberately kept loose with its wet oil brush strokes. Many of the Painter brushes will work for you as cloners, if you use the Cloner tool in the Color Picker palette. The options available to you are quite simply staggering.

Figure 11-61
Close-up of loose brush work with the Thick Wet Oils 30 brush

Figure 11-62
Completed "Red Geraniums in the Window"

Figure 11-63 illustrates a composition that was simplified, and the Nik® Burnt Sienna filter was used selectively.

I would suggest picking up a few good books on Painter. Focal Press has two excellent books devoted solely to Painter: Martin Addison's *Painter 11 for Photographers* and Jeremy Sutton's *Painter 11 Creativity.* They are both full of illustrations, step-by-step tutorials, and fine explanations.

This book was not meant to be a primer on the extensive programs available in Photoshop and Painter, but this chapter may by helpful in highlighting the basic skills that will make your task of collaging or digital painting a little easier. As always, I would encourage experimentation. Keep a notebook beside your computer for notes to yourself about tools, brushes, techniques, and more. Become familiar with your options, and you will have more artistic avenues to explore.

In closing, it is a joy, as an artist, to have more tools available for making art. The digital tools currently available to us warrant serious consideration as a legitimate art medium, equal to any other being exhibited today. Whether you are a photographer or a conventional artist, the digital art tools demonstrated in this book can add to your repertoire of art mediums to use. As you pursue creating art, brushes loaded with colored pixels can equal those loaded with pigment. It is, after all, all about making meaningful marks. I hope you enjoy exploring the possibilities.

Figure 11-63
"Hawaiian Surfer Sunset"

12

Resources

Suppliers: Equipment, Software, Tools, and Artist Materials

Adobe Systems, Inc.
www.adobe.com
345 Park Avenue
San Jose, CA 95110-2704

Alien Skin Software
www.alienskin.com
third-party Photoshop software (Eye Candy, Xenofex, Bokeh, Exposure, Blow Up, Snap Art, Image Doctor)

OPPOSITE PAGE: *"Peonies"*

Apple Computer, Inc.
www.apple.com
(408) 996-1010
1 Infinite Loop
Cupertino, CA 95014-2084

Auto FX
www.autofx.com
(205) 980-0056
(800) 839-2008
151 Narrows Parkway, Suite E
Birmingham, AL 35242
third-party Photoshop software

Auto Pan
www.autopano.net
panoramic system

Blurb Books
www.blurb.com
create your own book

Corel Corporation
www.corel.com
(613) 274-6373 (fax)
1600 Carling Avenue
Ottawa, ON K1Z 8R7, Canada
manufacturer of Painter

Craig's Actions
www.craigsactions.com
third-party Photoshop software

DASS Film and Super Sauce Concentrate
www.digitalartstudioseminars.com
supplies and instructional materials for alternative printing techniques

Digital Art Supplies
www.digitalartsupplies.com
(877) 534-4278
9596 Chesapeake Drive, Suite B
San Diego, CA 92123
digital printing supplies

Digital Film Tools
www.digitalfilmtools
plug-ins for Photoshop (EZ Mask, Light!, Ozone, Power Mask, Power Stroke, Snap, zMatte)

Epson America, Inc.
www.epson.com
(800) 463-7766
3840 Kilroy Airport Way
Long Beach, CA 90806
printers, scanners, projectors

Giga Pan
www.gigapansystems.com
panoramic system

Golden Artist Colors, Inc.
www.goldenpaints.com
(607) 847-6154
188 Bell Road
New Berlin, NY 13411-9527
inkjet coatings (Digital Grounds)

inkAID™ (Ontario Specialty Coatings Corp.)
www.inkaid.com
(888) 424-8167
16830 County Route 155
Watertown, NY 13601
inkjet coatings

John Derry's Artists' Brushes
www.johnsartistsbrushes.com
third-party Photoshop CS5 mixer brushes

Kolo®
www.kolo.com
(888) 636-5656
P.O. Box 572
Windsor, CT 06095-0572
photo albums, scrapbooks, journals

Lazertran LLC
www.lazertran.com
(800) 245-7547
1501 West Copans Road, Suite 100
Pompano Beach, FL 33064
transfer materials for photographers and artists (manufactured in U.K.)

Lineco, Inc.
www.lineco.com
(800) 322-7775
P.O. Box 2604
Holyoke, MA 01041
flexible hinge binding strips; books-by-hand supplies

Lucis® Pro 6 (Image Content Technology LLC)
www.lucispro.com
third-party Photoshop filters

Moab (Legion Paper)
www.moabpaper.com
inkjet papers

National Association of Photoshop Professionals
www.photoshopuser.com
(800) 738-8513
333 Douglas Road East
Oldsmar, FL 34677

Photo Tex Group, Inc.
www.phototexgroup.com
inkjet fabric with an adhesive backing

Photomatix
www.hdrsoft.com
high-dynamic-range software

Nik® Software Color Efex Pro™
www.nikmultimedia.com
(619) 725-3150
7580 Metropolitan Drive, Suite 208
San Diego, CA 92108
third-party Photoshop filters

SiteWelder
www.sitewelder.com
(800) 646-7483
10201 Meredith Avenue
Silver Spring, MD 20910
website construction for photographers and artists

Sony® Sweep Panorama
www.sony.com

Topaz Filters
www.topazlabs.com
third-party Photoshop filters (Adjust, DeNoise, Simplify, Detail, Clean, ReMask, DeJPEG, Fusion, Vivacity, Enhance, Moment)

Totally Rad
www.gettotallyrad.com
third-party Photoshop software

Wacom® tablets
www.wacom.com
(800) 922-6613
1311 SE Cardinal Court
Vancouver, WA 98683

Digital Collage and Painting Website

http://www.focalpress.com/companions/digitalcollageandpainting
This website contains images used in the tutorials and examples in
Chapter 11 of this book.

Index